THE
PREMONITION

ALSO BY MICHAEL LEWIS

The Fifth Risk
The Undoing Project
Flash Boys
Boomerang
The Big Short
Home Game
The Blind Side
Coach
Moneyball
Next
The New New Thing
Losers
Pacific Rift
The Money Culture
Liar's Poker

EDITED BY MICHAEL LEWIS

Panic

MICHAEL LEWIS

THE
PREMONITION

A PANDEMIC STORY

W. W. NORTON & COMPANY
Independent Publishers Since 1923

For information about permission to reproduce selections from this book,
write to Permissions, W. W. Norton & Company, Inc., 500 Fifth Avenue,
New York, NY 10110

For information about special discounts for bulk purchases, please contact
W. W. Norton Special Sales at specialsales@wwnorton.com or 800-233-4830

Manufacturing by LSC Communications Harrisonburg
Book design by Chris Welch
Production manager: Julia Druskin
Director of prepress production: Joe Lops

ISBN 978-0-393-88155-4

W. W. Norton & Company, Inc., 500 Fifth Avenue, New York, N.Y. 10110
www.wwnorton.com

W. W. Norton & Company Ltd., 15 Carlisle Street, London W1D 3BS

1 2 3 4 5 6 7 8 9 0

To my parents, Diana Monroe Lewis and J. Thomas Lewis.

Thank you for surviving this.

Every surgeon carries within himself a small cemetery, where from time to time he goes to pray—a place of bitterness and regret, where he must look for an explanation for his failures.

—RENÉ LERICHE,
The Philosophy of Surgery, 1951

CONTENTS

The Missing Americans

This book began with an unholy mix of obligation and opportunism. During the first half of the Trump administration I'd written a book, *The Fifth Risk*, that framed the federal government as a manager of a portfolio of existential risks: natural disasters, nuclear weapons, financial panics, hostile foreigners, energy security, food security, and on and on and on. The federal government wasn't just this faceless gray mass of two million people. Nor was it some well-coordinated deep state seeking to subvert the will of the people. It was a collection of experts, among them some real heroes, whom we neglected and abused at our peril. Yet we'd been neglecting and abusing them for more than a generation. That behavior climaxed with the Trump administration. My book asked: What happens when the people in charge of managing these risks, along with the experts who understand them, have no interest in them?

I had no clue what was going to happen next. I assumed

something was bound to happen. But it didn't—not really. For the better part of three years, the Trump administration got lucky. That luck ran out in late 2019, as a freshly mutated virus in China made its way toward the United States. This was just the sort of management test I'd imagined when writing *The Fifth Risk*. How could I not write about it? But as I got into it, and found these wonderful characters to tell the story through, it became clear that Trump's approach to government management was only a part of the story, and maybe not even the bigger part. As one of my characters put it, "Trump was a comorbidity."

Back in October 2019—nearly three years into the Trump administration, and before anyone involved was aware of the novel coronavirus—a collection of very smart people had gathered to rank all the countries in the world, in order of their readiness for a pandemic. A group called the Nuclear Threat Initiative partnered with Johns Hopkins and The Economist Intelligence Unit to create what amounted to a preseason college football ranking for one hundred ninety-five countries. The Global Health Security Index, it was called. It was a massive undertaking involving millions of dollars and hundreds of researchers. They created stats and polled the experts. They ranked the United States first. Number 1. (The United Kingdom was Number 2.)

Critics quibbled with the rankings. The complaints weren't all that different from the complaints you hear before every college football season. For years the University of Texas football team, with its vast resources and sway with voters, always seemed ranked more highly at the start of the season than at the end. The United States was the Longhorns of pandemic preparedness. It was rich. It had special access to talent. It enjoyed special relationships with the experts whose votes determined the rankings.

Then the game was played. The preseason rankings no longer mattered. Neither, really, did the excuses and blame-casting and rationalizations. As the legendary football coach Bill Parcells once said, "You are what your record says you are." At last count the United States, with a bit more than 4 percent of the world's population, had a bit more than 20 percent of its COVID-19 deaths. In February 2021, *The Lancet* published a long critique of the U.S. pandemic performance. By then 450,000 Americans had died. *The Lancet* pointed out that if the COVID death rate in the United States had simply tracked the average of the other six G7 nations, 180,000 of those people would still be alive. "Missing Americans," they called them. But why stop there? Before the pandemic, a panel of public-health experts had judged the United States to be more prepared for a pandemic than other G7 nations. In a war with a virus, we were not expected merely to fare as well as other rich countries. We were expected to win.

I like to think that my job is mainly to find the story in the material. I always hope that story will wind up being about more than what I think it's about—and that the reader will bring to it his own sense-making apparatus and find meanings in it missed by its author. But that doesn't mean that I don't form some opinion of what it's about. I think this particular story is about the curious talents of a society, and how those talents are wasted if not led. It's also about how gaps open between a society's reputation and its performance. After a catastrophic season, management always huddles up to figure out what needs to be changed. If this story speaks to that management in any way, I hope it is to say: There are actually some things to be proud of. Our players aren't our problem. But we are what our record says we are.

PART I

The Looking Glass

aura Glass was thirteen years old and entering the eighth
grade at Jefferson Middle School in Albuquerque, New
Mexico, when she looked over her father's shoulder to see what
he was working on. Bob Glass was a scientist at Sandia National
Laboratories, created in the mid-1940s to figure out everything
that needed to be figured out about nuclear weapons, apart from
the creation of the plutonium and uranium inside them. It was
Sandia's engineers who'd calculated how to drop a hydrogen
bomb from a plane without killing the pilot, for instance. By the
mid-1980s, when Bob Glass arrived, Sandia had a reputation as
the place you went with a top secret problem after everyone else
in the netherworld of national security had failed to solve it. It
attracted people who followed wherever their minds led them,
at the expense of pretty much everything else. People like Bob
Glass. When she peered over her father's shoulder, Laura Glass

didn't always understand what she was looking at. But it was never dull.

What she saw on this day in 2003 was a screen filled with green dots moving around, at random, it seemed to her. Then she noticed that a few of the dots were not green but red—and when a red dot bumped into a green dot, the green dot turned red. It was what was called an "agent-based model," her father explained. *You can think of these dots as people. There are a whole bunch of people on the planet. One of them is you. There are different types of people, with different types of schedules, and there are rules about how these people interact. I put together a kind of schedule for each person and then set them loose to see what happens . . .*

One of the things Bob Glass liked about this type of modeling was how easy it was to explain. Models were abstractions, but what this model was abstracting from was familiar: a single entity, which you could describe as a person, a piece of information, or any number of other things. As the green dots turned red, you could be watching gossip travel, a traffic jam, a riot start, or a species go extinct. "When you start talking about it this way, everyone can understand it immediately," he said.

His model was a crude picture of the real world, but it allowed him to see things in the real world that might be obscured in a more detailed picture. It also enabled him to answer the complicated questions that now routinely found him, most of which had to do with preventing some national disaster. The Federal Reserve Bank of New York just then was using him to help figure out how failure in one corner of the U.S. financial system might ripple into others. The Department of Energy wanted him to determine if a small glitch in the electric grid might trigger rolling blackouts across the country. Once you stopped talking about people and started talking about, say, money flows, the links between the little dots on the screen and the real world became harder for most people to follow. But not for him. "This is the crux of science," he'd say with enthusiasm. "All science is modeling. In all science you are abstracting from nature. The question is: is it a useful abstraction." Useful, to Bob Glass, meant: Does it help solve a problem?

At that moment Laura Glass had her own problem: that year's science fair. There was no question of skipping it. Science had always played a big part in her relationship with her dad; it was an unspoken Glass family rule that she and her two sisters would compete in the fair every year. And actually Laura loved it. "The kind of science I was able to do with my dad was very different from the kind of science I did in school," she said. "I always struggled with science in school." With her dad, science was this tool for finding cool new questions to ask, and answer. Exactly what questions didn't matter: her father had no respect for the boundaries between subjects and thought of all sciences as one and the same. They'd created one project on probability and coin flipping, and another on the differences in photosynthesis from one plant species to the next. Each year was more competitive than the year before. "When you got to middle school," recalled Laura, "you started to see the competition ramp up."

As she watched her father's computer screen, she thought, *It's almost like the red dots are infecting the green dots.* In history class she'd been reading about the Black Death. "I was fascinated by it," she said. "I had no idea. It wiped out a third of Europe." She asked her father: *Could you use this model to study how a disease spreads?* He hadn't considered using his model to study disease. "I thought, Oh God, how am I going to help her with this?" he said. His assistance was the only thing that neither father nor daughter questioned. Bob Glass was a "science dad," in the way other fathers were "Little League dads." He might not live through his daughters' science projects in the way those fathers lived through their kids' baseball games. On the other hand . . .

Soon they were deep into a new science fair project. That first year, the model was crude. The disease was the Black Death, which in Albuquerque, New Mexico, in 2004 felt a bit silly. Laura's village had ten thousand people in it, a fraction of the population of her school district. In what she called "Infect World," people gave the plague to each other simply by passing each other, which wasn't realistic. She was the one who had to stand beside her Styrofoam boards with their charts and graphs and answer questions from the science fair judges, so she was the most acutely aware of the limitations of her work. "The judges would always ask: How real is this situation? How can you take this and use it?," she recalled. Still. She was the only kid at the fair who had done epidemiology. Her project qualified for the state championships. Afterward she went back to her father and said: *Let's make it real.*

To make it real, she needed a more plausible pathogen. "I told my dad, 'It won't be the Black Death. It'll be something in the modern world. A flu-like thing.'" Whatever the pathogen was, she'd need to learn more about it, along with the society with which it would interact. "She came to me," recalled Bob Glass, "and said, 'Dad, it's not so great that they just pass each other and they get sick. Dad, another thing, people don't just walk around like this. They have social networks. I need to have social networks in here.'" Through 2004, Bob watched as his now fourteen-year-old child designed a survey and administered it to hundreds and hundreds of people in her school district: workers, teachers, parents, grandparents, high school students, middle school students, preschool students. "At first it was going to my peers and asking them questions," said Laura.

"How often did they hug and kiss? How many people? How many different people did they sit next to? How many minutes did they spend sitting next to them? Then I went from them to their parents." She mapped their social networks and their movements, and then mapped the interactions among the different social networks. She counted up the number of people each person spent in close enough proximity with to infect them with an airborne pathogen.

She'd become passionate about a science project, and her father loved it. The deeper she went, the deeper he went. "I treated her like a grad student," he said. "I'd say, Show me what you've done, and here are my questions." In order for it to help her, his own computer model needed to improve in ways that were beyond even his powers. The most gifted computer programmer Bob Glass had ever met was a guy at Sandia National Labs, Walt Beyeler. "Sandia's a really weird place," said Bob. "Los Alamos is full of people with pedigrees. Sandia hires the most brilliant people they could possibly find, and they don't really care about pedigree." Bob Glass was most people's idea of a brilliant mind, but Walt was Bob's idea of a brilliant mind. Asking him to help with a child's science fair project felt a bit like pulling LeBron James in to play on your pickup basketball team. Walt was game.

The model needed to include realistic social interactions. It needed to account for incubation periods, during which people were infected but not infectious. It needed people without symptoms but capable of spreading disease. It needed people to be removed from the network after they died or became immune. It needed to make assumptions about the social behavior of the ill, and about the likelihood of one person infecting another when the two came into contact. Father and daughter agreed that, given the nature of their own social interactions, children were twice as likely as adults to infect each other in any given social interaction. They also agreed to leave stuff out, for the sake of simplicity. "We didn't have college students in it," said Bob Glass. "There weren't all of these single-night stands or whatever."

Bob Glass was now seriously interested. To him, it felt less like a science project than an engineering one. Once you understood the way a disease moved through a community, you might find ways to slow it, and maybe even stop it. But how? He began to read whatever he could about disease, and the history of epidemics. He picked up *The Great Influenza*, a book by the historian John Barry about the 1918 flu pandemic. "My God, fifty million people died!" said Bob. "I had no idea. I started thinking, God, this is an important problem."

Father and daughter were both now alert to the real world of disease. They perked up when they read the news, in the fall of 2004, that because a single vaccine-making factory in Liverpool, England, became contaminated, the United States had lost half of its supply of flu vaccine. There was not enough vaccine to go around. So: Who should get it? United States government policy at the time was to administer the vaccine to those most at risk of dying: old people. Laura thought that wasn't right. "She said, 'It's young people who have all these social interactions and are transmitting the disease,'" recalled her father. "'What if you give it to them?'" They went to their model and gave the young people the vaccine, thereby eliminating the ability of young people to transmit the disease. Sure enough, the old people never got it. Bob Glass searched the literature for the infectious-disease specialist or epidemiologist who had already figured this out. "I can find only one paper that even suggested this," he said.

In the end Laura Glass, now a freshman at Albuquerque

High School, would win the Grand Award at the New Mexico state science fair. She was on her way to internationals in Phoenix, with two thousand other kids from around the world. Her big white foam boards now focused tightly on a question. "Flu strains mutate all the time," she'd written on them. "What would we do if we didn't have the right vaccine in time?" For his part, Bob Glass had now read or at least skimmed everything ever written about epidemics, and how to stop them. The disease in 1918 that had killed fifty million people had sprung from a handful of mutations in the virus inside some bird. By 2005, the seasonal flu had already achieved a few of these mutations. "We had a looming life-or-death problem of global proportions," he wrote later. Yet all the experts basically assumed that, in the first months after some killer mutation, little could be done to save lives, apart from isolating the ill and praying for a vaccine. The model he'd built with his daughter showed that there was no difference between giving a person a vaccine and removing him or her from the social network: in each case, a person lost the ability to infect others. Yet all the expert talk was about how to speed the production and distribution of vaccines. No one seemed to be exploring the most efficient and least disruptive ways to remove people from social networks. "I had this sudden fear," said Bob. "No one is going to realize what you could do."

ONE

Dragon

By the time Charity heard about the young woman, it was too late to help. The woman was on life support in a Santa Barbara County hospital. The doctors had just found tuberculosis in her brain. Before they could find anything more, she was dead. And that was just the start of the problem.

Dr. Charity Dean was the newly appointed chief health officer for Santa Barbara County. A health officer was a stopper of things, and the most important thing Charity was meant to stop, in her view, was people from giving diseases to their fellow citizens. *Mycobacterium tuberculosis* moves through droplets in the breath of the infected person, and is able to hang in the air for impressive stretches. "The vast majority of the risk is the first hour, but it may be there for two, three, four hours," said Charity. "No one actually knows." There were other things about TB that no one knew. Some TB patients infected no one, and others infected huge numbers: no one knew why. No one knew why some people were superspreaders: Was it their behavior? Their biology? The biology of their particular case of TB? The disease has been around basically forever; at the turn of the twentieth century it was the leading killer of human beings; and it remains, in many ways, a mystery. "It's the most intriguing infectious disease," said Charity. "My favorite infectious disease. It can do anything or be anywhere in the body. We've had TB of the uterus. Of the eye. Of the *finger*." Once, in Niger, she'd treated a man whose TB had started in his lungs, wormed its way through his chest wall, and finally oozed in pus down the side of his torso.

To move from one person to another, however, TB needed to invade the lungs. The young woman in the Santa Barbara county hospital had been diagnosed with tuberculosis of the brain, and, had the bacteria confined itself to her brain, it would have threatened no one. If it had found its way into her lungs, it had the power to kill. And 30 percent of the people who had TB in their brain had it also in their lungs.

Santa Barbara County had become almost famous, at least in disease control circles, for both the number and sheer terror of its tuberculosis cases. When people heard this, they didn't quite believe it. At first glance, the county was a tranquil Eden of beige boulders and golden grass and California oaks. Oprah lived there; Ellen lived there; the great estates in the foothills overlooking the sea blended into one another to form a single tapestry of American affluence. Even the ocean felt private.

But Santa Barbara County was both bigger and more complicated than it seemed. It had the highest rate of child poverty in the state. It sheltered maybe fifty thousand illegal immigrants in abject squalor. Plus all hell could break loose at any time: wildfires and mudslides and oil spills and mass shootings. Scratch the surface of paradise and you were plunged into the Book of Job.

The chief health officer of Santa Barbara County never knew

exactly where or when or how the next TB outbreak might occur. The young woman who'd just died in the county hospital illustrated the point: no one had any idea she even had tuberculosis until she was on her deathbed. She'd had a husband and children; she'd lived in a crowded neighborhood; she'd worked inside a massive open-plan office, alongside three hundred other people. If the TB had reached her lungs, anyone she'd been anywhere near was now in mortal danger. That was Charity Dean's immediate problem: to figure out who, if anyone, might be infected. She'd need to test tissue from the woman's lung. If the test came out positive, she'd need to call the company that employed the young woman and shut it down for long enough to test all three hundred of its employees, along with anyone they might have infected, along with anyone *they* might have infected—and on and on.

In short, she might need to alert and alarm a big chunk of Santa Barbara County. But who was *she?* A nobody. Hardly anyone in Santa Barbara County knew who she was, or what she did all day. She was invisible.

Three years earlier, in 2011, Charity had been a thirty-two-year-old resident in internal medicine, pregnant for the third time in five years, when the Santa Barbara County medical director had asked her if she'd consider filling an opening he had for a deputy health officer. The county required its health officers to possess both a medical degree and a master's in public health, and she had both. He also mentioned—in passing, but so that Charity heard it loud and clear—that the luxury she had of being married to a rich surgeon meant that she could afford to take the job.

The job had no obvious appeal, at least to a normal young doctor. It paid a third of what she could earn starting out in the private practices that had already asked her to work for them. Doctors of Santa Barbara already referred to themselves as "the working poor." Being a doctor in Santa Barbara without being paid like one—well, that was insane. "*Everyone* tried to talk me out of it," said Charity. "People couldn't believe it. They were like, 'You aren't seriously thinking of going to work for the county???' They thought it meant that I was going to be a doctor down in the shithole basement of the county clinic." The county clinic was where poor people without health insurance went for treatment. It was housed inside a decrepit facility erected a century earlier on the outskirts of Santa Barbara as a sanatorium for tuberculosis patients.

Charity still found herself drawn to the job. "I couldn't figure out why my heartstrings were tugged," she said. The medical director handed her a thick binder whose pages described the job in detail: "The Health Officers Authority in California." She read it closely. Health officers in California, like health officers across the United States and the rest of the free world, had a long list of responsibilities. Registering births and deaths. Inspecting restaurants. Counting bacteria in ocean water and swimming pools. Managing chronic diseases. None of that really interested her. Then she saw the phrase "Communicable Disease Controller." It was an official state role. Played by local health officers. Her mind lit up. "I don't really care about obesity or diabetes," she said. "I actually don't give a shit about chronic disease. What I like is a crisis."

What she more than liked was the kind of crisis that might be created by a communicable disease. She knew it sounded odd, but she'd been consumed by this interest since she was a small child. Disease had shaped history; disease had crippled societies—but that's not why, at the age of seven, she'd become obsessed with it. "It was gruesome death," she said. "It was the human powerlessness over it. I was interested in horrific disease that swept across huge swaths of the population, who were powerless to stop it, and died these awful deaths." In middle school she had created Styrofoam models of viruses and hung them from her bedroom ceiling "just so I could stare at them and think about them." She taught herself French so that, when the time came to move to West Africa to chase disease, as she assumed she one day would do, she'd have the ability to communicate. In college, as a microbiology major, she'd stay up late reading about yellow fever, tuberculosis, and Spanish flu. "My favorite microbes in college were the human pathogens that caused horrific disease," she recalled. "I mean, nobody cares about plant viruses." In medical school, at Tulane University, she'd ignored the derision of her fellow doctors and studied at the same time for a master's degree in public health, but only because Tulane, unusually, offered a degree with a focus on tropical disease. After that she'd gone to Gabon and Niger to work as a doctor, in part because the odds seemed to her pretty good that whatever disease was going to replicate the destruction of past plagues would come from Africa.

She knew that her obsession with pandemic disease was unusual, even off-putting. "I learned not to talk about it," she said, "because when I talked about it, people thought I was crazy." But the fact remained that, from a very young age, when she was feeling low, she had cheered herself up by reading books on bubonic plague. The ones with the grisly drawings she liked best.

She read more of the fine print in the binder describing the role of the local public-health officer. One sentence struck her as more important than all the others combined.

Each health officer knowing or having reason to believe that any case of the diseases made reportable by regulation of the department, or any other contagious, infectious or communicable disease exists, or has recently existed, within the territory under his or her jurisdiction, shall

take measures as may be necessary to prevent the spread
of the disease or occurrence of additional cases.

To minimize horrific death, and to chase disease, the state
of California had bestowed upon local public-health officers
extraordinary legal powers.

Charity accepted the job. She typed out that one sentence of
law and taped it to the wall of her new office. Once a TB quarantine room, her office still had the original grates in the wall
used to get fresh sea air into the patient's lungs. Sitting at her
desk in Building 4, she could hear the screams of the psychiatric
patients from across the courtyard in Building 3. In the halls,
cabinets as old as the building stored medical instruments that
belonged in a museum. The stairs led to a dank tunnel under the
building that went to the old morgue. It was her kind of place.

She had, in theory, incredible legal powers to prevent disease.
She soon realized how few people, in practice, knew the law.
Most of the citizens of Santa Barbara, including nearly all of the
public officials by whose pleasure she served, didn't even really
understand what a public-health officer was supposed to do. The
public-health officer had somehow come to be a recessive character. The other officials, and the public, expected her to lie low,
like a carrot in a school play, or the wife of a rich surgeon, until
called upon, usually to make some brief ceremonial appearance.
The law's words felt strong, but their spirit felt weak. By her second year on the job, she found herself quoting the law so often
that she asked her assistant to laminate a copy of that one passage, so that she might carry it with her in her briefcase. "I'm
in a meeting trying to explain to people that I actually do have
the authority to do something I need to do," she said. "I really
tried hard not to whip it out. But I pulled it out once a week."

By the time she got the call about the young woman with
tuberculosis in her brain, she'd read that one sentence aloud

more than just about any other in her life. Its lines weren't as easily performed as, say, the verses of the 23rd Psalm, which she also loved, but she could bring them equally to life.

> *Each health officer knowing or having reason to believe . . .*

"What does that mean??!!" she'd cry, and point her finger in the air. "It means *suspicion!* You only need to suspect!"

> *. . . that any case of the diseases made reportable by regulation of the department, or any other contagious, infectious or communicable disease exists, or has recently existed, within the territory under his or her jurisdiction . . .*

"*Any* disease!" she'd cry, and then parse the adjectives. " 'Contagious' isn't really a medical term, so ignore that—they just tossed in the kitchen sink there—but you *really* need to understand the distinction between 'infectious' and 'communicable.' " All communicable diseases were infectious, but some infectious diseases were not communicable. *Communicable* meant a person could give it to another person. You could get Lyme disease, for instance, but you couldn't give it to somebody else. *Communicable* diseases were the diseases that created crises. In an adjective she'd found a vessel for her life purpose.

> *. . . shall take measures as may be necessary to prevent the spread of the disease or occurrence of additional cases.*

" 'Shall'!" she'd exclaim. "Not a *may.* A *shall.* Not think about it. Not consider it. Not maybe get around to it one day if you feel like it. It's your *duty.* If you suspect disease, you can do whatever the hell you want."

Now she had a corpse with TB in a hospital an hour's drive north. She asked them to move the body to the Santa Barbara coroner's office, then called the coroner to ask him to send her a sample of the lung tissue. That's when the real problems started: at first he wouldn't even come to the phone. Once she had telephoned him into submission and he finally picked up, he simply refused to do it. Yet the law was clear. The coroner was meant to do with any corpse whatever she told him to do. Instead he explained to her why he wouldn't.

To her growing incredulity, this seventy-something coroner, who had contracted with the county to work part-time, and who clearly had only the vaguest idea of what he was talking about, began to lecture her about tuberculosis. Saying that it was both dangerous and unnecessary to extract the young woman's lung. Citing some study that purported to show that TB in a corpse subjected to surgery could become aerosolized and infect the surgeon.

Charity Dean was at this point the *chief* health officer of Santa Barbara County. She'd been promoted earlier that year. She was the youngest chief health officer in the history of California. She'd also spent three years running the county's TB clinic. She was legally responsible for every single case of TB in the county; fancy doctors who had supervised her residency now called her to ask for advice about the disease; for crying out loud, she was about to be named president of the Tuberculosis Controllers Association for the entire state of California. She tried to be civil with the old coroner, but it was hard. "I knew the study," said Charity. "It was a bullshit study. But the douchebag said he wouldn't do it—would not even allow someone else to come into his office and do it."

She hung up and called the sheriff. She explained the situation, sweetly, and asked the sheriff to require the coroner to cut the young woman open and extract her lung. The sheriff didn't know the law, either, it seemed, as he said he wouldn't interfere with the coroner's authority. At which point Charity lost her patience. "I couldn't believe he wasn't doing what I told him to do," she said. She wrote out a legal order and delivered it to the sheriff in person. "Then I waited for the phones to blow up."

The sheriff couldn't simply ignore a legal order. He phoned up the chief counsel for the board of supervisors to confirm his belief that a legal order issued by a local public-health officer carried no authority. Santa Barbara's chief counsel looked into it and, to his surprise, discovered that the sheriff was mistaken. The woman was right: the only person whose authority trumped the health officer's, in cases involving disease, was the governor of California. And then only if the governor had declared a state of emergency.

With that, Charity considered the matter settled. But the coroner's office called her the next day to say that it wasn't. "They said, 'Okay, we'll do it,'" she recalled. "'But we won't do it inside the office, because the building's old and lacks proper ventilation.' I said, 'Okay, could you do it outside?' They said, 'Okay, but only if you are here.'" Not for the first time she wondered what would happen in Santa Barbara County if there was ever a serious outbreak of communicable disease. "They won't even do an autopsy because they are worried about aerosolized TB," she said. "What the fuck are they going to do if it's aerosolized Ebola?"

It didn't help that this was all going down over Christmas. She'd just turned thirty-seven, was newly divorced from the rich surgeon, and was a single mother to three young boys. As she drove to the county morgue on the day after Christmas, she was unsure what awaited her. She sensed that the coroner and the sheriff and maybe some other people had grown irritated with her. Just how irritated became clear only as she rolled into the small parking lot beside the coroner's office. Seven people were waiting for her outside the morgue, all men. The coroner, the sheriff, and a bunch of his deputies. They'd clearly come for the show. She'd driven straight from cleaning up the mess under the tree, and so she wasn't in her usual battle armor of Talbots suit, pencil skirt, and grandma heels. Just a tacky Christmas sweater and blue jeans. All the men wore full-on hazmat suits. "They look like they're about to walk on the moon—the whole team," said Charity. "You'd have thought this *was* Ebola."

The morgue itself was even more appalling than the public-health office. Poking up from scrub oaks and dirt fields, it resembled more the bathrooms at a highway rest stop than an official public office. Not for the first time she wondered where they'd put the bodies if ever there were lots of gruesome deaths at once.

At some remove, on a picnic table, lay a body bag with the young woman inside. The coroner was now just angry. He explained all over again that the entire operation was unsafe and he was not going to risk opening up the body indoors. He cited the bullshit paper again—this time to explain why he hadn't even brought his bone saw with him, as the one known case of a surgeon becoming infected with TB by a corpse had involved a bone saw. Instead of the bone saw, he'd brought along a pair of garden shears. Now he offered them to her. Garden shears. They were brand-new and gleaming, with the word "ACE" on the red handles, for the hardware store. If the new chief health officer wanted to cut open the young woman and remove a piece of her lung she would need to do it herself, with garden shears. "I had thought I was just there to watch," said Charity. "And he turned it into a game of chicken."

Medicine had always felt to her a man's world. Especially in the places, like here, where it touched government. It was then Charity Dean realized: the real problem is that this man is frightened. *The douchebag is scared.* She'd been around terrifying diseases most of her adult life and had made a pact with herself not to fear them. "If you're a truck driver, you know you're going to get into an accident sooner or later, so you just learn what to do if you are in an accident," she said. "That's how you get over the fear. You just accept that you'll get the disease one day." Men weren't so accepting, she'd noticed, especially the big and supposedly brave ones. As a medical student she'd seen the fear—in the eyes of the New Orleans cops in the trauma center. "They'd haul in some guy with a gunshot wound, but when they found out he had hep C or HIV, they'd squeal and go take a shower in Clorox from head to toe." Over and again she'd seen mesomorphs with crew cuts who would happily run into a burning building to save a dog turn uncertain and uneasy in the presence of disease. Airborne diseases in particular seemed to spook them. "That was the number one reason I could not get TB patients arrested," she said. "The police would turn into these squeamish little girls. They'd sit in the car and let a nurse go get them."

Charity was not without her own fears, both real and imagined. The walls of her office and home bedroom were plastered with Post-it notes on which she had scribbled the mantras by which she hoped to live, most of them having to do with bravery.

There is no shortcut to courage.

Courage is a muscle memory.

The tallest oak in the forest was once just a little nut that held its ground.

Like most everyone else, she needed reminding. Unlike most everyone else, she reminded herself. Constantly. Her realization that the men outside the coroner's office were afraid in a way she was not led to a thought: *they don't think I'm going to go through with this.* Then another: *they don't think I will do it, because I don't look like a person who would do it.* Even in heels she was only five foot six, and slender. She had mixed feelings about her own looks, but men did not appear to share them. She'd gotten used to catcalls. She'd created a rule for herself: when entering a meeting with a certain kind of male, allow a thirty-second recovery period before attempting to convey information upon which that male might need to act. Men judged her by appearance—and were badly deceived. "The inside doesn't match the outside," she sometimes said of herself.

She unzipped the body bag and looked at the corpse. A bone saw would have allowed her to cut right down the middle of the young woman's sternum, but with garden shears she'd have to snap the ribs at the ends. She felt for the edge of the first rib. *Snip!* It was a sharp, thin sound, like a crab shell cracking. *Snip!* As she cut, she sensed the eyes inside the hazmat suits looking away. They'd left the young woman's face uncovered: that was the most unsettling part. Normally a surgeon saw only the tiny patch of flesh upon which she operated. The sight of the young woman's face made the operation feel personal. Disturbing. She felt woozy and nauseous. "I was just saying over and over in my head, 'Don't faint. Don't faint,'" she said. "And I was mad. This was such disrespect for her and for her family. But they were like, 'You want to see it, you get to do it.'"

Snip! The crab shell finally cracked. She tossed the garden shears to one side of the body and pulled apart the woman's ribs. "At that moment I had this feeling," said Charity, "this feeling of such grief for her husband." She didn't show any feeling at all to the men, though. She didn't want to give the douchebag the satisfaction. She needed a chunk of the woman's lung tissue to take back to Manny in the lab for testing. But as she reached into the woman with the garden shears, the coroner reached in, too. He wanted to . . . help. "Should we look in her belly?" he asked gently. *Right*, she thought. *If it was in her belly, then it was in her blood, and if it was in the blood, it was probably on her lung.* She felt around for signs of tuberculosis. Her internal organs were perfect. Lovely. "If the lungs were speckled and bumpy, I would know," she said. "And they weren't." Her hands sensed what the lab would later find: the TB hadn't ever left the brain. In the end, the coroner saved her the trouble of cutting out a piece of the lung with the garden shears, by showing her how to release the lungs. They did it together. It was as if her nerve had changed his view of the situation.

Now she held the young woman's lungs in her hands. This Jell-O. Outside the human body, lung tissue didn't hold its form. And now she could see just how sure the coroner had been that none of this would ever happen: he had nowhere to put them. The only container in sight was an orange plastic bucket from Home Depot. She grabbed the woman's lungs and placed them into it, then tossed the bucket into the car and drove away.

To the men she left behind, the entire scene would remain a vivid memory; to her it was almost just another day in her life as the local health officer. They had no idea of the things she had done, or what she was capable of. The coroner obviously hadn't even considered the possibility that she was a trained surgeon. "Men like that always underestimate me," she said. "They think my spirit animal is a bunny. And it's a fucking dragon."

TWO

The Making of a Public-Health Officer

Paige Batson had been a nurse in the Santa Barbara County Public Health Department for more than a decade when Dr. Charity Dean was named the new deputy health officer. Paige was surprised. Young doctors in Santa Barbara, as soon as they finished their residency and their obligatory tour of duty in the county clinic, usually ran as fast as they could from the poor. Health officers were usually the older doctors at the end of their careers with an interest in a life of quiet anonymity. "Before she came," said Paige, "if you took any hundred people in Santa Barbara—even if you had taken any hundred *health care workers*—I don't think one person could tell you what the public-health officer did. Or who he was."

Right from the start, Dr. Dean did stuff no other health officers had done. She spent huge amounts of time with the public-health nurses, for instance, and treated them not as subordinates but as teachers. She insisted on seeing patients directly, which was truly odd. Most health officers spent their days writing memos, or over at the county board of supervisors, or sitting in meetings in a suit. Dr. Dean—Paige never called her anything other than "Dr. Dean"—saw patients constantly, and not just in the county clinics. She'd pop over to the homeless shelter in downtown Santa Barbara for half a day every week, set herself up inside a tiny room, and treat whoever walked in the door. There were days when she would go straight from plucking maggots from the wounds of a homeless man to testifying on television in front of the board of supervisors. When the nurses asked her why she did that, she'd said, "When a doctor stops treating patients, they slowly start to forget. Seeing patients is how you develop a sixth sense." She wasn't simply doing good works, in other words. She was gathering intelligence.

But the most curious thing about Dr. Dean was the sheer number of strange events that occurred whenever she was around. "Things exploded the minute she came," said Paige. After Dr. Dean was promoted from deputy to chief, in early 2014, the pattern became even more pronounced. At one point Paige turned to her boss and blurted out, "You know, since you've been here, we've had the weirdest cases. It's been weird case after weird case."

In the beginning, Paige thought this was a coincidence. Later she realized that the weird cases didn't simply happen to Dr. Dean. They happened because of Dr. Dean. The hepatitis C case, for instance. A more ordinary health officer might well have ignored it. A woman had turned up at a hospital to donate blood and tested positive for hepatitis C. The hospital had sent the report to the public-health office, as it was required to do. The first nurse didn't know what to make of it. By 2016, hep C was killing more Americans than all the other infectious diseases put together, according to the Centers for Disease Control and Prevention, but it never made the list of diseases that required a swift response from the local health officer. It was blood-borne, which made it harder to contract, and easier to ignore. It didn't scream "Emergency!" In virtually all the hep C cases they saw in public health, the patients had contracted the disease long ago and were well past the acute phase—the phase when their eyes yellowed and their urine darkened and their stomach ached. "Usually you see chronic hep C and there's no way to figure out where they got it," said Paige. "They're just living with it, until they get liver cancer."

But this local woman who'd caught hep C was an unusual case. She happened to be a regular blood donor, and had given blood just a few months earlier, which meant that just a few months ago she did not have hepatitis C. Dr. Dean asked Paige to call the woman and ask her where she had been the past few months. It emerged that in that brief period, the infected woman had treated herself to an astonishing number of possibly infectious procedures. An improbable number of manicures and pedicures. Botox treatments. Dental work. Some kind of stem cell procedure. By the time Paige got off the phone, she had a list of ten places where a virus might have entered the woman's bloodstream. Dr. Dean asked her to go have a look around the places and report back.

*

In her first year of residency at Santa Barbara Cottage Hospital, Charity had worked under a doctor named Stephen Hosea. Dr. Hosea was a poor boy from Kentucky who had trained at Harvard in the 1960s and then spent a decade researching disease at the National Institutes of Health (alongside a young researcher named Tony Fauci) before coming to California to treat infectious disease. He was tall and easygoing and wore his learning lightly, but he had a genius for figuring out what was wrong with patients, and for training young doctors. Each morning, he'd take the new doctors with him to visit patients whose illnesses remained undiagnosed. "The Dr. Hosea Show," the young doctors called it. "He said you should always put your hands on the patient," said Charity. "He'd get right in close into the patient's space. You know there are people who stand a little too close. He'd be like that." Soon the patients would be babbling on about their travels, their love lives, their workplaces, their extended families. It could seem like a natural conversation, but it never was. "The patients were all like, 'Oh, he wants to know all about me,'" said Charity. "But not really. He was digging into the parts that helped to inform his differential diagnosis."

The differential diagnosis was Dr. Hosea's mental list of the infectious diseases that might have caused the symptoms, along with his best guess of the odds of each being right. Over and over again, Charity watched the older doctor tease out possibilities missed by the younger doctors, just by getting patients to talk about the relevant parts of their lives. Or, as Dr. Hosea put it, "What have you been doing that I haven't been doing that puts you at risk for whatever the hell you've got?" A college student turned up one day with a dramatic and mysterious rash on his torso. The younger doctors had spent some time puzzling over it when Dr. Hosea appeared and led the kid on a tour of his social life. "When's the last time you were in a hot tub?" the doctor finally asked casually. (Charity noted that he hadn't asked: "Were you ever in a hot tub?") *A few days ago*, the kid said. *Anyone with you?* asked the doctor. *Yeah*, said the kid, *a few friends. Any of them have a rash?* asked the doctor. *Actually, yes*, said the kid, *my roommate does, just not as bad.* "It was classic *Pseudomonas*," said Charity, "a bacteria you can get from hot tubs. But Dr. Hosea wouldn't just say it. It was infuriating! He wouldn't tell you what the diagnosis was. He'd just lead you to it with the questions he asked the patient."

This wasn't how she'd been taught in medical school. As a

medical student, she'd been shown how to follow a checklist to get the life history of a new patient. She'd spend forty-five minutes asking questions and yet scarcely touch on the patient's social relationships. Communicable disease required a different approach. "It's one person spreading it to another person," said Charity. "It's not what you ate or smoked or something you did with yourself. It's something you have to get from another person. It's 'Who lives with you in your home?' It's 'What kind of sex do you have and how often?' It's 'Have you ever lived in a homeless shelter?' Steve Hosea burned into my mind that the most important part of the medical history isn't the medical history. It's the social history."

Charity had taken away other lessons from Dr. Hosea.

The simplest explanation is usually the best. If the patient turns up with two separate symptoms—say, a fever and a rash—the cause is more likely than not a single underlying disease.

If there is the faintest possibility of a catastrophic disease, you should treat it as being a lot more likely than it seems. If your differential diagnosis leads to a list of ten possibilities, for instance, and the tenth and least likely thing on the list is Ebola, you should treat the patient as if she has Ebola, because the consequences of not doing so can be calamitous.

When something doesn't quite seem right about your diagnosis, respect the feeling, even if you can't quite put your finger on why the diagnosis might be wrong. A lot of people had died because doctors had allowed their minds to come to rest before they should.

A doctor needed to be a detective for the patient: that was Dr. Hosea's big message. Charity had grafted it onto her job as health officer. Her patient was Santa Barbara County. To keep it healthy, she needed to think about it the way Stephen Hosea thought about his patients. She needed to keep her hands on it. To be its detective.

When Paige Batson returned from her tour of the hep C patient's life, Charity could feel that something was slightly off about her—in the same way she occasionally felt something was slightly off after a diagnosis failed to explain a symptom. Paige was usually a chatterbox; now she'd gone quiet. "I don't know, Dr. Dean," she said. "Something didn't feel right." She'd gone to all the places on her list, but only one of them left her feeling unsettled: the stem cell clinic. The Thomashefsky clinic, as it was called. It offered a treatment for joint and back pain, platelet-rich plasma therapy, in which blood cells were removed from the patient, whipped around in a centrifuge, then reinjected into the patient. Dr. Thomashefsky charged up to forty-five hundred bucks a pop for a procedure that wasn't covered by medical insurance, as its actual usefulness was still a matter of dispute. Thomashefsky was old and established. His clients were rich. Some, like the professional athletes who drove up to see him from Los Angeles, were even famous.

Paige had visited the place, but informally, like a cop without a search warrant. Dr. Thomashefsky had been welcoming and had shown her around. He seemed proud of his work. On her brief tour of his office, she'd seen things that troubled her. Vials of patients' blood without names on them. Multidose vials of painkillers with no dates on them. But Paige was hesitant to make a stink. Thomashefsky had been in practice for more than thirty years; his clients were a Who's Who of Santa Barbara. And never in her fifteen years on the job had the public-heath office taken it upon itself to investigate a case of hepatitis C. "I honestly thought Dr. Dean was going to say something like 'We need to provide them with education and support,'" said Paige. Instead Dr. Dean grabbed her purse and said, "We're going back there."

The Thomashefsky clinic was inside a squat beige building

right behind Cottage Hospital. They arrived to a stone-cold stare from the young woman behind the reception desk, and a reception area full of patients. The doctor feigned good cheer and said that, yes, of course, the chief health officer of Santa Barbara County was welcome to look around. But Paige sensed a tension in the air that hadn't been there on her first visit. That was because the chief health officer was more like a cop with a warrant.

Charity had always found it odd what was regulated and what was not: "You can just suck fat out of somebody's belly, whip it up, and inject it back into their knee and no one can say a thing about it." The Medical Board of California had the power to remove his license, of course, but neither the board nor anyone else was paying this doctor any mind. The doctor's office building had once been apartments, and even his operating room had a lived-in feel to it. Charity walked around and took it all in. The business card that described him as a "specialist in orthopedic medicine." That's what doctors called themselves when they weren't actually trained as orthopedists. The contents of cupboards and drawers. She found these thick four-inch needles Thomashefsky used to inject the plasma into people's joints. She saw that he wasn't relying entirely on painkillers but putting patients under with full-on anesthesia, without tracking their vital signs. On the sink in the room where he performed procedures lay the doctor's toothbrush and toothpaste. The fridge in which the patients' blood was stored also contained the doctor's lunch.

Charity asked the doctor's receptionist if there were other employees, and she replied that, no, it was just her and the doctor, and that she did other stuff in addition to sitting behind the front desk. Charity asked her to demonstrate what that other stuff might be. The young woman explained, for example, how she used the centrifuge to spin the patients' blood. "Show me," Charity said, and the young woman walked over, removed a vial of blood from the fridge, and used the centrifuge. Charity saw that Thomashefsky had the ability to treat two patients at a time, which meant that his receptionist might need to remove two vials from the fridge at the same time.

How do you keep track of which vial goes with which patient? she asked.

Oh, I just put them on different sides of the sink and then I remember, said the young woman.

The vials of blood she'd removed from the fridge were undated. As the receptionist handled the specimens, Charity noticed that she hadn't donned gloves. She asked the young woman about her education. She didn't have a medical license, the woman admitted. But she was a beautician.

Charity then asked Dr. Thomashefsky if she could observe him while he treated a patient. He'd be on his best behavior, she knew, but she also thought doctors, especially older doctors, had trouble hiding who they were. "Doctors get into habits in the way they flick their wrists. How they turn, how they spread things out on a table." This doctor didn't wash his hands or use gloves. As he worked, she saw that he had no clear rules about where he put things: dirty vials and syringes wound up on the same table as the clean ones. "In surgery you always have a clean area and a dirty area," she said. "He just mixed it all together." When she pushed him on this, he said, still cheerily, that he had been doing things this way for thirty years.

Preventing infection was all about creating barriers: between patients; between dirty needles and clean ones; between work spaces and life spaces. That's why all the rules existed, but the doctor was following none of them. "There's a culture of infection prevention that he had missed entirely," said Charity. The most likely source of infection, she thought, was a contaminated vial, but really the problem could be anywhere. Charity knew how to run a centrifuge, and it was tricky. If the beautician didn't balance the liquids just so, the centrifuge could become contaminated. "I thought, Oh my God, he may have been infecting people for thirty years," said Charity. "I thought, If these are the things I am seeing when they knew I was coming, what are the things I'm not seeing? At that moment I wasn't worried about hep C. Hep C was the least of my worries. I was worried about HIV."

Paige Batson, public-health nurse, watched all this with interest, as she'd never seen anything quite like it before. She watched Dr. Dean tell this important doctor, on the spot, that she was issuing a health order to shut him down. What struck her was the total absence of apology or hesitation in Dr. Dean's voice. "You know how some people kind of look away when there's conflict," she said. "She doesn't do that. It's straight eye contact, and very direct. 'Effective today, you're closed. Here's what we need to do.'" The two women then drove together back to the office, where Dr. Dean called the chief counsel of Santa Barbara County to let him know what she had just done— and that he should maybe expect a shitstorm from the doctor's important patients. Then she asked Paige to take the list they had removed from the doctor's office, of the several thousand people he had treated over the prior eighteen months, and mail a letter to each of them, to let them know that they might have been infected with hepatitis C, and that the county would pay to have them tested.

At which point Charity needed to let the California Department of Public Health and the Centers for Disease Control in Atlanta know what she'd done. That was the moment she sensed just how far out on a limb she had climbed. "The CDC was aghast," she said. "They were aghast that I hadn't asked their opinion. They said no local health officer in the history of local health officers has ever issued an order to close down a doctor's office based on a suspicion." They tried to argue that, as a mere local health officer, she lacked the authority to close a doctor's practice. Charity didn't understand, first, that the CDC could not know just how broad her authority was—but then she too had only just learned that the power in most of the rest of the United States resided with the state health officer rather than the local ones. California was unusual in having conferred on its county health officers the same powers that, say, Texas and Mississippi reserved for their state health officers. Yet even after the CDC people conceded her authority, they refused to condone how she'd used it. "They told me that if I'm wrong I'm going to get fired," she said.

That threat actually wasn't all that original. As Kat DeBurgh, head of the Health Officers Association of California, put it, "To do the job of local public-health officer, you basically always need to be willing to lose your job." To be a public-health officer—to really own the role—you needed to be prepared for your only appearance on the front page of the local newspaper to be in a story about a call you got wrong. That might be the only time anyone ever looked up and noticed who you were: the moment they chopped off your head.

Apart from the uninsured poor she treated in the clinics and homeless shelters, few citizens had any clue what Charity did—until she did something that infuriated them. "Rich white people would look at me like I was a relic from the past when I explained my role," she said. "Like they'd stumbled across a candelabra from the *Titanic*. How lovely—but what does one need it for today?" The illness you prevented, and the lives you saved, went unnoticed by the people sitting on top of society. That's why her role was, every year, less well funded than the year before. The fax machine was the new tech in the office that still kept its records on paper and filed the paper in red manila envelopes. "If I wanted to send a letter, I needed to fill out a form, and the form had to be approved—all to use a county-funded stamp," said Charity. "I was the county health officer, and I wasn't allowed to use a stamp. But that's okay! I learned to live within the system."

That system was the front line of defense against disease, not just in the county but in the whole country. Seventy percent of Santa Barbara's cases of communicable disease came through one of its five public-health clinics, overseen by the health officer. The math was the same everywhere. But because people who had health insurance thought it had nothing to do with them—that it was just *government*—the society had starved the system of resources. "People don't realize what it is until something bad happens," said Charity. "It's protecting the entire society, the whole economy." The economy, for its part, understood her role only in its own narrow financial terms. "I learned the way to make the argument to elected officials for money for disease control was not 'It is the right thing to do to take care of the most vulnerable in our community,'" she said. "Rather, make the case of the dollar return on investment to prevent the disease from spilling over into the rest of the community." Yet even then—even after she showed a return—the investment often went unmade. It had taken *years* to get the money to buy a machine that allowed her to test quickly for tuberculosis, and to prevent some number of new cases. "The cost of a single TB case is between thirty and a hundred thousand dollars," she said. "Higher if it is drug-resistant TB. So why are we haggling over a seventy-two-thousand-dollar machine?"

She'd grown used to the lack of material support. But in her investigation of the Thomashefsky clinic, the total absence of moral and practical support from the state and federal governments mystified her. "I kept waiting for the feds—the CDC, maybe the FDA—to say, 'Dr. Dean, we got this.' And no one ever said that." On the other hand, she had to admit that this wasn't a smallpox outbreak. The Thomashefsky clinic wasn't going to cripple society. The situation was entirely ignorable: a doctor to the rich and famous and a single case of hep C. If she were wrong, they'd have to fire her. Hell, if she were wrong, *she* would fire herself. "I was like, 'Fuck, I don't have to be doing this. I leaned too far forward this time.' "

The odd thing about it, to Charity, was how docile Dr. Thomashefsky had been, from the moment she'd turned up. It was as if he had been waiting for her. She returned twice more to the shuttered stem cell clinic, to poke around and see if there was anything she had missed. "I was terrified that I would not find the things I needed," she said, "and if I didn't find it there would be twenty more cases of something out there." On her subsequent trips to the clinic, she discovered that Thomashefsky was prescribing Versed—one of the drugs that killed Michael Jackson—and that he was making house calls to inject it into rich old ladies in the hills. She found a great many more multidose vials of medicine than the doctor claimed to have used. She figured out that when the doctor used one of his multidose vials of painkiller on different patients, he changed the needle but not the syringe—and to prevent the spread of disease you needed to change both. She found that Dr. Thomashefsky had a second clinic, in Oregon, in which he performed the same procedures. Behind a door, which she had at first assumed led to a closet, she found a bedroom, which clearly had served as both a recovery room for patients and a crash pad for the doctor. And she learned that the cold young receptionist and beautician was actually the doctor's daughter.

It took a few months for the test results to arrive. When they finally did, four more of Thomashefsky's patients were found to have been infected with hepatitis C. All had been treated by the doctor on a single day, September 4, 2014. None of them knew each other, but their new virus shared the same genome, which proved they'd all been infected by the same source. The culprit turned out to be a single syringe the doctor had used on all the patients. Charity expected the state medical board to dig deeper. They never did. "I called them and said, 'We thought you were launching an investigation.' They said, 'We are. But it consists of you telling us what you've found.' " The subsequent report by the Medical Board of California explained that Dr. Thomashefsky had violated a great many standard operating procedures. The state of California stripped him of his license to practice medicine, and he eventually was asked to close his practice in Oregon. With that, his career in medicine ended.

By then Charity Dean knew that, in her quest to stop the spread of disease, she was more or less on her own. She had her friends and allies. The public-health nurses, for example, who were among the more impressive human beings she had ever known. She was also growing to adore Santa Barbara's chief counsel, who kept handing her enough rope to hang herself, by confirming that, yes, the law allowed her to do whatever the hell she thought needed doing to protect the public. She felt a deep connection to the fifty-seven other California county health officers—though they were, she had to admit, a mixed bag. Some were ancient doctors who viewed the job as a sinecure; some were part-timers who didn't even seem all that interested in the job. "There's no defined career path to becoming a public-health officer, and that's a problem," she said. "You get the retired anesthesiologist who is spending most of his time as a professional dog breeder." But some of her fellow local health officers, like Charity herself, were so deeply committed to the job that they experienced it more as a mission. These people she loved best. But their needs and issues were too diverse for them to function as a single, powerful unit. And they weren't in a position to have her back in a crisis.

The larger apparatus of American public health was very different on the inside from how Charity had imagined it from the outside. The Centers for Disease Control, the apex authority, wasn't of much practical use to her. The distance they had put between themselves and her when she closed Thomashefsky's clinic was of a piece with their general behavior. She'd repeatedly seen the tendency to flee when conflict arose.

At the end of 2013, for instance, as she was promoted to chief health officer, she had a call from a local hospital saying that a nineteen-year-old student-athlete at the University of California–Santa Barbara had just been brought in by friends with symptoms of meningitis B. He was now in the intensive care unit in a state of shock. The disease was rare but still terrified student health doctors, as it attacked healthy young people and could kill them in hours. "It's one of the most feared diseases for student health doctors," said Mary Ferris, UCSB's medical director. "We knew right then people's lives were at risk." No one knew exactly all the ways the disease might spread, though one known path was through saliva. There was no agreement on what actions to take on a college campus in the event of an outbreak. "We spoke with the CDC and asked them what to do," said Dr. Ferris. "But the CDC initially wasn't too impressed. We rely on them for advice on what to do. And their advice was to do nothing."

The initial problem was that there was no clear diagnosis. The attending physician in that first possible case was none other than Dr. Stephen Hosea, who had taught Charity Dean much of what she knew about diagnosing disease. The young man's legs, Dr. Hosea told her, were purple. But the lab test of the young man's blood and spinal fluid had come back negative for meningitis B, and essentially eliminated the possibility that he was carrying a dangerous communicable disease. Diagnosing an infectious disease is like following a path, with clues along the way. The Gram stain—the test that came back negative for meningitis—was the first clue: it told you in which of two big buckets the bacteria you were dealing with belonged. "It's very reliable," said Charity. "And it's hard to fuck it up." But at the same time, Dr. Hosea said he was standing there looking at the mottled purple legs of the young man. To stop the infection from moving farther up his body, he could already see, they'd need to amputate both legs.

What do you think? she asked him.

What do you *think?* he asked back, which threw her. She couldn't figure out if he was testing her, the way he'd done when she was his student, or treating her as a colleague.

I think the Gram stain is wrong, she said.

As it happened, he'd already asked the lab how often the Gram stain had been wrong, and they had said never. But the Gram stain was to him mainly of academic interest. He was already treating the young man for meningitis B, just in case.

I know what it means for me to ignore the lab report and assume it is meningitis B, he said. *And it's very different from what it means for you.* In other words, a misdiagnosis carried no professional risk for him. For her, the risk was massive.

What do you think? she asked again.

I think the Gram stain is wrong, too, he said.

The Gram stain was indeed wrong—but that would take a day and a half to figure out. They didn't have time to wait for another test. If one kid had the disease, others surely did, too. If six kids had it today, twelve kids might be infected the following week. And if twelve had it next week, twenty-four might have it the week after. And if . . . well, it wasn't long before she'd have an epidemic on her hands. "I knew I had to stay ahead of it," said Charity. "Because ninety percent of the battle is in the first few days. But in the beginning it's always quiet, and you are quietly making decisions, and you're a nut job."

And so the intervening calls with the CDC were maddening but, she soon learned, always the same. An email would go out to set up the call, and there would be twenty people inside the CDC copied on it. The email addresses were people's initials, so she never knew most of their names. On the call itself, she'd find herself talking to the CDC's resident expert on meningitis outbreaks—with a dozen or more others on the line. "It's very eerie," she said. "It feels like it's a movie, and you think you're in a one-on-one conversation, but there's a wall that's two-way glass with twenty other people lurking behind it. It was almost like he was playing a role for the twenty people behind the glass." After each call she'd go online and look up the CDC org chart, to try to figure out who these people were and which division they were in, but she couldn't find them anywhere. They were an invisible mob inside an ivory tower. The calls themselves irritated rather than informed her. "They'd do mental masturbation," said Charity. "Mental masturbation is actually an important concept. It's when you talk in circles for an hour and reach no decision. But at the end of these sessions I had to make a decision."

The first decision was to scour the student population for cases that had gone undetected. Charity instructed the Santa Barbara medical community to test any young person who turned up with a low-grade fever. "It's not those people with mild symptoms you worry about," she said. "It's the people they infect, and the exponential growth." As the CDC dithered, three more UCSB students tested positive for meningococcal disease. Each case presented differently. One student, with only a rash, had been diagnosed initially with chicken pox; the other two had slight fevers and had been initially misdiagnosed as having nothing special. "None of them lived together," recalled Dr. Ferris, UCSB's medical director. "It was really sort of hard to understand why we had these random cases." Within days the school had set up hotlines to field calls from panicked parents, along with complaints from citizens of Santa Barbara who thought that the school's twenty thousand students should be confined to their rooms.

Charity stayed up nights staring at the whiteboards in her office, on which she had charted the social relationships of the infected UCSB students. At the top of the board she had written "Cross-Pollination," a term of art she'd picked up from Dr. Hosea. "It's when you don't want to say 'he had sex with her' and what kind of sex they had," she said. "But I was basically trying to figure out who had shared saliva with whom, and where they'd shared it." All signs pointed to the Greek system. She decided to shut down the college sororities and fraternities and give the twelve hundred students in them a prophylactic drug. "With meningitis B you have a very narrow window to give the prophylaxis," she explained, "and it was a weekend. You had to do it fast and all at once, or else the pathogen just keeps circulating."

She got on the phone with the main guy at the CDC and his silent crowd. The guy strongly disagreed with her doing anything. "What he actually said," recalled Charity, "was, 'That decision is not supported by the data.' I said, 'Oh, really—there *is* no data.'" She outlined a plan she'd created: thin out the dorms by moving some of the students into hotel rooms; shut down the intramural sports teams; and administer a vaccine that had been approved in Europe but that the FDA had not yet signed off on. "The CDC guy said, 'We're not going to do any of that, and if you do that, we're going to put it in writing that it was your decision and we disagreed with it,'" Charity recalled.

There followed other calls with the CDC, each more dismissive of her than the last. After one of them, Paige Batson turned to her boss and said, "Dr. Dean, I've never heard anyone at the CDC speak to someone like that!" But in the end the campus ignored the CDC and did everything Dr. Dean recommended. "It was kind of a stern order," said Dr. Ferris, "and it had never been done before. But after she stopped all the parties and administered the prophylaxis, we had no more cases." From start to finish, what Dr. Ferris and everyone noticed was that, as Dr. Ferris put it, "the CDC wasn't pleased with her. The CDC kept saying, 'There is no evidence to back it up.' They didn't have any evidence, because there is only one case every four years."

The root of the CDC's behavior was simple: fear. They didn't want to take any action for which they might later be blamed. "The message they send is, We're better than you and smarter than you, but we're letting you stick your neck out to take the risk," said Charity. "They would argue with me about how kids behave in fraternities and sororities. And I had been president of Kappa Delta!" In the middle of the crisis, Charity figured out what it would take to appease the nation's highest authority on infectious disease. "It was when they said, 'If any of this works, you won't know which one worked,'" she recalled. "They said, 'You need to do these things one at a time and gather evidence.' They wanted to learn from this meningitis outbreak, and I wanted to stop it. My goal was to stop it, and that was not their goal. They wanted to observe it as if it were a science experiment on how meningitis moves through a college campus. And I was like, 'Are you kidding me: a kid just lost his feet.'"

Charity never would know which of the measures she took

had controlled the disease; she knew only that all of them together had. To her, all that really mattered was that the disease had been contained. The job of the public-health officer— or at least *her* job as the public-health officer—was a series of intense firefights. There was no standard operating procedure for many of the situations in which she found herself: usually, they were sufficiently different from anything that had ever before happened. If she waited until she had enough evidence to publish in a scientific journal, the battle would be over, and she'd have lost. Kids would lose limbs, or die. The decisions she was forced to make were less like, say, those made by a card counter at a blackjack table, and more like the ones made by a platoon leader in combat. She never had all the data she wanted or needed when making her decisions—enough so that afterward she could defend them by saying, "I just did what the numbers told me to do."

The hard truth was that there was never time to wait for more data. The moment an infectious disease appeared, decisions cried out to be made. The longer you waited, the more likely it was that people would die waiting for you to decide—or waiting for you to gather the data you needed to cover your ass if your decisions proved wrong.

Two years after the UCSB meningitis outbreak, the CDC finally published a report on how to deal with a meningitis outbreak on a college campus. On its list of best practices were most of the things Charity had done at UCSB. After that, from time to time, someone would call her from the CDC and ask her if she'd please get on the phone with some college health officer somewhere in the United States and describe how she handled the UCSB outbreak. But by then Charity had washed her hands of the CDC. "I banned their officers from my investigations," she said. The CDC did many things. It published learned papers on health crises, after the fact. It managed, very carefully, public perception of itself. But when the shooting started, it leapt into the nearest hole, while others took fire. "In the end I was like, 'Fuck you,' " said Charity. "I was mad they were such pansies. I was mad that the man behind the curtain ended up being so disappointing."

In theory, the CDC sat atop the system of infectious-disease management in the United States. In practice, the system had configured itself to foist the political risk onto a character who had no social power. It required a local health officer to take the risk and responsibility, as no one else wanted to. Charity could see that the CDC's strategy was politically shrewd. People were far less likely to blame a health officer for what she didn't do than what she did. Sins of commission got you fired. Sins of omission you could get away with, but they left people dead. The health officer's job was to choose, all by herself, the direction in which to err: do too much, or too little? "I did not sign up to be that kind of brave," said Charity. "That wasn't my plan. I was always saying to the CDC, 'This is your job! Do your job!' But after the UCSB outbreak, my motto was, 'Stop waiting for someone to come and save you. Because no one is coming to save you.' "

*

Paige Batson could not spend seven years playing Watson to her boss's Holmes without being at least dimly aware of how much of her boss remained an unsolved mystery. The year after she'd arrived in the public-health office, back in 2012, Dr. Dean had left her husband—a Santa Barbara surgeon who had wanted her to quit to be a stay-at-home mom. Dr. Dean would refer to her private life as a "dumpster fire," and Paige sensed that was just a way for her to put it all in a box, to be stored. There was a void inside her boss, she thought. Yet somehow, in the midst of everything, she was raising three boys while working eighty-hour weeks. "She was on call 24/7," said Paige. "She'd take calls at two in the morning telling her that a man with four-plus tuberculosis had just been released from county jail." (The number was a measure of infectiousness.) In the end, Paige decided that it wasn't really her place to intrude upon Dr. Dean's private life, as she herself never allowed that life to intrude upon their work. "There was never a blip," she said. "Wherever she parked it all, she parked it all."

The big thing about her boss, Paige thought, was that an American public-health officer, at some risk to herself, had taken the job of protecting the public's health as seriously as it had ever been taken.

The Montecito mudslide was the final case in point. It was one of those Book of Job–like events in which Santa Barbara County specialized. On December 7, 2017, a fire swept down from Ventura County. It grew big enough to earn its own name: the Thomas fire. Then it grew even bigger, into the largest wildfire in the recorded history of California. In the dead of winter, in a county of less than half a million people, more than a hundred thousand people had to be evacuated. The ash that fell in downtown Santa Barbara was not the light dusting they usually got. It rose above the street curbs. It became dangerous to breathe, and impossible to tell what colors the cars had been. When the county's emergency response team went looking for a precedent for how to deal with the volume of ash, the only one they could find was the eruption of the Mount St. Helens volcano back in 1980.

But the Thomas fire was just the opening act. It burned the vegetation in the Santa Ynez Mountains, above the town of Montecito, so there was nothing to grip the soil and rock. The National Weather Service forecast for January 8, 2018, was for heavy rain. A team from the federal government created a forecast for a possible landslide. The county issued a mandatory evacuation of the hills around Highway 192, the road on which Oprah lived, and where Ellen was buying. The houses were huge, many of them second homes of the distant rich.

Matt Pontes saw right away how hard it was to persuade people that the mountain in the distance might more or less collapse on them. Pontes had been a firefighter in the U.S. Forest Service until he blew out his knees one too many times, after which he'd gone into emergency response. When 2018 came around, he was assistant CEO of Santa Barbara County, and dealing with a problem that didn't arise from wildfire. Californians had experienced wildfire; often they could actually see it coming. When a fire was bearing down on them, you didn't need to holler at people to get them to evacuate. This was a different beast. People had never seen a mudslide, and in truth the event was hard to imagine. "It's blue skies," said Pontes. "It's something that's never happened before, at least not in memory. It was, 'Hey, something's coming. It's not a fire. We got to get you out of here.' And they said no."

The storm on January 8 was even worse than the forecast had led residents to believe it might be. It rained more than half an inch inside of five minutes, and an inch and a half in a single hour. Around three in the morning of January 9, the mountain that looms over Montecito in effect melted and rushed down upon the town. The water and mud moved at such speed that boulders the size of automobiles skipped along their surface. Cars parked up in the hills were caught and dragged down for miles until finally deposited in the ocean. Over the next week or so, first responders dug out twenty-three bodies from the mud. Two were never found. Some of the dead were never honestly counted, including the bodies of old people found weeks later, still in their armchairs, depleted oxygen tanks beside them.

The mudslide forecast proved incredibly prescient: the mountain moved exactly as the experts had predicted. "It could not have been more accurate if they had cheated," said Charity. Her first job, she realized, was to figure out what was in the mud. Over Christmas break, before the big rains came, she'd declared a public-health emergency, to enable crews to go onto the private property of the absent rich and clear the debris from the fire. "There is this hazardous pile of toxic goop. You have just set all the chemicals in your garage on fire. Now you are about to put a hose on it and spread it into the waterways." The cleanup crews made only a dent in the mess before the rains, and now the mess was everywhere. "I needed to know what microbial pathogens are there—to know which vaccines do you give the first responders and utility workers." No one seemed to have any idea. She tried to educate herself. "No one had ever published anything on wading through mud in an urban setting," she said. "It's so rare." The federal and state governments were now helping with the response, and the director of the California Department of Public Health, Dr. Karen Smith, suggested that Charity try to figure out what was in the mud on her own. "So I said, 'Okay, I'm gonna make a list. I'm going to guess what's out there." She started with the likely bacteria (*E. coli*, *Clostridium tetani*—the cause of tetanus), before moving on to viruses, like hepatitis B, and, finally, other single-cell organisms. "The one that really scared me was *Vibrio cholerae*," she said. "This was a ripe setting for cholera."

She tracked rashes. When first responders came off their shifts, she'd pull up the legs of their pants and inspect their skin. "That's the only way to know what diseases they might be coming back with," she said. "We had no surveillance system. I *was* the surveillance system—seeing what disease emerged from the muck." She went on local television to tell anyone with a rash to call her. What turned up she first mistook for chemical burns. Then she figured it out: the oil from poison oak had mixed with liquid and blended into the mud. They ended up giving it its own name: the Montecito rash.

By then almost everyone in Montecito had cleared out. However, for some reason Charity could not fathom, people were still wandering around Casa Dorinda. Casa Dorinda was a rich person's old-age home. Julia Child famously had ended her days there. Now it was the sort of place to which billionaires sent their mothers. A second big storm was about to hit. The same forecasters who had predicted with such fantastic accuracy where mud would flow the first time around thought the most likely path of the next mudslide was right through Casa Dorinda. And no one was doing anything about it.

Late one afternoon, a week after the mudslide, Charity drove up as close to Casa Dorinda as she could. She had brought with her another doctor ("to check my judgment") and the county counsel ("because I didn't want there to be two versions of the conversation"). What she really needed was a map and a compass. She had a terrible sense of direction and was forced to guess where she was going. Street signs had vanished, along with the streets. She drove as far as she could and then parked and walked through the mud. The sights were shocking; the video she and everyone else had seen, taken from helicopters, didn't do justice to the destruction. "It looked like a war zone." A tsunami of rushing mud, in places fifteen feet high, had taken out massive homes. A few of them hung from trees. Giant septic tanks littered the ground, like fallen fruit. The doors of the houses in which bodies had been found were marked with a red X.

The mud was the most incredible thing: what would turn out to be 4.5 million wheelbarrows of toxic debris wasn't simply going to be returned to the mountain. She realized that she'd need to help them figure out the safest place to put it, and that people wouldn't like the answer. "The public-health officer is like the garbage disposal," she said. "Whatever issue can't be filed into someone else's box or slot winds up in the health officer's."

Casa Dorinda itself sat in the middle of the devastation. At the gates outside, the first responders were extracting a body from the mud. But on the other side of those gates was a sight Charity couldn't believe. Hundreds of people, many of them ancient, carried on as if nothing had happened. Their garden was pristine. The mud from the first slide had missed the fancy old-age home. It was as if their money acted as a magic bubble. "I'm thinking, Shoot, I'm wrong," said Charity. "This place looks perfectly preserved. I've overreacted."

Then the sun went down. She watched as Casa Dorinda went dark. It had no power. "I get up to the door and they have camp light," Charity recalled. "They had one backup generator and were using the swimming pool for drinking water." When she found the medical director and asked what he thought he was doing, he said that some of the residents were too frail to be moved. The math, to Charity, wasn't complicated. The forecasters put the chance of another mudslide wiping out the place, and the hundred or so people inside, at 20 percent. The medical director estimated that there was a 100 percent chance that five of the residents would die if forced to evacuate. It was like that famous problem taught to college freshmen in ethics classes across the country. You, college freshman, are driving a train. Ahead on the tracks you spot five people. Do nothing and the train will run them over and kill them. But you have an option! You can flip a switch and send the train onto a siding, on which, unfortunately, there stands a man named Carl. Do nothing and you kill five people; flip the switch and you kill Carl. Most college freshmen elect to kill Carl and then, *wham*, the professor hits them with the follow-up. Carl has five healthy organs that can be harvested and used to save the lives of five people in need of them. All you need to do is shoot Carl in the back of the head. Would you do that, too? If not, explain the contradiction . . .

It can take a week for a college ethics class to sort through that one. Inside Casa Dorinda, Charity had thirty minutes. "I knew what I had to do," she said. "I didn't want to do it. I was asking myself: Is there any way out of this?" The answer came back: no. She looked around and found that the fire sprinklers didn't work—and that alone, she told the medical director, was grounds for shutting the place down. "I told them, 'We can do this the easy way or the hard way,'" said Charity. "They were very upset, but they decided to do it voluntarily. Sure enough, there were seven deaths. Their medical director sent me a scathing email saying, 'Their deaths are on you.' He was right." The second mudslide never came.

A lot of people were now watching her. One of them was the guy running the disaster response. "I thought, Where in the world did she come from?" said Matt Pontes. "She was just different." She was especially different from anyone he'd known in government. "Her receptors were just very keen," said Pontes, "and she processes information fast and it spits out decisions and it makes people get nervous. And it makes government people *really* nervous. You don't find people like her in government. It felt almost like an accident that she was there." She'd made the right decision to evacuate Casa Dorinda, he thought, but it was a decision that she could have avoided if she had wanted to. "There are two ways to be a health officer," he said. "One is to pretend it's not happening. She didn't do that."

Someone else who'd become a Charity Dean watcher was Dr. Karen Smith. After the mudslide, she called Charity to ask if she'd move to Sacramento to serve as her deputy at the state Department of Public Health. "There needed to be another person who can step in as the state's health officer if I get hit by a bus," Dr. Smith said later, "and it was clearly her." Charity, at forty, was a generation younger than Smith, and young for the job. It paid fifty thousand dollars less than she was now making—and never mind the seventy-two thousand dollars in student loan forgiveness she'd be putting at risk. And the offer took her by surprise.

Why me? she asked Dr. Smith.

Because you make decisions, said the doctor.

The deeper why of it all went unexplored. Why did she make decisions? Why had she self-consciously cultivated the ability to do it? She'd long ago stopped telling people why she did what she did for a living—or at any rate she didn't tell them the whole story. Something was coming: she felt it. She'd obsessed about it since childhood and had learned not to talk about it, because other people thought she was kooky when she did. But as she drove into Sacramento, one subject was at the front of her mind. And not long after she arrived, toward the end of 2018, a journalist asked her about it. "What scares me most and what I think about most," said Charity, "is our ability to respond to a new pathogen, maybe one we've never seen before, or an old pathogen, like influenza that's just mutated. The H1N1 pandemic of 1918 was over 100 years ago now. The world is overdue for a pandemic like that, whether it's influenza or something else. And in public health, we know that we have to be prepared for that."

THREE

The Pandemic Thinker

As it happened, the United States of America had a plan to fight a pandemic. The first draft had been written back in October 2005, by a man named Rajeev Venkayya, in the basement of his parents' house in Xenia, Ohio. He'd given himself just a weekend to write it, but even that felt to him like too much. The president was waiting, and not patiently.

The story of how the United States more or less invented pandemic planning began when George W. Bush, in the summer of 2005, read a book. Written the year before, it was the same volume that had dropped Bob Glass's jaw: John Barry's *The Great Influenza: The Story of the Deadliest Pandemic in History*. Bush was the modern president perhaps most frequently reminded that freakishly terrible events can and do happen. He presided over the deadliest ever attack on American soil and the deadliest American natural disaster in a century. Hurricane Katrina was still in his thoughts, and on his daily schedule, when he picked up Barry's account of the 1918 Spanish flu. Inside of eighteen months, a virus had killed somewhere between forty and sixty million people around the world, but Barry focused on the American carnage. At least half a million Americans, most of them young, had died. A similar culling of the far larger population in 2005 would kill a million and a half Americans. If anything like Barry described were to occur again, it would distort American life in the most fantastic ways, and leave it forever changed.

Bush returned to the White House from his summer vacation with a new interest in pandemics. His concern led to a meeting in the Oval Office, on October 14, 2005, to which Rajeev Venkayya was invited. Though he was the junior person in the room, Rajeev's medical training had invested him with a nebulous authority—which was funny, as he'd never really wanted to be a doctor but had let his father talk him into going to med school. "Even during school I know I'm not going to sit in an office seeing patients," said Rajeev. "I'm not going to be in a lab. I knew I wanted to do something bigger. I just didn't know what that was." In the end he'd used his medical degree as a ticket to the border of medicine and government. He'd landed a White House Fellowship back in 2002, at the age of thirty-five, and then worked his way into an obscure unit of the Homeland Security Council that dealt with biological threats to the American people. The Biodefense Directorate, it was weirdly called. In the summer of 2005 he'd been named the unit's head.

The Homeland Security Council was staffed mainly by military types who spent their days imagining and preparing for attacks by hostile foreigners. Even the Biodefense Directorate was mainly consumed by anthrax and ricin, and fantasies of terrorists injecting themselves with smallpox and then wandering around the United States infecting people. There was neither status in nor congressional funding for worrying about the flu. "The hard-core biodefense types didn't like to talk about it because it isn't interesting to them," said Rajeev. "H5N1 [a flu strain] appears in poultry in Hong Kong. Who the fuck wants to talk about chickens?"

Even at the time, the distribution of worry struck Rajeev as a bit odd. In 2003, a new strain of flu found in geese and other migratory birds had jumped into 120 humans and killed half of them. Migratory birds migrated. That same year, a new coronavirus had moved, probably from an animal called a masked palm civet, into humans, infecting eight thousand people and killing eight hundred. A mutation here or a mutation there, and either one of these viruses could have wreaked havoc on American life. Yet in national security policy circles the threats posed by nature remained someone else's problem. Then Bush read John Barry's book, and asked, *What's our strategy?* "We didn't have a strategy," said Rajeev.

Instead they had an unsatisfying document. Recently generated by the Department of Health and Human Services, it laid out plans, in the event of a pandemic, to speed up the production of vaccines and stockpile antiviral drugs. That was the reason for the Oval Office meeting: Bush had read it and hated it. "The president said, 'This is bullshit,'" Rajeev recalled. "'It's just health. We need a whole-of-society plan. What are you going to do about foreign borders? And travel? And commerce?'" And how were you going to stop hundreds of thousands of Americans from dying while they waited for even a speeded-up vaccine? If anything like the 1918 flu occurred, the basic functions of the society would come to a halt, and no one in the federal government seemed to have worried about it. "The point," said Rajeev, "was that the president was pissed." At the end of the meeting, Fran Townsend, the homeland security adviser, told President Bush that they'd have a plan for him in two weeks.

It was new and a bit odd for the White House to put itself in charge of creating a new strategy for disease control, especially as there was an entire federal agency down in Atlanta called the

Centers for Disease Control. "The CDC was frustrated," said Rajeev. Plus it was not at all clear what the new plan might be. Various White House staffers with various ideas sat down and tossed them around. "We wasted the first week," said Rajeev. "It was smart people trying to create the thing by consensus. You can't write a strategy by committee." He decided he'd just take the notes he'd made in the White House meetings with him back to his parents' house in Ohio and write it himself. The house was on the seventh fairway of the Country Club of the North. But for the occasional golf ball crashing through his parents' living room window, he'd have peace and quiet. "I wrote the whole thing in six hours on Friday night," he said.

The federal government had a well-earned reputation for moving slowly. Rajeev marveled at just how fast it could move—when the president was pissed. He returned from his parents' house on October 23, 2005. Five days later, all of the cabinet secretaries had signed off on his twelve-page document. Four days after that, on November 1, Bush gave a speech at the National Institutes of Health, announcing the new strategy. It had three parts to it: to detect outbreaks overseas so they might remain there; to stockpile vaccines and antiviral drugs; and, finally, to "be ready to respond at the federal, state and local levels in the event that a pandemic reaches our shores." Whatever that meant. Bush did not elaborate much, because Rajeev hadn't, either. The twelve pages he'd written on his own amounted less to a plan than a plan to have a plan. "It was written for an audience of one: the president," said Rajeev. "To get the president off the ledge."

Eleven days after Rajeev sat down in his parents' basement, Bush asked the U.S. Congress for $7.1 billion to spend on his three-part pandemic strategy, and Congress gave it to him. To staffers on the U.S. House Appropriations Committee, John Barry's *The Great Influenza* became known as "the seven-billion-dollar book."* But the book offered no advice about what to do with the seven billion dollars. The book, truth be told, left the reader feeling that there was little that might have been done to prevent all those people from dying. But the memo that Rajeev had bashed out in his parents' basement was vague enough to allow the White House to do whatever it wanted, and now he had seven billion dollars with which to do it. "The plan gives you cover to do all sorts of things," said Rajeev. "It gave us license to go and figure things out."

The whole enterprise felt not just new but audacious. "The United States took this on as a national priority before anyone in the world," said Rajeev. "We want to use all instruments of national power to confront this threat. We were going to invent pandemic planning." Yet he was still more or less on his own. And he needed to produce an actual plan, one that explained what exactly needed to be done and who was going to do it. He asked for and was given permission to hire seven people, from relevant federal agencies, to help.

His first pick was Richard Hatchett, another doctor who had stopped treating patients and moved into government service. Richard belonged to a dying species: the romantic southern man of letters who travels north and there makes an uneasy

---

* The first John Barry heard of any of this was when Bush was asked at a press conference in September 2005 what he'd done with his summer vacation, and he mentioned reading Barry's book. Barry later learned that Stewart Simonson, a senior aide to Mike Leavitt, the newly appointed secretary of the Department of Health and Human Services, had handed his boss the book and said, "When we have a pandemic, there's going to be a 9/11 Report, and you're going to be the bad guy in it. So you'd better read this." Leavitt had read it and asked Simonson for fifty copies, marked up to highlight the important bits, one of which he gave to Bush. "It was an inflection point," said Simonson. "Up till then there was no money for this. People would say, 'Oh, it's just the flu.'" To this day, Barry has never heard from Bush.

home for himself. He'd grown up in Daphne, Alabama, and in 1985 had gone off to Vanderbilt University, where his poetry caught the eye of the eminent poets in residence Donald Davie and Mark Jarman. They'd picked him to represent Vanderbilt at a national collegiate poetry competition, in which he finished second. A judge, the future Pulitzer Prize—winning Irish poet Paul Muldoon, singled out one of his poems as the work of a young poet of promise. When asked why, instead of pursuing a career as a poet, he had gone to medical school, Richard would say simply, "Writing is too hard."

In September 2001, he was working in the emergency room at Memorial Sloan Kettering Cancer Center, in New York City, and preparing to start a fellowship in oncology. On September 11, he moved to a field hospital that arose spontaneously in Stuyvesant High School, where he ran triage for the rescue workers at Ground Zero. Years later he wrote a letter to his newborn son describing the feelings of that moment.

> What positive I remember about that day and the weeks that followed was the profound social cohesion and solidarity of communities and the desire of individuals to serve and contribute. That sounds, superficially, like patriotism and in a sense it is patriotism of the best sort but in fact, at least for me, it was more complex than that. What we experienced had more to do with communities coming together than it did with a sense of national identity. It had more in common with the social cohesion that occurs after a tornado or hurricane, at least for the first few days, than it did with the nationalism of people at war.

The call for doctors and nurses after the 9/11 attacks struck Richard as so haphazard that afterward he wrote a crisp memo to the people who ran the Alfred P. Sloan Foundation, arguing that they should use whatever political clout they had to push for a national medical reserve corps. A week or so later, a nurse interrupted him while he was dealing with a fever in a patient on chemotherapy. Someone was on the phone and insisting on speaking with him personally. Richard was irritated, as fever could kill you when your blood count was low.

"This is Noreen Hynes, from the vice president's office," said the voice on the other end of the line.

"How can I help you?" bristled Richard, while thinking, *Vice president? Vice president of what?*

"General Lawlor has read your medical proposal," she said.*

It took Richard a moment to realize. "Oh, Vice President *Cheney*," he said.

"There's another vice president?" she asked.

The people at the foundation, without telling him, had sent his memo to someone in Washington, who had sent it to someone else, and so on, until it reached the White House. In his 2002 State of the Union address, President Bush would call for the creation of a reserve medical corps. Richard would move to Washington to help set it up inside the Department of Health and Human Services. By the time they'd finished, the medical reserve corps had one hundred offices and two hundred thousand medical volunteers.

In the bargain, Richard entered the subculture of federal emergency response. A pair of recent events had pushed the threat of bioterrorism to the front of the minds of the people who worked in and around national security. One was the series of anthrax attacks on Capitol Hill in October 2001; the other was an exercise conducted a few months before those attacks,

---

* General Bruce Lawlor, a member of the Bush White House team that wrote the plan to create the U.S. Department of Homeland Security. Noreen Hynes is an infectious-disease specialist then posted to the White House.

called Dark Winter. In the summer of 2001, a bunch of smart people in and around the U.S. government gathered at Andrews Air Force Base and thought through a bioterrorist attack on the U.S. population. In the imaginary attack, on shopping malls in Atlanta, Philadelphia, and Oklahoma City, three thousand Americans are infected with smallpox. The disease had been eradicated in the 1970s, vaccine was scarce, and so the U.S. population was vulnerable to any new introduction of the virus. The imaginary exercise did not end well. Just a few months after the hypothetical attack, three million Americans were infected. A million were dead.

Then came the real attack, of September 11, 2001—and, following it, the Bush administration's weird shifting of public attention and fear from the Saudis, who had actually led the attacks, onto Iraq and Saddam Hussein. The last big smallpox outbreak had occurred in Iraq in 1972, when Saddam was in power. Saddam took an obvious delight in biological weapons.

The possibility that Saddam Hussein had preserved the smallpox virus preoccupied the Bush administration. Richard had no obvious place in the national security conversation and was surprised that when the conversation turned to bioterrorism his new colleagues assumed, because he was a doctor, he might have something to offer. "I was going to stuff I didn't really belong at," he said. "I would be going to these meetings at the White House or the Homeland Security Council. There'd be a bunch of generals and some question comes up and they're all looking down the table at me. I'm like the doctor at the table." By January 2003, Richard found himself giving a talk at the Pentagon on how the country might minimize illness and death if terrorists seeded it with smallpox. He didn't really think that terrorists would attack the United States with smallpox. "I was never really able to suspend my disbelief. If you are a terrorist, there are better ways to achieve what you want to achieve." But at the request of the Defense Department, he thought through a smallpox attack, all by himself. From the ground up. "The way I solve a hard problem is not to start with the conventional wisdom, but to start over." He began to make drawings on napkins, using little dots to represent people, and circles to represents networks of people, and before long he was off and running.

The problem, as he framed it for the Pentagon, was how to slow the spread of a communicable disease until you can produce a vaccine. As communicable disease spreads through social networks, Richard reasoned, you had to find ways to disrupt those networks. And the easiest way to do that was to move people physically farther apart from each other. "Increasing Effective Social Distance as a Strategy," he called it. "Social distance" had been used by anthropologists to describe kinship, but he didn't know that at the time, and so he thought he was giving birth to a phrase. ("But I don't think I turned it into a gerund," he'd later say.) What he also didn't realize was that he was giving new life to a dead idea: that apart from isolating people who were ill, you needed to do anything you could to slow the spread of a disease before you had drugs to help. "I was this emergency room doctor," he said. "I didn't know that people said all this stuff had been tried in 1918 and it hadn't worked. I wasn't rejecting anything. I just didn't know any better."

When Rajeev Venkayya called him, in late 2005, Richard was running a program at the National Institutes of Health to study and treat radiation exposure. He'd been asked, by a person in the White House working on medical countermeasures in the event of a nuclear attack, to help prepare for one, but he sensed that the real value in his work might wind up being in the treatment of cancer. If you could figure out ways to prevent tissue damage during radiation therapy, you could use it more safely—and so maybe use a lot more of it on the cancer cells. "I viewed the likelihood of an atomic bomb going off in an American city as essentially zero," said Richard. "I was taking this job to work on another threat I didn't believe in. But at least I could develop products that could have a broader value."

Like Rajeev, Richard thought that the United States government was paying too much attention to the threats posed by people and too little to those posed by nature. Like Rajeev, he believed that some new strain of flu, or some similar respiratory virus, was an accident waiting to happen. And so when he heard Rajeev's offer to create a pandemic plan for the country, he was all in. His employer, on the other hand, was not. The National Institutes of Health didn't want to let him go. "It caused some bitterness when I asked for him," recalls Rajeev. "We had to ask Tony Fauci for permission."

Rajeev didn't know the other six people he was about to bring into the White House. He'd sent out requests to the relevant agencies for a certain kind of person: quick learner, good teammate, trusted by the top brass inside their agencies. The task at hand was so unusual that he also asked for people who could think "outside the box." Soon he had a team. The State Department sent him someone to think through how to coordinate with foreign governments—to find and contain new viruses before they even got to the United States. The Justice Department sent him someone to create a strategy for safeguarding law enforcement and the courts. And so on. All these people were of a certain Washington type. Smart. Schooled in the inner workings of the federal government. Experienced in the crafting of national policy. They were all insiders. Even, by then, Richard Hatchett.

The guy sent by the Department of Veterans Affairs was the glaring exception. Rajeev had figured that he needed someone from the VA, as it ran the nation's largest hospital system and, during a pandemic, might be tapped both for hospital beds and for data about what was going on around the country. The VA sent not a policy person, not a Washington person, not a person who knew anything about pandemics, not a person who looked all that happy wearing a suit and tie, but a doctor from Atlanta named Carter Mecher. As it turned out, he would make all the difference.

*

Carter Mecher had only ever wanted to be a doctor, but the world kept finding other uses for him. He'd grown up in a big, working-class family in Chicago. Though his father hadn't finished the ninth grade, he had a highly successful career as a tool and die maker, and as a parent. He encouraged his children to tackle problems with the same confidence that he shaped steel. "If some other dumb fuck can do it, so can you," he liked to say. He'd said exactly that when Carter asked him if he thought he could become a doctor.

Carter loved his father's ability to make anything out of steel, and inherited his father's gift. Working with his hands, Carter became perfectly focused; otherwise, his mind refused to sit still. "I think I have ADD," he'd say. "I have something like that. I wander all over the fucking place." By the time he reached college, he'd grown so used to not paying attention in class, and instead thinking about whatever he wanted to think about, that he would just make note of whatever book the professor was talking about so that he could go read it on his own later. There were exceptions, though. Times when Carter's mind would lock into a problem, in the same way it did when he was fixing a car engine. That was when he was at his best, and most himself.

An inability to pay attention to anything except that which you find totally riveting might not sound like the most promising trait in a medical student. But almost by process of elimination, it led Carter to his calling: critical care. Just about everyone found their first hours inside the intensive care unit of the hospital jarring and upsetting. Patients who survived often suffered from post-traumatic stress disorder. In the ICU, medical students were most likely to discover their fears. Long stretches with nothing but the faint beeping of machines against a quiet background hum: then, *bam*, lights flashed and alarms screamed, and someone was dying. Code Blue. You could no longer watch and wait and admire the problem. Your thoughts and actions were suddenly the difference between life and death.

From the moment he walked into an ICU, Carter sensed it was where he was meant to be. The ICU rewarded his handiness: he could intubate anyone. "There are two skills you have to have in an ICU," he said. "You need to be able to put an IV into anybody, and you got to be able to stick a tracheal tube into anybody. You can't do that, and you are going to lose a patient." The ICU also grabbed his attention, and kept it. "I loved it," he said. "The alarms would go off, and it was like someone gave me Ritalin. Everything else is cut out and I can see the problem. I felt like I was my best when the shit hits the fan. I focus like a laser when everything is going to shit."

There was this other thing he liked, too—the feelings the ICU left you with. If you didn't allow yourself to become numb, the place kept you alive to the complexity of life, and its sanctity. When Carter first started teaching medical students, in the early 1990s, he was working in a VA hospital. Most of the patients were blue-collar guys who had fought in the Second World War. All you saw as a doctor, or medical student, were these dying old men. But if you got them talking, you'd hear the most amazing stories—how they once flew their fighter plane under the Golden Gate Bridge, how they had taken Iwo Jima. "All of us are like a story," he'd tell students. "You're seeing the last two pages of the book. You know so little about him. He was once a little kid. He was your age once."

And if you needed reminding of the benefits of life, you only had to watch people cling to it, even after they claimed they did not want to. Carter would never forget one crusty old World War

II vet with incurable lung disease, and a tube down his throat. He'd been able to communicate only by writing on a whiteboard. *I want to die*, he'd written one day. The nurses brought Carter over. *I want you to take me off this goddam machine and let me die*, he wrote to Carter. Carter told him that if he really wanted to die, he could die, but maybe they should sleep on it, as death wasn't one of those procedures that was easy to reverse. The old vet wrote, *If you don't pull this tube out, I'm going to yank it out.* "He was in a rage," said Carter. "They brought in the chaplain and the family." Carter decided to change the subject.

"What can we do to make you more comfortable?" he asked.

The old vet studied him a beat and then wrote on the board, "Beer."

"What kind of beer?" asked Carter.

A few minutes later Carter was at a gas station buying a six-pack. He gave it to the ICU nurse along with a formal prescription: one can of beer a night. "I hand him the beer and he has a smile on his face," said Carter. "And he went to sleep." The old World War II vet decided he preferred to live, and he lasted a surprisingly long time. "People have this strong will," said Carter. "You feel it. You see it. It really was spiritual being in the ICU."

Carter didn't spend a lot of time thinking about himself, and about what made him different from other people. His mind naturally turned not inward but outward. But he couldn't help but notice that very few medical students shared his enthusiasm for human beings on the brink of death. They felt the pressure; the pressure led to mistakes. Carter wound up hearing about a lot of these mistakes, but the first one he witnessed impressed him so deeply that he never forgot it. He was in Los Angeles, finishing his residency inside a county hospital ICU. They wheeled in an older woman suffering from both lupus and pneumonia, and rapidly losing her ability to breathe. Carter intubated her and put her on a ventilator. At the end of his shift, he left thinking she had a fair chance of survival. "I came back the next day," he said, "and the bed's empty." He found the doctor who had followed him on duty. The guy was in shock. The woman had died after her lung had collapsed, he said.

Right away, Carter knew what had happened. Every so often, the pressurized air pumped in by the ventilator escaped the lungs and entered the cavity that held the lungs. The air had nowhere to go, and the cavity expanded like a balloon, squeezing the lungs down. The pressure in the chest can grow so intense that it cuts off the flow of blood to the heart.

He also knew what the doctor should have done. Puncture the cavity in which the lung resided, to release the air. You needed to feel for the top rib and then push in a needle hard just above it, through the chest wall. "Didn't you stick a needle in her chest?" Carter asked, then regretted having asked it. The guy was a mess. He knew he'd choked. He'd asked for an X-ray so he could see what was happening inside the woman's chest. By the time he had the picture, and the comfort of certainty, she was dead. "We used to tell ourselves, 'You're going to make a mistake,'" said Carter. "The sin is making the same mistake twice. The best is to learn from other people's mistakes."

Carter didn't make mistakes in the ICU, at least none that mattered. Other people's mistakes, however, had a way of finding him. By 1991, he was running the ICU at the North Chicago Veterans Affairs Medical Center, a massive, thousand-bed hospital, when a cluster of patients in other units died from what appeared to be the mistakes of doctors. One old vet had turned up with back pain, for instance, and the VA doctor had prescribed Motrin and sent him home. Twenty-four hours later, the vet was back at the hospital with a ruptured aorta. His back pain had been caused by an aneurysm, missed by the VA doctor. The vet died in surgery. Several other bad outcomes in the hospital's surgery rooms triggered an investigation by the Department of Veterans Affairs, followed by a damning report.

Mistakes in private-sector medicine often never saw the light of day. The grievances they spawned could be resolved quietly, by insurance companies. Mistakes inside a VA hospital had to be reported to Congress, where members of whichever party did not control the White House would set about blaming the president for mistreating veterans. "It became a pile-on," said Carter. "It became a game of finding everything that's wrong." None of what happened implicated him, but he couldn't escape it. The people who ran North Chicago were fired or reassigned. The VA banned the hospital from performing surgeries. Doctors and nurses left in droves, so as not to be associated with the mess. The media was incessant. The *Chicago Tribune* ran a piece on the front page with the wife of a World War II veteran clutching a photo of her dead husband, under the headline "Widow Says VA Treated Man Like a 'Lamb Led to Slaughter.'" Carter would emerge from the ICU to speak with the family of some new patient, only to find them watching a television report on the many ways North Chicago was killing everyone who walked through its doors. "I can't tell you how humiliating it was," he said. "You feel it. And you don't forget it."

Carter didn't want to leave. He'd never been the leaving type. He liked the vets. That's why he hadn't pursued higher-paying jobs in the private sector: these old blue-collar guys reminded him of his dad and his uncle. "I felt I was one of the last ones left," said Carter. "Everyone was kind of deserting. The whole place is in turmoil."

Plus he knew that what had happened in the surgery was complicated. The VA's patients tended to be old and fragile. The *New England Journal of Medicine* had just published a study of medical mistakes. It showed that for every thousand people admitted to a hospital in the United States, three would die from error. The Veterans Health Administration treated a quarter of a million Americans a day: it was the second-largest provider of medical care in the world, behind the UK's National Health Service. The entire scandal could have been a statistical artifact: in such a vast system, there were bound to be, as a matter of pure chance, clusters of error. He also knew that the VA surgeons were doing their best; and all of them could have made more money in private practice. "They don't come to work with the intention of harming anybody," Carter said. "People make mistakes." But whatever the reality, the perception overwhelmed it. The U.S. Congress held hearings to grill officials from the VA about its mistreatment of veterans in North Chicago. "People are walking around with their heads down," recalled Carter. "Surgeons, like these really confident guys, were totally destroyed."

At the end of World War II, General Omar Bradley had taken charge of the Veterans Administration and forged strange and brilliant partnerships between its hospitals and local medical schools. The connections now ran so deep that, in North Chicago, it fell to the dean of the Chicago Medical School to sort out the mess. The dean found his way to Carter's ICU. *We have a crisis, and we need someone to fix it,* the dean said to him. *I have zero interest,* said Carter. He sensed he had been picked by process of elimination. He was thirty-six years old and had found his calling in critical care. He'd feel about a desk job, he suspected, the way he often felt about college lectures: there'd be nothing there to keep his mind from wandering all over the fucking place. The dean pressed Carter until he agreed, but only after his mind made a little leap. "My strength is taking care of really sick patients," he said. "We've got an entire medical center that is a really sick patient. It's a dying hospital. That's how I approached it: How do I stabilize it?"

He brought in a friend from his residency, Jim Tuchschmidt,

to help him. Together they set about rebuilding the reputation of the hospital, a patient at a time. "So here I am," said Carter. "I'm really young, I'm really junior. I'm head of the hospital. It happened so fast. And I had no idea what to do." He replaced what had been an impersonal system with personal health care teams for each of the thirty thousand or so veterans in North Chicago's care. He then measured everything that might be measured about the quality of the care given by each team: acute bed days, emergency room visits, length of hospital stays, and so on. Once you had the data, you could see weaknesses more quickly and fix them. Prime Health, they called the new system. The new logo was the iconic image of U.S. Marines raising a flag over Iwo Jima, and the new motto, below the logo, was: *So exclusive you fought to get in.* By the time Carter left, in 1995, four years later, North Chicago was receiving awards for health care excellence.

How exactly they did what they did is relevant here mainly because of where it led Carter Mecher. It led him to take an interest in medical error, and that interest soon became an obsession. It led also to a new job, after the VA, having seen this miraculous turnaround in North Chicago, asked him to move to Atlanta and serve as chief medical officer for an entire region. "Each time I moved, I felt like I was walking up stairs and the view was getting bigger," said Carter. "Atlanta was like the next veranda. It was the first time in my life that I got to see things at a national level. That was when I started to see the world differently. To see systems."

In Atlanta he oversaw nine big hospitals across three states, with no end to the mistakes that might be made inside of them. Often it was the thing you most took for granted that proved most deadly. The hot water, for instance. Taking steam as their heat source, VA hospitals heated water to very specific temperatures, hot enough to kill certain bacteria but cool enough that it didn't scald. To make sure the water didn't emerge too hot, they'd installed special valves on the bathtub faucets. The mechanism that heated the water had broken, however, and the water was coming out too cool. To compensate, the nurses set a valve on the tub to a hotter setting. That valve had inside it a kind of failsafe: it shut off the hot water above a certain temperature. All of which seemed fine until, one night, plumbing engineers came and fixed the heating mechanism, without telling the nurses.

Normally the special valve on the tub would have prevented the water from filling the tub, but, unbeknownst to all, as the tub had not been used while the pipes were busted, the special valve was also busted. Normally, you could rely on the patient to let you know the water was too hot. But there was one patient in the VA hospital, an old guy with mental health problems. No matter what the nurses did for him, he screamed. The nurses would always bathe him first, to relieve the pressure on the next shift. And so it happened that, after the engineers fixed the pipes, the man who screamed when treated was the first patient to be given a bath. "The nurses don't know the valve doesn't work," said Carter. "They don't know the engineers have set the temperature too high. And the first person they bathe screams no matter what you do. When they put him in, he screamed." An hour later, the man's skin was peeling away, and he was dying of thermal burns. And Carter was fielding calls from various people to let him know that the system he oversaw had boiled someone alive. The nurses were devastated, but to Carter's way of thinking they were victims, too. The environment in which they worked, and which they had been encouraged to trust, had failed them. "When you go into the details of the cases, you see it's not bad people," he said. "It's bad systems. When the systems depend on human vigilance, they will fail."

In medical error he'd found a subject that focused his attention as sharply as a Code Blue in the intensive care unit. To keep patients safe, he felt he needed to know all the details of anything that had gone wrong, in a way that was odd for a person in his position.

Not long after he became its supervisor, the VA hospital in Charleston, South Carolina, identified an issue. The patients in their care were dying in higher numbers than elsewhere from colon cancer. A shocking percentage of the cancers were being found only once they had reached the stage at which they were untreatable. No one could figure out why. Carter visited the hospital to poke around. He now had a rule: if you visit a hospital to investigate some problem, visit more than once, as on the first visit the locals assume that you have come merely to find fault and assign blame rather than to enlist them as partners in the hunt for the flaw in the system. He'd learned that from some field anthropologists whom he had sought out. "They taught me how important it was to have a second visit when they visited villages," said Carter. "The second visit made a statement to the villagers, and it usually wasn't until the second visit that trust emerged." Not until his second visit to Charleston did Carter start asking how they treated certain high-risk patients, how they scheduled colonoscopies, and so on. He made a point of asking questions in plain English, and less in the manner of a doctor than a child. *Why do you do it this way? Can you show me how you do that?* Putting things simply made it easier to ask important questions that, if put in doctor-speak, might sound silly.

By his third visit, the nurses were walking him through every stage of the colon-cancer detection process. "I never told them what I would do," said Carter. "I was allowing them to open the curtain and take a look. You see *so* much. If people would just spend their time and observe. You don't need any advanced degrees." Touring him around, the nurses realized something they'd missed: the hospital's patients were surprisingly unlikely to mail back their colon-cancer test kits. The Charleston hospital, like other hospitals, mailed out these test kits with little cards on which patients were meant to capture a stool sample. To ensure that the test kits made their way back to the hospital, the hospital enclosed pre-addressed envelopes.

Carter had asked if they could go see where the test-kit envelopes arrived. They took him to the mailroom, where someone dumped the sack with that day's mail onto a table. A bunch of test kits were in the pile, but each envelope bore the same red notice: *Insufficient Postage: Return to Sender.* ("Thank God the post office delivered them anyway.") One of the nurses said: I wonder how many of them were returned to the sender? "Bulbs went off in everyone's head," said Carter. It had occurred to no one that the colon-cancer test kits might require two postage stamps. "Who the hell would know that you need more than one stamp to send it back to the medical center? I would have done the same thing." People were dying, for a stamp. The Charleston VA began to send out pre-addressed envelopes with two stamps, and within a year had leapt to the front of the pack in its detection of colon cancer. "I loved that moment," said Carter. "It was so commonsense."

One way to reduce medical error, he thought, was to redesign the environment to make it more difficult for bad things to happen. "You cannot put a 120-volt plug into a 240-volt outlet," he said, by way of analogy. "Why? You can't do it! You can't fit it in!" In medicine there were too many 120-volt plugs that fit into 240-volt outlets. The ease with which a nurse might give one patient medicine intended for another, for example. When he heard that a nurse at a VA hospital in Topeka, Kansas, had the bright idea of using bar codes on patients and medications to match them up, Carter grabbed it and spread it across his entire system.

He also set out to learn everything he could about the inner workings of the human mind, and where and why it was prone to err. He found a book called *Human Error*, by a British psychologist aptly named James Reason. "It was like reading the owner's manual of the human mind," he later recalled. "Not the usual owner's manual, but an owner's manual that pointed out all the peculiarities and idiosyncrasies of how we operate— especially under conditions of stress." The ICU was a stressful and complicated place; Carter had experienced what Reason described. He was struck especially by Reason's argument that the best way to guard against error is to design systems with lay- ered and overlapping defenses. There was an image of Reason's that Carter loved, of slices of Swiss cheese being layered on top of one another, until there were no holes you could see through.

All of which was to say that when he was handed his new job in Atlanta, his mind behaved a bit the way it did when he was a kid, sitting in the classroom, and the teacher said something that caused him to think of something else. He was always less interested in answering the question he'd been asked than in finding a more interesting question to answer. So, while running a bunch of hospitals, he was also now making himself expert in all sorts of seemingly irrelevant subjects. Aviation safety, for instance. Whenever two planes almost collided, the Federal Avi- ation Administration knew about it and investigated. But when a nurse screwed up and gave a patient medications intended for another, no one made a note of it unless the patient died. "That stuff resonated with me like crazy," said Carter. "You can keep mistakes from happening if you can identify the almost mis- takes. This kind of changes how I view everything."

He felt strongly that Veterans Affairs should attack the mis- takes that happened inside its hospitals in a more systematic way, by scouring the system for almost mistakes. Near misses. "It was the natural place to explore medical error, because unlike a sim- ilar situation in the private sector, you can't hide it," he said. He implored his bosses in Washington, DC, to create a "safe space" in which people felt comfortable admitting the bad things that had almost happened. He wrote long memos to the other twenty-one chief medical officers in the VA system, pushing them to press for change. "We need an incident reporting system in medicine," he wrote in one. "We focus on the bad event. We ignore what didn't happen. We crucify whoever was in the bad event and ignore the others. And that's not how you fix the system."

It wasn't easy to create a safe space with members of Congress gazing over your shoulder, looking for mistakes to publicize for political gain. Carter sensed that his memos weren't having the desired effect in Washington. "I felt like we were not having a serious conversation," he said. Instead of an incident reporting system, in 2001 the head office created a Lessons Learned website, which allowed anyone in the VA system to log in and post. Most of what was posted, however, was not confessions of medical error, or stories of near misses, but ideas and insights that reflected glory upon the author. The VA website quickly became a suggestion box stuffed with thinly veiled personal advertisements. "The hope was that employees would go onto the website and adopt these great ideas," said Carter. "But nobody did. Leaders were not happy."

By then the leaders had a sense that their chief medical officer in Atlanta was a bit different from the others, and had a taste for tackling unusual problems. They asked Carter to create a committee to find the five best new ideas on the VA website and spread them throughout the system.

Once again, the teacher had unintentionally said something that interested Carter Mecher and caused his mind to wander. Specifically, he wondered: If these ideas on the Lessons Learned website are so good, why haven't any of them taken off? And why were all these other ideas spreading inside the VA without anyone's help? For some reason, this caused him to ponder the wheelie bag. One day everyone is humping their luggage around the airport; the next, everyone's got a wheelie bag. The wheelie bag was what a good idea looked like. It just sort of took off on its

own. Then he asked himself: Why did some ideas attract attention while others did not? Why did he have this stack of unread
back issues of the *New England Journal of Medicine* piled up in
his office and making him feel guilty? What caused him actually to open the *New England Journal of Medicine?* For that matter, why did so much of what he learned in life come from doing
some job, and so little from school? And why . . . well, from there
his mind became totally engrossed, but not with the problem his
superiors had asked him to solve. "I did pull a group together,"
said Carter, "but the task I gave the group was to figure out why
the idea of a Lessons Learned website didn't work."

He spent the next year making himself expert on why, and
in what circumstances, people learned—and why, and in what
circumstances, they did not. He read many books, hunted down
many authors in person, and picked their brains to see what else
might be inside of them. He wrote a long report for the people
at the top of the Department of Veterans Affairs about, in effect,
why its Lessons Learned website was dumb. The gist of it was
that people don't learn what is imposed upon them but rather
what they freely seek, out of desire or need. For people to learn,
they need to want to learn. "How many times have you traveled
by air?" Carter began, in his report to his superiors.

> . . . Dozens, perhaps even hundreds of times? A common
> aircraft you might have flown on is a Boeing 757. Boeing has
> produced nearly 2,000 of these aircraft and Delta Airlines
> alone has over 100 of these aircraft in its fleet. It is rather
> likely, given the frequency with which you travel, that you
> have flown on this type of aircraft. During the pre-flight
> safety instructions you were treated to a multimedia event.

He described all the ways that airlines try to hammer safety
information into the minds of the passengers, then asked, "How

many times have you been exposed to this sort of 'training'? Dozens? Hundreds of times? Try answering the following questions."

How many exits are on a 757? Four? Six? Eight?

What does orange and red lighting identify?

How do you remove the life vests under your seats?

And so on. There were thirty pages more like this and an argument for creating, inside the VA, a new kind of institution that he called a Learning Exchange. "People in an organization learn," said Carter. "They're learning all kinds of things. But they aren't learning what you are teaching them. You go to a formal meeting. The important conversation is not in the meeting. It's in the halls during the breaks. And usually what's important is taboo. And you can't say it in the formal meeting."

He was trying, among other things, to create ways to admit the conversation from the hallways into the formal meeting. But of course the people running the meeting had their reasons for keeping it out. "We handed in the report," said Carter. "They didn't know what to do with it. They asked us if we could please just pick the four or five best ideas on the Lessons Learned website and spread them throughout the system."

In late October 2005, the VA received a request from the White House. The request was submitted to a VA doctor named Lawrence Deyton, who had played a leading role in the treatment of HIV. He was just then creating a program, which would prove successful, to wean veterans off cigarettes. The White House was looking for an unusual person, and a chief medical officer type, to help think through a big national health problem. Dr. Deyton walked the request down the hall to the office of Odette Levesque, who knew maybe better than anyone the twenty-two chief medical officers in the VA medical system.

Levesque was a nurse by training, and the human link between the VA head doctors in the field and headquarters. "If I needed help on a certain issue, I knew who to call," she said. She looked at the White House request. "They wanted someone who could think 'outside the box,'" she said. "There was only one name that came to mind, and that was Carter Mecher."

*

Carter was surprised by the call from the White House, and even more surprised by what they wanted him to do. He'd learned a lot about infectious disease by treating it in various intensive care units. He knew nothing about pandemics, and hadn't given any thought to how to plan for them. "But it was the White House calling," he said. "I figured, Yeah, yeah, what the hell."

In late November 2005 he went to Washington and, with the six other members of the new team, was installed in a room at the end of a corridor on the fourth floor of the Old Executive Office Building, next door to the White House. It had ten workstations, just computers with desks and chairs and no partitions, but it did have a lovely view of the Rose Garden and the Marine One landing pad. In the room adjacent to them, people were cleaning up the mess left by Hurricane Katrina. From the moment he convened with his new team of pandemic planners, Carter sensed that one of these things was not like the others, and that that thing might be him. To their first meeting, the other six members of the team wore suits. Carter had thought he was dressing up by putting on a sports coat, and, right afterward, he went to Jos. A. Bank and bought five suits, which he wore in rotation. Even then he didn't get it quite right. "Your first impression of Carter is, yes, he's now bought a suit, but he's wearing combat boots with it," said Ken Staley, who worked for Rajeev Venkayya and supervised the pandemic planners. "You ask him why and he says someone gave them to him and he thought they were cool."

Richard Hatchett watched Carter with interest, too. "We were all sort of thrown into a room with people from across government who we didn't know," said Richard. "It took a while for Carter to unfold. To feel comfortable with us and to be willing to go where his head goes." Carter's head, at first, had no idea where to go. "We all had the same title," said Carter. "It was like a bullshit title. But I'm kind of the doofus from the VA. Everyone else is from DC, and they're all policy people. And I never did this crap before." As they divvied up responsibilities, Carter had trouble following what they were talking about. "It's like starting a new school and everyone else is ahead of me," said Carter. "It's all new. It's all different. They're using acronyms. The words they are using aren't words that I normally use." *APHIS... FBO... CBO... HSPD... PCC. Interagency.*

That last one wasn't an acronym, but Carter didn't really know what it meant. The entire federal government felt to him like some gigantic black box. One of the people on the team was from the Department of Agriculture, and everyone else seemed to know exactly what that department did. Carter had no real clue. The others kept referring to "the NRP," until finally Carter leaned over and asked Richard, "What the hell's 'NRP'?" *The National Response Plan,* said Richard. *It lays out how the federal government organizes itself during an emergency.* That sounded important to Carter, and so he went and found a copy and read all four hundred pages of it, and felt no wiser for the experience. "It's all government language," he said. "They're just saying the same thing over and over."

The other six members of the team each had some obvious narrow role to play. The woman from the Department of Homeland Security would write the chapter on transportation and borders; the guy from the Agriculture Department would write the chapter on protecting the health of farm animals. The other doctor in the room, Richard Hatchett, had somehow already

been given the job of writing the key chapter in the plan, chapter 6, which would be the strategy for minimizing illness and
death in humans. The divvying up of the plan was a bit like
musical chairs, and when the music stopped, everyone but Carter had a seat. As he recalled, "Rajeev just said, 'Richard, you're
going to work on chapter six, and, Carter, you'll help Richard.'"

Once Carter saw how government reports got written, he
understood why no one ever really wanted to read them. Richard was a natural writer, but there was no place in the process
for a natural writer. "There were all these stupid rules," said
Carter, whose first job was making sure that whatever Richard
wrote conformed to the U.S. government's style manual. "Like
you need to put countries and states in alphabetical order, so no
one is offended. You can't say 'over' three hundred bucks—you
have to say 'more than.'" The bigger obstacle to clear prose was
the sheer number of people invited to complain about whatever
Richard wrote. Anything that implicated any federal agency
had to be sent to that agency for approval. "So we'd send it to,
like, the EPA," said Carter. "And it wasn't one person at the EPA.
It was ten. There were times I had five different comments on
the same sentence all wanting me to change the sentence a different way." The process drove Richard Hatchett nuts. "It just
gets dumber and dumber," he'd say.

Richard and Carter thought in slightly different ways about
the problem of stopping a deadly disease as it swept through
the population. Richard's mental model was warfare, with an
enemy that resembled a network of highly connected nodes.
Identify the nodes with the most connections and take them
out: that's how you won the war against a virus. Carter's first
analogy was with medical error. He'd designed systems to minimize the likelihood of mistakes being made by doctors and
nurses. He was now designing a strategy to minimize the likelihood of a bug jumping from one person to another. What their

views had in common, he suspected, was the absence of a magic bullet. The solution would be a layering of multiple strategies, sort of the way you laid slices of Swiss cheese on a sandwich, so that the holes did not align. He began to write memos to the group about the Swiss cheese strategy.

Inside their room in the Old Executive Office Building, both Carter and Richard saw that there was more than one thing going on. There was this official plan that they were dutifully hammering out, from which all joy and flair had been squeezed by a mad editorial process. Then there was what the plan might allow them to do. In other words, the plan wasn't really the plan but a plan to have a plan. (And the original twelve-page document that Rajeev had created now looked more and more like a plan to have a plan to have a plan.) The actual words that ended up in the chapter they wrote would remain vague enough to justify doing any number of things. There was, most importantly, a passage that suggested what the federal government might do, at the start of a pandemic, before a vaccine was available. It would, they'd written, *"provide guidance, including decision criteria and tools, to all levels of government on the range of options for infection control and containment, including those circumstances where social distancing measures, limitations on gatherings or quarantine authority may be an appropriate public health intervention."*

It was hard to imagine anyone wading into that passage voluntarily, much less giving it a second thought. The words mattered less for what they said than for what they could be made to say. Like the words in the Holy Bible or the U.S. Constitution, they invited the problem of how they might be interpreted, and by whom, and for what purposes. As read by Richard Hatchett and Carter Mecher, those words gave them cover to answer the most important medical question they'd ever faced: How do you save lives in a pandemic before you have the drugs and vaccines to do it?

FOUR

Stopping the Unstoppable

One day some historian will look back and say how remarkable it was that these strange folk who called themselves "Americans" ever governed themselves at all, given how they went about it. Inside the United States government were all these little boxes. The boxes had been created to address specific problems as they arose. "How to ensure our food is safe to eat," for instance, or "how to avoid a run on the banks," or "how to prevent another terrorist attack." Each box was given to people with knowledge and talent and expertise useful to its assigned problem, and, over time, those people created a culture around the problem, distinct from the cultures in the other little boxes. Each box became its own small, frozen world, with little ability to adapt and little interest in whatever might be going on inside the other boxes. People who complained about "government waste" usually fixated on the ways taxpayer money got spent. But here was the real waste. One box might contain the solution to a problem in another box, or the person who might find that solution, and that second box would never know about it.

Sandia National Laboratories had been created back in the mid-1940s in part to help the people stuck in various boxes to think outside them. Even by the high standards of the Sandians, Bob Glass was a gifted thinker whose mind naturally belonged in no one box. Yet by the spring of 2006 he felt trapped. In the two years since its conception, his fifteen-year-old daughter's science fair project had spun up into this grown-up model of disease control. He'd found data from the long-forgotten flu pandemic of 1957–58, estimated to have killed more than a hundred thousand Americans, and used it to test his model. Given the broad facts about the disease, the model had basically reproduced that pandemic. The illness and death that had occurred in each age group in real life recurred in the model, for instance. Bob Glass had now read enough about epidemiology to know that his daughter's project was an original contribution to the field. "I asked myself, *Why didn't these epidemiologists figure it out?* They didn't figure it out because they didn't have tools that were focused on the problem. They had tools to understand the movement of infectious disease without the purpose of trying to stop it." With the help of the computer programming genius at Sandia Labs, he and Laura had built a tool that might stop a disease.

He was stunned by how difficult it had been to get anyone to use it or even notice it. Some months earlier, the White House's Homeland Security Council had asked Sandia Labs to help it prepare for a tabletop exercise on pandemic flu: What questions should they address? What should they think about that they might not have considered?* But the group inside San-

---

* The same Oval Office meeting that led to the creation of a pandemic plan also spawned this brief exercise. The exercise occurred on December 10, 2005, just as the planning got underway. It had no effect on the planning.

dia assigned the task wasn't Bob Glass's group. Glass talked a friend into slipping a note about his model into the packet they sent to the White House, but the homeland security people had ignored it. "There's a natural inclination towards certain narratives," said Glass. "Instead of worrying how to stop this thing, they got wrapped up in a thing from outside the country that was coming in. And so they spent all their time talking about closing borders. Which is exactly what does not work. It also immediately shuts down all economic flows."

The only way to get attention for this new tool for disease control, Glass decided, was to write it up in a paper for an academic journal. The scientists at Sandia National Labs worked under the highest security clearance in the federal government, called "Q clearance," and were prohibited from revealing their work without first seeking approval. The work was his kid's science fair project, but he was now taking it as seriously as anything he did at Sandia. So he explained the situation to his superiors and wrote up a long paper, which, at length, they allowed him to publish. He sent it to *Science* and *Nature* and to other, more obscure journals of medical science. "Every one of them just returned it to me unread because I wasn't known in their field," he said. "So then I got really worried." When asked about himself, which he seldom was, as he spent so much of his time alone in thought, Bob Glass described himself as "an extreme introvert." It violated his nature to reach out personally to people in the field of communicable disease and seek their help. But he did it anyway. He found the names of professional epidemiologists who claimed to be using computer models to study disease spread and sent them his paper, along with a note. "They wouldn't even return my emails," he said. "They just didn't respond. So then I got pissed. I had this fear: a pandemic will occur, and no one would do anything right. I thought I was dead. I thought we were all dead. Then I remembered the guy at the VA."

A year and a half earlier, Laura had gone to Washington, DC, to visit her aunt. Over dinner one night, she told her aunt's boyfriend, an infectious-disease specialist who worked for the Department of Veterans Affairs, about her science fair project. "You should write that up and publish it," he said with enthusiasm. He said he'd never heard of anything like it. When she returned home, she told her father about the dinner. "I thought, 'Jeez, this is going to take a lot of work,'" he'd said, but he agreed to turn the science fair project into a serious academic paper on disease control, authored jointly. The VA guy had already had one big effect on their work, Bob Glass thought; maybe he could have another. It troubled him deeply to use his sister's boyfriend to get attention for a scientific discovery, but he didn't know anyone else in the federal government in Washington, DC. "You just don't do this in science," Glass said. "But I said, I'm going to do something someone my age never does. I'm going to go around the system. I write him an email and attach the paper and ask: 'Do you know anyone who needs to see this?'"

At that point, he'd spent the better part of six months trying to get the attention of experts in disease control. Inside of six hours, he had a call from Richard Hatchett. "He said, 'We're in the White House,'" recalled Bob Glass. "'When can you come and talk to us?'"

*

As it turned out, the guy at the Department of Veterans Affairs who had once dated Bob Glass's sister actually knew Carter Mecher, and had emailed him everything Bob had sent. "When I first saw it, I was like, What the hell is this?" said Carter. "Most things you get in the White House are kind of bullshit stuff." His mind still hadn't shaken free of his project at the VA, which revealed to him how poor official channels could be for the transfer of information, and how rich the unofficial ones could be. Richard had become obsessed with the idea of using models to shape their pandemic strategy, and so Carter had forwarded him the whole package—the VA guy's email, together with all the stuff Bob Glass had attached.

Richard was nearly alone in his interest in models. The National Institutes of Health had funded three academics to build models of disease, but it was unclear how useful they would be. The new models were complicated and slow and expensive to run. If you asked a simple question—for instance, "What happens to the spread of a certain disease if you insist that people work from home?"—it could take days to get an answer. Even then, you felt faintly suspicious, because the models' complexity made it nearly impossible to see what was going on inside them. Richard invited the academics for a meeting so that he could pick their brains. He liked them more than Carter did; Carter thought they were pretentious. After the meeting, Richard compiled a spreadsheet with hundreds of columns, in an attempt to describe the features of each model. Each made assumptions about the nature of the new disease attacking the population—how it spread, how likely an infected person was to infect another person, how likely it was to kill, and so on. There were even more assumptions about the population under attack: age distribution, living arrangements, employment, vaccination rates, and so on. Compiling the spreadsheet was tedious, but Richard sensed that the models offered the only hope of finding some new strategy.

Working alone on his spreadsheet, he had one of the most curious experiences of his life. As a small child, he'd suffered a horrific accident; he'd never quite shaken its aftereffects. It had happened when he was on vacation with his parents. They were visiting Bushkill Falls, in Pennsylvania, and walking along a path carved into a steep cliff. Richard dropped a pack of Life Savers he'd been clutching, then chased them under a fence—and off the cliff. He plummeted seventy feet into a creek. By the time his father reached him, he was facedown in the water, not breathing. He was bleeding from a deep gash in his forehead, and his jaw was locked. His father, a banker with no medical training, by sheer chance had just learned a bit about pediatric life support, from a friend who was taking a course on the subject. Unable to pry open his son's jaws, he knew to breathe into his nostrils. He did this until Richard once again began to breathe.

Growing up in Alabama, Richard heard that story over and over. "It always ended with my parents saying that I had been saved for a reason," he said, "and I think my father, and maybe my mother as well, actually came to believe it. So that was a kind of heavy thing to grow up with." He'd achieved enough along the way to feel that maybe he had some special destiny, but he never really thought what it might be or spoke of it. Grandiosity mortified him; he really was, at his core, a southern gentleman poet. And so it was strange indeed that, as he sat there in the White House compiling this extremely boring spreadsheet about these possibly useless models, he was overcome by feeling. "It hit me like a lightning bolt," he said. "This is it; solving this problem is why I'm here. I'm the only person in the White House who cares about this stuff, and if I don't pursue this, it won't happen. And I mean it really hit me like a thunderclap. Like, the only time ever in my life that I had something like that happen."

Later, he made sense of that feeling. In the moment, he was aware mainly of just how nearly alone he was in the view that there might actually be ways to stop a new disease once it began to sweep through the population. A powerful conventional wisdom held that there was only one effective strategy: isolate the ill, and hustle to create and distribute vaccines and antiviral drugs; that other ideas, including social interventions to keep people physically farther apart from each other, had been tried back in 1918 and hadn't worked. America's leading disease experts—the people inside the CDC, and elsewhere in the Department of Health and Human Services—agreed on this point. Richard was by then friends with the most famous of them all, D.A. Henderson. Donald Ainslie Henderson was maybe six foot two, but in Richard's mind he stood twelve foot six and loomed even larger in his field. Among other achievements, he was known as the man who, in his work with the World Health Organization, had eradicated smallpox.* He'd been dean of the Johns Hopkins School of Public Health and held other titles, but he was, when Richard arrived there, on assignment at the Department of Health and Human Services.

Back then, Richard had listened to D.A. vent about the newest idiots at fancy universities who thought they could capture anything meaningful about disease control in a computer model. "He thought they had no idea what they were talking about," said Richard. They'd not spoken about the subject, but Richard could guess what D.A. would make of what he was now up to. D.A. had been in charge of the federal government's response back in 1957–58, when that new strain of flu had killed more than one hundred thousand Americans. He'd advised doing no more than isolating the ill, and waiting for a vaccine, as the costs of any other strategy exceeded any possible benefits. Richard couldn't understand his certainty, or the weird conventional wisdom that

---

* "Never before has man set out to eradicate a disease and succeeded," D.A. told one interviewer. Obviously, no one has ever singlehandedly eradicated a disease. The former head of the CDC, Tom Frieden, introduced another former head of the CDC, William Foege, to me as "the man who eradicated smallpox." At any rate, the last known case of smallpox was a twenty-three-year-old Somalian, who was diagnosed on October 26, 1977.

had coalesced. "One thing that's inarguably true is that if you got everyone and locked each of them in their own room and didn't let them talk to anyone, you would not have any disease," he said. "The question was can you do anything in the real world."

The new models of disease, slow and unwieldy though they were, gave Richard hope. D.A. Henderson, and the people at the CDC, along with pretty much everyone else in the public-health sector, thought that the models had nothing to offer; but they were missing the point. They, too, used models. They, too, depended on abstractions to inform their judgments. Those abstractions just happened to be inside their heads. Experts took the models in their minds as the essence of reality, but the biggest difference between their models and the ones inside the computer was that their models were less explicit and harder to check. Experts made all sorts of assumptions about the world, just as computer models did, but those assumptions were invisible.

And there was every day fresh evidence that the models inside the minds of experts could be seriously flawed. In professional sports, for example. For decades, former players went unquestioned as experts in the evaluation of both players and strategies. Then came the statistical revolution. Complete outsiders, armed with mathematical models, had made a mockery of the experts. The market forces that punish ignorance were far more intense in pro sports than they were in disease control; the mistakes made by epidemiologists didn't cause their teams to lose and their bosses to waste tens of millions of dollars. If models could improve predictions about some basketball player's value in a game, there was no reason they couldn't do the same for the value of some new strategy in a pandemic.

Richard believed that if the country was suddenly overwhelmed by some strain of flu for which there was no vaccine, there nonetheless existed strategies to prevent illness and death. He also wanted to believe that the benefits of these strategies could exceed their costs. He even thought it might be possible to eradicate a new virus without a vaccine. The trick there would be to lower the disease's reproductive rate: the number of people each infected person in turn infected. Drive that number below 1, and a disease would flicker and die. But as few disease control experts believed any of these things, and so would not explore possible strategies in a real-life pandemic, he needed the models, to explore the strategies in an artificial world. And so when he opened the email from Carter and looked at what Bob Glass had done, it took him no time at all to realize that the White House needed Bob Glass.

Once Carter saw Richard's enthusiasm, he, too, opened what Bob Glass had sent and started playing around with it. The math he understood. The thinking was clear and simple. All the rules the guy and his daughter had used to describe the social lives of kids and grown-ups felt plausible. Ditto the rules governing the spread of the disease. The only problem was that the model's output was just a bunch of numbers listed in these mind-numbingly long tables. "Most people can't read tables," said Carter. "They need to see it graphically." Carter turned the numbers into a graph. The picture shocked him.

The graph illustrated the effects on a disease of various crude strategies: isolating the ill; quarantining entire households when they had a sick person in them; socially distancing adults; giving people antiviral drugs; and so on. Each of the crude strategies had some slight effect, but none by itself made much of a dent, and certainly none had the ability to halt the pandemic by driving the disease's reproductive rate below 1. One intervention was not like the others, however: when you closed schools and put social distance between kids, the flu-like disease fell off a cliff. (The model defined "social distance" not as zero contact but as a 60 percent reduction in kids' social interaction.) "I said, 'Holy shit!'" said Carter. "Nothing big happens until you close the schools. It's not like anything else. It's like a phase change. It's nonlinear. It's like when water temperature goes from thirty-three to thirty-two. When it goes from thirty-four to thirty-three, it's no big deal; one degree colder and it turns to ice."

He and Richard didn't let themselves get too excited at first. "We said, 'Okay, this is just a toy model, so now we need to go and talk to the really sophisticated modelers,'" recalled Carter. They had the three academics with their big, complicated models more or less on call. When you fed into those models the question "What happens if you do nothing but close schools and reduce the social interaction of minors by 60 percent?," they responded, slowly, but as one: *that works.*

It was now April of 2006. With the exception of a tedious final chapter about the practical business of keeping big institutions open during a pandemic, the official strategy of the United States was as good as finished, and less than a month from publication. It detailed all the actions, big and small, for federal agencies to take. Most of the line items didn't much interest either Carter or Richard. For example:

> Educating Bird Owners: We will expand our multilevel outreach and education campaign called "Biosecurity for the Birds" to provide disease and biosecurity information to poultry producers, especially those with "backyard" operations. (p. 11)

There were hundreds of these kind of things, and someone in the federal government would do them. (The Department of Agriculture, in this case.) But it wasn't until *after* the plan had been written that Carter and Richard felt real excitement.

By now it was apparent that the two doctors on the pandemic planning team were leaving everyone else behind. They were no longer working normal hours, even by White House standards.

"You'd see Richard on the phone late at night explaining to his wife when he might be coming home," recalls one White House colleague. "He was like cheating on his family for pandemic preparedness." The intensity of their partnership caught their new colleagues by surprise. "The odd couple," Ken Staley, who worked in Rajeev's bioterrorism unit, called them. Richard played chess and quoted Borges; Carter took apart pickup trucks and put them back together. Much of what Richard loved doing could be done in a white linen suit. Much of what Carter loved doing left his hands black. Richard liked to borrow a phrase, Carter a tool. Richard was top-down—he conversed easily with the fancy academics and important policy people, and they with him. Carter was bottom-up—there was no fact, and no person, trivial enough to evade his curiosity. Richard left every classroom he entered at or near the top; Carter often just left the classroom. Carter poked fun at the way Richard walked around saying important-sounding things, like "All models are wrong; some of them are useful," but he felt the alchemy in their interactions. "Richard has the part of my brain I don't have," he said. "Richard is a philosopher type," said Rajeev, who had brought them both into the White House. "He's good at putting things into a bigger context. Carter is good at putting things into a smaller context."

Richard viewed models as a check on human judgment and as an aid to the human imagination. Carter viewed them more as flashlights. They allowed him to see what was inside a room that, until now, had been pitch-black. Each day, the two doctors cooked up ideas and questions and sent them on to Bob Glass. In the beginning, the questions concerned this model he'd built with his teenage daughter. How much did the results change when you tinkered with the severity of the disease? Or when you made different assumptions about how real-world Americans interacted? Or when those Americans only partly complied with whatever you asked them to do? Once they were satisfied that this very simple model somehow captured a lot of truth about the social lives of Americans, and that it generated roughly the same answers even after you tinkered with the specifics, they bombarded it with their full curiosity. What happened when you closed just bars and restaurants? Or just public transportation? Or made people telework? What happened when you combined every possible strategy they could think of, in every possible combination? How many cases of the disease could you have in a community and still hope to contain it by closing schools and making kids spend 60 percent less time in one another's company? What else might this model reveal?

A few days after Richard first called him, Bob Glass installed a bed on stilts beside his computer in a shed in the backyard. Each night in Albuquerque, he ran computer simulations of various pandemics, and various responses to them, so these guys he'd never met could have answers when they arrived at work in the morning. He'd been promoted, basically overnight, from the world's most ignored pandemic modeler to the world's most important pandemic modeler. He didn't tell his daughter that he was moonlighting at the White House with her science fair project. "Kids get stressed," he said. He didn't ask his superiors at Sandia National Labs for permission, because he already knew the answer. "They kill people for doing that," he said. "They would flip and put people in between me and them, and I wouldn't be able to do anything."

Everyone could see that kids played a role in disease transmission. No one imagined they would have the effect that they had in the Glasses' model. That didn't mean the model was right; but it might be. "It showed me where to dig," said Carter. "I said, 'I'm going to dig deep right here. Is there something about kids and schools that I don't know enough about and haven't thought about?'" To Carter, digging meant gathering data, and no place on earth collected as much of it as the United States government. In federal databases, he discovered that the majority of Americans employed by state and local government were employed in education, and he thought, *No wonder those unions are so powerful.* He learned that there were more than one hundred thousand K–12 schools in the country, with fifty million children in them. Twenty-five million rode a bus to school. "I thought, Holy crap, half the kids in the U.S. hop on a school bus." There were seventy thousand buses in the entire U.S. public transportation system, but *five hundred thousand* school buses. On an average day, school buses carried twice as many people as the entire U.S. public transportation system. A lot of the talk in the White House pandemic planning room had been about grown-ups: how they worked and traveled. "We'd been talking about the New York subway and the DC Metro," said Carter, "but for every person hopping on public transportation in one day, there are two kids taking the school bus."

How kids got to school was one issue; what happened once they were there was another. The Department of Education dug out blueprints of America's schools that enabled Carter to calculate just how much space each kid had. He did some math and reckoned that each elementary school child spent the day in a space with a radius of just three and a half feet, which, when they reached high school, expanded to four. That can't be right, he thought, it's too small—but then it had been a long time since he had been in school. "I called my wife," he recalled, "and told her, 'I want to go to school.'"

Carter had married his high school sweetheart. Both he and Debra had come from families with six children, and they had six children of their own. They'd remained in Atlanta during Carter's White House deployment; Carter commuted back and forth, so that he was now home only on weekends. He'd of course attended parent-teacher conferences. He'd never been to one with the goal of studying the spacing of the children. Now he asked his wife to arrange a meeting with a teacher while school was in session. That whole day, from the moment they got in the car, he viewed the world through a new lens. *Look!* he said, as they passed children waiting for the school bus. *Look at the way kids stand at the bus stop. When adults stand at a bus stop, they give each other space. Kids are like those close talkers on* Seinfeld. He and Debra entered the school. *Look! It's just a sea of humanity. I could almost walk across their heads!* He watched the way they horsed around and jumped on each other's backs and behaved in ways that he no longer did. *Look! They're so different. They're not little adults. They have a different sense of space.*

At length they reached the classroom, where the teacher waited. Carter had always disliked how they made you sit at one of the kids' desks during the parent-teacher conference, but now he didn't mind, as it allowed him to get a feel for how jammed together the students were during class. As the teacher spoke, he reached out his arms in either direction. *Look!* he said to himself. *It's three feet. I can touch the person next to me.* Leaving the school, he saw a bus and boarded it, with a tape measure. The seats turned out to be forty inches long. "They estimate kids' hips are thirteen inches across so they can put them three to a seat," he said. The aisle was narrower than a normal bus; paramedics knew not to bring a normal-sized stretcher onto a school bus, he later learned, because it wouldn't fit down the aisle. "I couldn't design a system better for transmitting disease than our school system," he said after his visit.

Until that moment, no one had really seen what was unusual about schools, at least from the point of view of the pandemic strategist. It had taken the Glasses' model to point it out. *Why?* Carter wondered. *Why hadn't they seen it?* Then it struck him. *They saw it all with adult eyes. They forgot the world that their kids live in, and that they once lived in.* Adults imagined their spaces smaller than they were and children's spaces larger than they were. Experts who'd passed through the White House pandemic planning room sometimes brought up how dense the modern workplace was, and the possible need, in a pandemic, to move to working from home. "These are really smart people," said Carter. "People who are national leaders in disease and epidemiology. Right away they'd say, 'Of course we need to do things in the workplace. Telework.' But even with all these damn cubicles, offices are nowhere near as dense as a classroom." After a while, he decided that the problem was the human mind. "They'd forgotten childhood," he said. "Adults just forget what it feels like to be a kid."

To illustrate this point he created a picture, of a 2,600-square-foot home, but with the same population density as an American school, then turned it into a slide. "The Spacing of People, If Homes Were Like Schools," read the top. The inside of the typical American single-family home suddenly looked a lot like a refugee prison, or the DMV on a bad day. "There is nowhere, anywhere, as socially dense as school classrooms, school hallways, school buses," said Carter.

The more Carter and Richard learned, the more excited they became. "Imagine if we could affect the weather," Carter wrote, in one of his long memos. "Imagine if we had the capability to reduce a category 5 storm to a category 2 or a 1 . . . Now although the Federal Government is not at the threshold of significantly reducing the potency of a hurricane, it is at the threshold of doing just this to another natural disaster—pandemic influenza." For his part, Richard began to deliver talks to small groups of important people about the way the model confirmed their hunch that there were things you could do to buy time before a vaccine. He'd coined a phrase for their strategy: Targeted Layered Containment. TLC.

TLC's basic idea was the same as that underpinning Carter's approach to medical error. No single intervention would stop a flu-like disease in its tracks, just as no single safety measure would prevent a doctor from replacing the right hip when it was the left hip that hurt. The trick was to mix and match strategies in response to the nature of the disease and the behavior of the population. Each strategy was like another slice of Swiss cheese; enough slices, properly aligned, would hide the holes. With any flu-like disease, the closure of K–12 schools was going to be one of the slices, but there were others. "The thing that Bob's model let us do was to test our intuitions and see which of the tools we had could be successful," said Richard. *"Tell me if this works. Tell me when it breaks."* Where their strategies failed was when a virus had a reproductive rate above 3*—when each infected person infected more than three others, or when the society's rate of compliance fell below 30 percent. "If you dial up the infectiousness to such an extent, you can overwhelm the interventions," said Richard. "But Bob's model showed us that we had this huge margin of error."

Carter was now digging furiously into the issue of school closure, and when Carter started digging, he usually stopped only after he'd reached China. This time, as he dug, a lot of people started hollering at him. "When I started learning about schools, I was already hearing objections," said Carter. *"This is never going to work. Kids are going to start hanging out in shopping malls. Crime rates will skyrocket. Poor kids will starve. People won't be able to work with their kids at home."* Here they were,

---

* "R naught," or R_0, is the shorthand for the idea. It's defined as how many people are infected, on average, by each infected person at the start of an epidemic, before any attempts have been made to intervene, either with drugs or social distancing. R naught will change if people change their behaviors, say, or as people achieve immunity. There is a need for a second concept: "effective R naught." Effective R naught is the term for the reproductive rate at any moment in time. To put an R naught of 3 in context: the flu strain that caused the 1918 pandemic had an R naught between 1.8 and 2.1.

inside the White House, doing exactly what the president of the United States had asked them to do, with money allocated to them by the U.S. Congress. But it turned out they still needed to persuade a lot of skeptical people in public health and education and emergency management and other corners of the U.S. government of their strategy's wisdom. The strategy would never work if it sat on some shelf in the White House. Lots of people had to believe in it, and lots of people already didn't. "I'd give them things," said Bob Glass. "They'd turn them into graphs and go give talks and get laughed out of the room."

*

At some point Richard and Carter realized that they'd need to change the minds of everyone working in and around public health, and that this meant first changing people's minds inside the Centers for Disease Control. The CDC sat at the top of the country's system of public health; in some ways it sat at the top of the *world's* system of public health. Leaders everywhere looked to it for guidance. But there had been a reason Rajeev hadn't asked the CDC to join the team creating a new pandemic strategy. Whatever strategy the White House dreamed up would necessarily be original, he thought, and the people who already saw themselves as experts in the field would be least capable of original thought. They'd be constrained by their sense that they already knew everything worth knowing about disease control, and would be threatened by the possibility that in fact they did not. And that might have been true. But it created a tension between these two doctors who were making it up as they went along and the people who regarded themselves as the world's authorities on disease control.

As they finished the plan, Carter got the first whiff of the CDC's condescension. There'd been one final chapter to write, on how to keep big institutions, public and private, running during a pandemic. Somehow everyone on the team had agreed that it needed to be written into the plan, without anyone's agreeing to write it. One day Rajeev stopped by and asked Carter about what everyone now just referred to as "chapter nine."

"There's nothing in chapter nine," Carter said.

"You write it," said Rajeev.

"I don't know shit about it," said Carter.

"Write it anyway," said Rajeev. "No one else knows anything, either."

Carter thought, *This is the boring crap. That's why I'm getting stuck with it.*

He wrote it up anyway. He ran what he wrote through a software program he'd created that spotted any inconsistencies with the U.S. government's grotesque style manual, then sent it on to the relevant agencies for comment. It came back, fast. Every sentence marked up in red and disputed. "The only thing that hadn't been crossed out was the title," said Carter. He paged through the comments and saw that most came from just one person, inside the CDC. Her comments were not warm and encouraging. Carter handed them to Richard, and Richard went off and phoned her, then came back and said, "She wouldn't even talk to me." Usually when you said you were so-and-so calling from the White House, the person on the other end of the line treated you with at least a smattering of respect. "Who is this bitch?" said Richard. "I don't know," said Carter, "But I'm going to find out."

The following week, instead of flying back to Washington, Carter visited one of the campuses occupied by the Centers for Disease Control. He'd lived in Atlanta for nearly a decade, but he'd never been inside the place or met anyone who worked there. On the way, he'd calmed down a bit and reread the CDC woman's comments. Maybe twenty people from around the federal government had offered criticisms of what he'd written, and hers were the only ones that suggested actual knowledge of the subject. "All the comments from other people were stupid things, like changing 'happy' to 'glad,'" he said. "Everything she said make sense." He was surprised by just how far down in the CDC she was; when he called, they passed him to her rung by rung down this long ladder. But she still had a name: Lisa Koonin.

*

Lisa Koonin had grown up in Atlanta in the 1960s. When she was fourteen, a doctor removed her appendix, and she decided there and then that she wanted to be able to do that kind of thing for others. She confessed her ambition to a school guidance counselor. The counselor told her that if she wanted to have a family, she couldn't be a doctor but might become a nurse. She became a nurse. After nursing school, she'd run a pediatric nursing unit at Douglas General Hospital and pursued a master's in public health. Her thesis established that mistakes by anesthesiologists were killing women during childbirth. It was wholly original, and it led the CDC to offer her a job in a unit that studied maternal mortality. Over the next two decades, she had moved around some inside the CDC, but she never rose as high as she might have, had she been a doctor. She remained just one of twelve thousand foot soldiers there. She loved the place and admired its people. But she was shadowed by a life she hadn't lived.

By the time Carter came to see Lisa, she was running an unfashionable unit inside something called the Division of Partnerships and Strategic Alliances. She worked with big companies to get them to nudge their employees to better health by, say, paying for their flu shots and their Nicorette gum. She'd been recently assigned to create a checklist of things companies should do to prepare for a pandemic. She couldn't make anybody do anything, but the prestige of the CDC was such that, by and large, people welcomed her phone calls. The checklist gave her a view of the challenges companies might face if a serious disease ever swept the country. After she'd finished it, she got a call from her boss asking her if she'd review a paper related to her checklist that had just come in from the White House. "Already there is something odd here," she said. "Usually CDC is creating the strategy."

She saw that the White House document had been passed down, rung by rung, inside the CDC by people who didn't want to deal with it, until it had finally, and a bit surprisingly, reached her. "I was a nobody," she said. "I had no position or stature." She opened it and marked everything she found wrong—which was, basically, everything—and sent it back to her boss. "I was kind of a typical CDC person. Everything was no, no, no. Everything had to be right. And it had to be so right that it was not wrong."

When one of the document's authors rang her up directly, she suspected it was some kind of prank. "He says, 'This is Richard Hatchett from the White House.' I was, Yeah, right. I guess my self-image was no one from the White House is going to call me." So sure was she that she was insufficiently important to receive this kind of attention that she'd hung up on the guy. "I was not friendly," she said. Now the White House was visiting, in the person of Carter Mecher, so Lisa Koonin couldn't really deny that the White House wanted to speak with her. Yet she was prepared to remain unfriendly. She had an unflattering preconception of "guy from the White House." Blue suit. Self-important. Stuck-up.

Three hours later, she'd more or less agreed to write chapter 9 for Carter Mecher. "I just liked him instantly," she recalled. "He wasn't some slick White House dude. He was like a guy in a t-shirt with motor oil under his fingernails. He wasn't a bastard." Lisa thought that doctors who stopped treating patients and went into public health needed to go through a transformation. "They go from taking care of individual people to taking care of the entire society," she said. "Not all of them can make that jump in their minds, but Carter had. You could tell that what he really cared about was saving lives." Carter also had real humility about him. "He said, 'I don't know about these things, and I think you do, and I need your help.' " I'd been working for a long time with a lot of people for whom I'm nothing but chopped liver. So I said, *He's trying to do good things. I'm going to help him.*"

Not long after Carter's visit, Lisa was asked by one of her bosses to help out with an awards ceremony. The CDC felt more like an academic institution than a government bureaucracy. "The culture of the CDC is to be super-humble and never brag on yourself, to an extent that is sometimes ridiculous," she said. The CDC had a shabby courtliness about it, with people in khakis and Birkenstocks graciously awaiting quiet recognition. Status in disease control came not from puffing out your chest but from getting your name on scholarly papers. At this particular ceremony of quiet recognition, Lisa's role was to hold the plaque while the CDC director explained the importance of the person about to receive it. As she was standing in the shadows at the back of the stage, her BlackBerry began to buzz. Embarrassed, she tossed it offstage to a colleague. "He starts going nuts," said Lisa. " 'It's the White House!!!! It's the White House!!!!!' " Lisa stepped off the stage and looked at Carter's message. "I want to invite u to meeting at WH this Thursday afternoon," it read. "I need to explain."

Arriving a few days later at the White House gates, she was so nervous that she called Carter from outside and said, "I've never been here! You've got to meet me on the street and walk me in!" That first meeting was actually a little awkward. A big shot from the CDC—sort of her boss's boss's boss—also was there. "He looked at me when I walked in and said, like, 'What the hell are you doing here?' " She wondered that, too. There were only a few people in the room, but they seemed important. They'd all come to hear Richard explain what he and Carter had been up to. Carter had only given her the faintest outline; now she heard the full story. "It blew my mind," she said. "The specific thing that blew my mind was using multiple semi-effective strategies together. There was no silver bullet. Right then I say, 'This is important. This has legs. It's not my job. I don't give a shit. I'm working on this.'"

Soon she was flying back and forth from Atlanta to Washington. The team of Richard and Carter became the team of Richard and Carter and Lisa. In Lisa they'd found their first real connection to the CDC. She knew just how radical their ideas were, and how hard these ideas would be to sell to the Americans who, in the event of a pandemic, would be charged with implementing them. "There was the CDC way of doing things," she said. "It was vaccinate and isolate. And this wasn't that." No one in the CDC was thinking about how, in the event of a deadly pandemic, the government might move people apart from each other in this way or that.

The week of the plan's publication, Carter asked Lisa to fly up for a meeting at the Department of Health and Human Services. This was the first time Richard would sell the idea of Targeted Layered Containment outside of the White House. His audience included people who had written the original pandemic plan that had enraged George Bush, vaccine experts from various agencies, people from the CDC, and, most alarmingly, the legendary D.A. Henderson. They didn't even pretend to be polite. "They just beat the shit out of him," said Lisa. Never mind Bob Glass and his toy model: the people inside the American government who would be charged with executing various aspects of any pandemic strategy thought all models of disease control were bullshit. They thought closing schools was a stupid idea. They believed none of these so-called non-pharmaceutical interventions would contribute anything but economic loss. "The argument was that we had no real-world data," said Richard. "That this was all just models." The subtext of every criticism was: *we're experts and you are not.* After the meeting, Lisa gave Richard a nickname: Piñata.

By then, the other people on the original pandemic planning team had left the White House and returned to their old jobs. Now Richard thought it might be better if he returned to his work studying the effects of radiation on the human body. "I had become overidentified with the arguments," he said, "and it was too easy to attack me as the crazy guy with the crazy arguments." Carter, on the other hand, had somehow remained uncontroversial. He'd been in the White House for six months, edited the entire plan and written big chunks of it, and helped dream up a strategy for disease control that seemed to piss off every agency in the federal government. But he had this curious ability to remain invisible. Rajeev, too, thought Carter had the best chance of selling a new idea. "People would object to what he'd write," he said, "but he'd already have thought it through and anticipated the objections. He doesn't dismiss your issues. He accepts that this is somebody else's reality."

On the heels of the plan's publication, Rajeev accepted an invitation from Harvard University to sit onstage and discuss the 1918 pandemic with John Barry, the author of the definitive book on the event. The day before the discussion, he asked Carter to go in his place. Carter, for his part, did not fully grasp why all of a sudden he was being thrust into the limelight. "I said, 'Fuck, I never read the guy's book,' and so I ran to a bookstore, bought a copy, and read it that night." As he read, he saw that much of the carnage it described had occurred in Philadelphia, then the nation's third-largest city. In just five weeks in the fall of 1918, twelve thousand people died. Corpses were stacked like cordwood outside the city morgue; corpses rotted in the streets. Philadelphians closed schools and banned public gatherings and wore masks—and suffered the highest death rate in the country. That's why everyone now thought that social distancing was a waste of time. But what struck Carter now was how slow Philadelphia's leaders had been to respond, even after they knew a deadly virus was racing out of control in their city. Yet he also saw that other cities had had radically different outcomes. The disease had swept through St. Louis, too, for instance, but had killed people at about half the rate that it had in Philadelphia. Why was that? No one seemed to know. Medical historians had surmised that St. Louis and other cities might have experienced a milder version of the virus the previous year and been left with some immunity.

Carter went onto the panel with John Barry the next day. "I had an interesting discussion with John Barry today," he wrote to his White House superiors afterward. "Barry doesn't buy into the modeling and thinks that school closure would be ineffective." But, he went on, "I saw things in his book that I would have never noticed had I read it prior to our thinking about community shielding." Carter then said he wanted to see what he could find out on his own about what actually happened in America in 1918. "Let me play with this."

The next day he sent, not just to Rajeev but also to Richard and Lisa, a single-spaced, thirteen-page memo, "Analysis of Philadelphia Outbreak 1918." He'd gone back over some of Barry's original sources—academic papers, old newspaper articles, and so on—to tease out at what point various local leaders had imposed restrictions on social life. "I felt very much like a paleontologist who found a bone fragment and was trying to reconstruct the entire animal," he wrote. "The most complete 'fossil record' that Barry provided was for Philadelphia. Yet even that record was pretty sketchy . . . I was able to uncover additional 'fossil records' by searching the internet for additional clues." In the end he plotted both the deaths and the restrictions imposed to prevent them, and saw that the earlier the restrictions imposed in any given outbreak, the fewer the deaths. In the case of Philadelphia, he wrote, "the closing of schools and churches, banning of public meetings, and banning of large public gatherings occurred relatively late into the epidemic"—nearly one month after the outbreak began and just a week before its peak. He wondered if other cities had reacted more quickly, and if their specific reactions might explain the huge variation in the death rates from city to city.

Two days later, he wrote to Lisa and filled her in. "Others use the stories in Barry's book to support the position that the infection control and social distancing measures would probably be ineffective," he wrote. "On the flight back to Atlanta I went thru Barry's book carefully and tried to reconstruct the events in a particularly hard hit city—Philadelphia . . . The bottom line is that anyone using the 1918 Philadelphia experience to argue that infection control and social distancing measures would be of little help needs to recognize how ineffective the overall response was in Philadelphia and how late the measures were instituted (within one week of the epidemic peak and after tens of thousands and perhaps hundreds of thousands were already ill)."

Carter and Richard were once again off and running, with Lisa now beside them, though without the knowledge of her superiors at the CDC. "She always said, 'Please keep it quiet,'" recalled Carter. "All of us had taken a blood oath—we absolutely had to trust each other." Soon Lisa was racing back and forth between her CDC day job and her night job, combing through archives of local newspapers that she paid out of her own pocket to access to find out what, exactly, had happened back in 1918. "I felt like I was on a treasure hunt," she said. "Gold was any mention in the newspapers of closing schools, or closing saloons or asking people to stay home." Richard moonlit from his new job in the stacks of the Library of Congress, but then he decided that they should bring in someone who knew how to compose an academic paper. "Carter and I were just a couple of buffoons who didn't know how to do a statistical significance test if it bit us in the ass," said Richard. Carter invented a name for what they were doing. "Redneck epidemiology," he called it.

It took just a few months for them to piece together what had actually happened in 1918. Their paper appeared in the May 2007 issue of the *Proceedings of the National Academy of Sciences.* A coauthor and friend, the Harvard epidemiologist Marc Lipsitch, did the statistical work and the other stuff that made it seem as if it were written by proper scholars.* Titled "Public Health Interventions and Epidemic Intensity during the 1918 Influenza Pandemic," the piece revealed, for the first time, the life-or-death importance of timing in the outcomes of 1918. Cities that intervened immediately after the arrival of the virus experienced far less disease and death. The first reported flu cases in Philadelphia had been on September 17. The first case wasn't spotted in St. Louis until October 5—which also happened to be the day the United States surgeon general, Rupert Blue, finally acknowledged the severity of the disease and rec-

---

* Lipsitch, whose name was on the paper, found the invitation to collaborate fun, if a bit off-the-wall. "No one was really thinking about the subject," he said. "You only ask a question when you have a reason." Later, a lot of people would have a reason to ask the question. As of October 26, 2020, of 86,622 papers ranked from the *Proceedings of the National Academy of Sciences*, the paper came in as the eighth most-cited. Lisa Koonin was an author on the early drafts, but for her name to appear on the final publication, she required the CDC's approval. At some point it became clear that the CDC's approval process would delay publication for so long that the academics Richard had initially brought in to help them, and who had set off in competition with them, would beat them to publication. That drove Lisa nuts: the whole idea had been Carter's. And so she asked Carter and Richard to remove her name. "We thank Lisa Koonin for invaluable and indefatigable assistance," they wrote at the paper's end. "Her name should have been on the paper," says Carter.

ommended that local leaders take action. The death rate in St. Louis was half that of Philadelphia because St. Louis's leaders used the cover provided by the federal government to distance its citizens from one another.

That didn't mean that everyone in St. Louis appreciated what had happened. "We're reading the newspapers in St. Louis," said Richard, "and they know for a fact that they are having a better experience than other cities, and they still couldn't keep their interventions in place for more than four to six weeks." The paper analyzed the effects of that inability, and showed that American cities that caved to pressure from business interests to relax their social distancing rules experienced big second waves of disease. American cities that didn't did not. The paper offered a real-world confirmation of what Bob Glass and the other mathematical modelers had discovered in their fake worlds. However you felt about the strategy of Targeted Layered Containment, you could no longer say there was no data to show that it had any effect. "Until then, the people who hated our ideas could throw up smoke screens about modeling," said Richard. "They couldn't throw up smoke screens about what had happened in 1918."

The paper's more subtle message appeared between its lines: people have a very hard time getting their minds around pandemics. Why was it still possible, in 2006, to say something original and important about the events of 1918? Why had it taken nearly a century to see a simple truth about the single most deadly pandemic in human history? Only after three amateur historians studied the various interventions, and the various death tolls in individual American cities, did the importance of timing became obvious. Carter wondered why this had been so hard to see. A big part of the answer, he decided, was in the nature of pandemics. They were exponential processes. If you took a penny and doubled it every day for thirty days, you'd have more than five million dollars: people couldn't imagine disease spread any better than they could imagine a penny growing like that. "I think it's because of the way our brains are wired," said Carter. "Take a piece of paper and fold it in half, then fold it in half again, for a total of 50 times folding it in half. If a piece of paper is 0.004 inches thick to begin with, by the time you fold it 50 times, it is more than 70 million miles thick." Again, it feels impossible. The same mental glitch that leads people to not realize the power of compound interest blinds them to the importance of intervening before a pathogen explodes.

It was seven months before the United States public-health system fully bought into the power of social distancing. The story of those months was dear to Lisa Koonin. She saved every email and every version of the fifty or more presentations she and Carter made—to everyone from the Department of Education to state and local public-health officers who filled hotel ballrooms. She thought she might one day write a book about it.

The big theme of her book would be the power of storytelling. It had taken Lisa, Richard, and Carter some time to see that they were in a war of competing narratives, and that whoever had the best narrative would win. Public-health people who did not actually know all that much about the subject, for instance, would insist that if you closed schools, all sorts of bad things would happen: crime would rise with kids on the streets; the thirty million kids in the school-lunch program would lack nutrition; parents wouldn't be able to go to work; and so on. American society now leaned on schools to care for children in a way that would have bewildered Americans of an earlier age, as that other institution, the family, was failing at the job. "The sub-rosa conversation was that families weren't safe places for children," said Lisa.

To refute knee-jerk arguments about the costs of social distancing, Carter had marshaled so much data from so many corners of the U.S. government that a senior public-health official who passed through the White House called him Rain Man. He'd show his critics that crime rates actually fell on weekends, for instance, when kids were out of school. *The FBI keeps all these stats*, he'd say. *Juvenile crime peaks at 3:30 p.m. on weekdays. Because they've been cooped up all day and they're just going nuts.* He'd show his critics exactly how many households would need help minding their children—and it was not nearly as many as they had assumed. During the summers, only 2.6 million kids used the school-lunch program: Did that not suggest that the number of kids without access to proper nutrition was far smaller than the number of kids using the program? He showed them a survey that Lisa Koonin commissioned, of parents with children who used it: just one in seven, or 2.8 million, said they'd have trouble feeding their children if schools could not. If schools were closed, Carter concluded, the problem was not 30 million kids but fewer than 3 million; they could be fed with supplemental food stamps.

He did that kind of thing over and over: take some problem others thought insurmountably huge and shrink it until it seemed manageable. And yet he had no effect on people's deep feeling that it wasn't worth the cost of closing schools, or intervening in American social life in any other way, to slow a pandemic.

There'd come a moment when he and Richard had both almost given up. Afterward they'd decided that, rather than try to change people's minds, they ought to try changing people's hearts. Or, rather, that the way to change minds was by first changing hearts. Carter ceased his appeals to reason and began to appeal to emotion—which is to say that he stopped making an argument and began to tell a story. His story, at its core, was about the hole left when someone dies, especially when the death is preventable, and the someone is a child. He'd ask his audience to reimagine the last great pandemic, but as an emotional event. He'd put up on a screen a heart-tugging photograph of a nine-year-old girl in 1918, smiling and dressed for church. Then he'd describe how she and other small children would end up as bodies, stacked liked cordwood. He'd even put up a picture of his mother as a child and tell the story of her next-door neighbor. The woman who lived next door to his mom had given birth to four children. After the third had died of flu, the undertaker had told the woman that if the fourth child died, he'd bury him for free. Carter's mother hadn't actually been born until 1928, but he was pretty sure the story was true.

The story that Lisa planned to tell in her book would build to a tipping point, a meeting that ran for two days, December 11–12, 2006. It amounted to a final showdown on this new, but also ancient, strategy for disease control. Public-health officers from around the country had gathered, along with assorted big shots from the private sector and academia, among them D.A. Henderson, in a big room in a crappy hotel near the Atlanta airport. The local public-health officers had been the most critical of social distancing and especially of the idea of closing schools. They would have to implement the strategies and deal with their fallout.

By then several inside the CDC were on board, including the CDC's head of global migration and quarantine, Marty Cetron. Their support was conditional, however. The condition was that the people in the big room in the crappy airport hotel buy into the strategy.

Carter spoke for thirty minutes to the assembly and then ceded the floor to Marty, who, after all, was the expert on disease control. After Marty had finished speaking, the local health people began to voice the usual list of objections. It was then that Carter leaned over to Marty and whispered: "Ask them what they would do." He'd prepped Marty for just this moment. *How many of you have children or grandchildren?* asked Marty. Nearly all hands went up. *If there's a pandemic anything like the one in 1918, how many would send your kids to school?*

One guy from someplace in Florida raised his hand, then saw that he was alone and quickly lowered it. "So it's only poor kids who need school lunch who should risk illness and death to go to school," Carter said. "Why don't we just find another way to feed them so they can stay home, too?"

That was the moment that Lisa sensed people *felt* it. They stopped thinking like social justice warriors and became parents. Of course if there was a real risk of disease killing their children they'd keep their kids home from school! That, thought Lisa, was the moment she and Carter looked at each other and said, "We won!" That was the moment the CDC accepted various forms of social distancing as a viable tool in any future pandemic, because they saw that everyone else would.

That was also when Carter fully infiltrated the Centers for Disease Control. The morning after the hotel meeting, he dressed in what amounted to a CDC costume: Birkenstocks, a loose-fitting shirt, and khaki pants to match—or not. He drove to a CDC campus in Atlanta; there Lisa badged him in and led him to Marty Cetron's office. Marty had left for a ski trip in Europe. Carter sat at a desk and, consulting with Richard over the phone, wrote the CDC's new policy, which called for social distancing in the event of any pandemic. The nature of the interventions would depend on the severity of the disease, of course. The CDC recommended that schools close, for instance, only when some new communicable disease was projected to kill more than 450,000 Americans. But school closure and social distancing of kids and bans on mass gatherings and other interventions would be central to the future pandemic strategy of the United States—and not just the United States. "The CDC was the world's leading health agency," said Lisa. "When the CDC publishes something, it is not just the CDC talking to the U.S. but to the entire world."

Back at the White House, they couldn't quite believe what

had happened. The people who worked on biodefense policy watched as the CDC, and other U.S. government agencies
with a stake in pandemic response, went from being closed and
defensive about the idea of school closures and social distancing
to open and accepting. Ken Staley, who had supervised the pandemic planners, fielded a call from the CDC in late December
2006. "They call and say, 'We just want to make sure you guys
are okay with us doing all this,' " Staley recalled. "They were
asking us if it was okay to do it—like it was their idea all along.
I'm asking, 'How did this happen?' They say, 'Well, we're here
with Carter . . .' " Later Staley realized what had happened.
"Carter went like undercover," he said. "He's sort of a goof-
ball, and he does this thing where he just burrows in and they
forget he's even from the White House." When Staley and the
others read what the CDC wanted to publish, the only change
they could detect was in the title. Instead of "Targeted Layered
Containment (TLC)," the CDC wanted to call the new strategy "Community Mitigation Guidance." "Carter could give a
shit about the name," said Staley. "He let them change it so it
becomes their idea."

Long after Carter had left the building, Lisa Koonin remained
incredulous. "He was from the White House!" she said. "And
people forgot he didn't work here. I have never seen that. I have
never seen any other outsider get himself so on the inside of the
development of some CDC policy." Carter's trick was that he
never reminded people where he was from, or for that matter
told them anything else about himself. "He just went incognito,"
said Lisa. "People didn't even know how to say his name. They'd
pronounce it *MEE-cher* or *METCH-er.* They were always getting it wrong. Carter would never correct them." (It's pronounced
MEH-sher.) After he'd left, people seemed to forget he'd ever
been there. By February 2007, when the CDC published the new
strategy, if you asked anyone inside the place who had written it,

they'd have given you the name of a man inside the CDC. Marty Cetron, or maybe someone who worked for him.

This bothered Lisa. If one day in some future pandemic the new strategy saved millions of lives, no one would ever know where it came from. She thought they should know. And so, on the cover of the CDC's official publication, in print so tiny it needed to be magnified many times before it became visible, she stenciled *TLC*. And she saved Carter's emails. "It is funny how life unfolds," he'd written to her in one. "I always felt a bit like a child in all this but having the eyes of a child and a sense of awe and no firmly held perspective to begin with was how I could help in some small way. I never had anything to unlearn."

*

Two months after the CDC published its new pandemic strategy, Laura Glass, now sixteen years old, returned to Washington, DC, for her final science competition. The Young Epidemiology Scholars Competition, this new contest was called. Her mom had somehow found out about it and suggested she enter her science fair project and make a trip of it. On her giant foam boards, she'd honed her mission statement. "Could the oldest of strategies, social distancing, be designed to target specific age groups and zones of high infectious contact within a social contact network and thus limit the spread of disease?" she'd written. On her boards, she walked the science fair judges through all the work she had done. She explained the computer model she had helped to build, the surveys she'd done of the citizens of Albuquerque, New Mexico, and the insights that her work had led to, with the help of the model. "I found that if schools are closed AND preschoolers, children and teens are restricted to the home epidemics that would have infected 65% of the population COULD BE REDUCED BY NEARLY 80%," she wrote.

"If adults also restrict their contacts within non-essential work environments epidemics from such highly infective strains can be ENTIRELY THWARTED!"

Somehow they didn't give her a prize. The judges never explicitly criticized her for collaborating with her father. She just felt an undertone of disapproval. It bothered her father more than it did Laura, but still she found it unfair. Everyone who made it to the highest levels of science competition had some grown-up mentor. Hers just happened to be her father. "I don't have any bitterness about it," she said. "I just remember they asked me lots of hard questions, and that I didn't answer them as well as I should." A year later, she went off to college and decided that she belonged less in science than in the humanities. By then science perhaps didn't need her as much: the insights at the heart of her project had become the official policy of the United States government, and were spreading rapidly from the CDC to the rest of the world.

FIVE

Clairvoyance

Carter watched the people inside the Bush White House slip out the back door, one by one. "At the end of the second term, they know it's over," he said. "What I learned later is that all the smart people leave early to get jobs." Richard and Rajeev had left long before the election. Then James Lawler left. Lawler was a young navy doctor who had joined their little group toward the end of the Bush administration. His job, among other things, was to make fun of their situation. Outside the office, he'd posted cartoons that, as he put it, "captured the way people viewed us." The picture of Richard was of Mr. Know-It-All from *Rocky and Bullwinkle*. Carter's was a guy in a river wearing a loincloth: John the Baptist, of pandemic response. Once Lawler left, the cartoons were all that remained of the old group. And after Obama's election, the entire building was basically drained of humanity.

Still, Carter remained. He wasn't quite sure how it happened, but his name wound up on a list of experts asked to stick around for a few months to advise the new administration in case of emergency. To sell the new pandemic strategy and stay on in the White House beyond his original six months' leave of absence from the Veterans Health Administration, he'd been forced to surrender his job running hospital systems. That had been a painful but necessary sacrifice that left him without a role at his former employer. "I didn't have anyplace else to go," said Carter, "so I said sure."

And so there he sat, nearly invisible, in the same room in the Old Executive Office Building he'd been in since he arrived, with its excellent view of the Rose Garden, and the takeoffs and landings of Marine One. He watched the new people flood into the White House to replace all the old people who had flooded out. "It felt like going to your old high school after you graduated," he said. "The buildings are all the same, but the people are totally different." All the work he'd done had been swept away, too. He'd had three computers on his desk: top secret, secret, and normal. "They came through and took away all the hard drives and put in new ones," he said. "They take all of your crap. All your old files just get packed up and removed. You can't even keep your old emails."

He marveled at the inefficiency of his government. All of this stuff, lost. Thousands upon thousands of files, including all the work he'd done selling the world's first pandemic strategy, simply vanished. "I was shocked," he said. "No wonder you want people to stay behind. All that's left of the work is what's in their heads."

Even that was not put to use. He'd never been so idle in his life as he was during those first few months of the new administration. He entertained himself by watching the new people learn their way around the office: the new Office of Management and Budget director brought his girlfriend to see his grand new office with its grand fireplace, and built this huge fire for her, only to discover that the flue had been welded shut. The building filled with smoke. Carter walked around with newspaper pictures of the new people and, like a bird-watcher, tried to identify who was who. For the first time in his career, no one really wanted him to do anything. He wasn't a political appointee, but he was linked to the previous administration and so assumed to be beside the point. "I would be considered—what do you call it?—the deep state," he said. "I was part of the old crowd." There was no hostility, merely indifference. The new class knew he'd be gone in a few months, so why bother?

The official newly in charge of him, Heidi Avery, who came from some deep place in the intelligence community and was now called deputy assistant to the president for homeland security, told him that the Obama administration had decided to dissolve the Biodefense Directorate and fold it into something called the Resilience Directorate. For Carter personally, it just meant swapping out one bullshit job title he could barely remember for another. In terms of pandemic response more generally, he thought it was a big mistake: henceforth disease would be managed alongside all the other existential threats to American life, and, along with other, less sexy threats, be shoved into the background. George Bush's moment of terror after reading John Barry's book had led his administration to break with tradition and create an office that did nothing but worry about pandemics. Now Obama was about to do away with it. "She was a real hard-ass," Carter said of his new boss. "She told me that if I thought it was a bad idea, I should write a memo explaining why it was a bad idea."

He wrote the memo knowing that the Obama people would dismiss it, which they did. After that, to the vast amusement of Duane Caneva and Dave Marcozzi, two younger doctors in the office that was being dissolved and moved to someplace else, Carter occupied himself by writing the third annual review of the original pandemic plan. "They kept saying, 'No one, not a single person in all of human history, is ever going to read that,'" he said. Each year for the next four years, he wrote one of these progress reports. The relevant government agencies had been given three years to implement the hundreds of actions the pandemic plan required of them. It might take mere months for the Department of Agriculture to, say, educate bird owners to behave in ways that minimized the chance of some bug jumping from their backyard chicken farm into their children. It would take years for the Department of Health and Human Services to renovate the nation's vaccine supply chain so that the country wasn't dependent on chicken eggs to grow a vaccine for bird flu.

One night in April 2009, weeks before he was scheduled to leave the White House, and as he was finishing his annual review, Carter got a phone call from a friend. His friend worked in the Department of Health and Human Services and had news that he thought Carter should hear: a second person in Southern California had tested positive for what appeared to be a novel flu virus. The first case had occurred two days earlier, but it was more than a hundred miles from the second, and the two people involved had no connection to each other. At the same time, there were disturbing reports of a flu in Mexico City killing young people. If those deaths had been caused by the same new pathogen that had turned up in California, they took on new meaning. Old strains of flu caused sporadic illness; a new strain of flu could kill millions. Carter asked his friend if the virus in California was the same as the virus in Mexico City. "He said, 'That's a complicated question,'" recalled Carter. "I said, 'Ah, c'mon, can you just give me a complicated answer, then?'" He wouldn't, so Carter called Marty Cetron at the CDC, and Marty explained that the Mexicans had sent samples of the virus not to the CDC but to the Canadian government, and that the Canadians had just analyzed them and figured out that, yes, young Mexicans had died of the same new strain of flu that had just turned up in California. And actually Texas, too. Two more cases had just been reported.

Carter hung up and called Heidi Avery. He told his new boss that a pandemic had begun and should be viewed as an imminent threat to national security. She gathered senior White House people for a meeting at seven the following morning and asked Carter to brief them. The day after that, he popped over to the West Wing, to John Brennan's office, and, feeling a little funny about the presumption, suggested to the homeland security adviser that he call an emergency cabinet meeting to signal how seriously the president was taking the disease, and Brennan agreed. On April 17, Obama had returned from a trip to Mexico City, where he had shaken hands with a man who died just days later of what some suspected, wrongly as it turned out, to be swine flu. Now Obama wanted to speak with Carter.

What's the worst case? asked the new president.

Nineteen eighteen, said Carter.

What happened then? asked Obama.

Thirty percent of the population was infected, and two percent died, said Carter. *In the current situation, you'd be looking at two million dead.*

Then he explained to the president the pandemic strategy. That strategy assumed that the virus would first emerge a long way away, likely in Asia, and that the United States would have time to prepare. *It's totally jumped ahead of our plan,* Carter explained. *It's already here.* He felt a little bad dumping all of this on Obama, as the president was just then dealing with a global financial crisis, two foreign wars, and a domestic fight to the death over his proposed health care plan. As he was speaking, Rahm Emanuel, Obama's chief of staff, looked up and said, "What's next, locusts?"

After sounding the alarm, Carter had told Heidi he wanted to call Richard Hatchett and bring him back to the White House. She said that she'd have Richard badged up and cleared to work the next day. "As soon as the pandemic hit, she trusted me," said Carter. "I don't know why."

*

I first saw the news stories of a new strain of swine flu a couple of days ago, but am so far from my flu-fighting days, and had become so inured to false alarms that I didn't even read them . . .

Richard had promised himself that he would keep a journal of his life during the first years of the lives of each of his children, to give to them as adults. He'd written one for his first child and then procrastinated with his second, who was three years old in early 2009, when Richard finally got to it. Over the next year he'd write a thousand words every night, in longhand, without ever needing to scratch one out and replace it with another. It was as if he walked around with fully formed paragraphs in his head, which he might later dictate to himself. His entry from that Friday in April 2009 continued:

This morning I woke up to find a terse email from Carter Mecher, now director of Medical Preparedness Policy in the White House, saying 'If u r up call me' and providing his cell phone number; the e-mail had been posted at 11:20pm last night.

What happened was that during the day it had emerged that a serious outbreak of respiratory illness in Mexico, associated with at least a thousand cases and perhaps as many as 60 deaths, mostly in young adults, had been identified as influenza and not just influenza but swine influenza, identical to the swine influenza in Texas and California. This virus was an odd

combination of known North American human and bird flu and
Eurasian swine flu. Presumably some pig in Mexico, perhaps
in the vicinity of Mexico City, had served as a mixing bowl in
which this unprecedented recombination event had occurred.

Richard's journal was meant to be an account of domestic life. After Carter's email, it became a real-time fine-brushed picture of the inner workings of the United States government confronting a new virus. The story ended seven months later with Richard, in the Oval Office, being asked for a postmortem on the response to the pandemic by President Obama. By then, people would be saying that the country had dodged a bullet. "It isn't that we dodged a bullet," Richard would tell the president. "It's that nature shot us with a BB gun."

A couple of months into the swine flu pandemic, Richard sensed that his journal might be a valuable historical document. Once it became clear that swine flu would come and go, like a massive hurricane that dissipated before making landfall, it became something else. A message in a bottle. A premonition. A warning. Richard emerged having absorbed dozens of small lessons and two big ones—the first being just how different a real pandemic was from an imagined one. "The entire epidemic has been characterized by nothing so much as ambiguity—and in particular about the number of people infected," he wrote on May 9, nearly three weeks after he'd moved back into the White House. All they had were these reports, possibly exaggerated, of young people dying in Mexican intensive care units. "The ICU is like a funnel," said Richard. "It concentrates all of the badness." But that badness only told you so much; you needed to see the goodness, too. The infection fatality rate had not just a numerator (deaths) but also a denominator (infections). If you didn't know how many people had survived infection, you couldn't say how deadly the virus actually was.

We are now two weeks into our response to the virus and we still have no idea how heavy a blow it could deliver. There are reasons for optimism and reasons for concern and a thousand reasons not to trust the evidence of one's senses. We've seen the beast's dorsal fin once, in Mexico, but now it has submerged again, and the cases now stacking up say more about where the virus has been than where it is going.

The Mexicans, interestingly, had taken the new pandemic strategy of the United States and run with it. They'd closed schools, and socially distanced the population in other ways that, studies would later show, shut down disease transmission. The CDC, by contrast, sent the message that each American school should make its own decision, which was a bit like telling a bunch of sixth graders that the homework was optional. A few schools closed, but the vast majority did not. The local public-health officials with the power to close the schools had no political cover to do what needed doing. In that moment it was clear to Richard and Carter that there'd be no cohesive national strategy.

Carter and I argued as hard as we could for a 'tactical pause'; CDC felt we "didn't have enough data." It was an argument about the precautionary principle v. the scientist's desire not to make a mistake, coupled with risk aversion that was all too characteristic of public health bureaucrats. It was literally driving Carter nuts.

Richard had helped to invest with credibility the whole idea of using mathematical models to forecast disease, and the forecasters were becoming accepted experts. On May 4, the White House invited Neil Ferguson from Imperial College London and Marc Lipsitch from Harvard to present their work. "They are the world's best—literally the world's best—at doing this sort of real-time analysis," said Richard. "They showed not only what you don't know but why you don't know it." The two epidemiologists had gathered the data from the Mexican outbreak. They estimated the attack rate—the percentage of the population likely to be infected—at somewhere between 20 and 30 percent, and the so-called case fatality rate at between 0.1 and 1.8 percent. That was the difference between a slightly worse than usual flu season and more than one million dead Americans, some large number of them children. With that little information, decisions had to be made.

The new pandemic strategy insisted upon the need to close schools before more than 0.1 percent of the population had become infected. That amount of disease was virtually impossible to detect with the naked eye: in a city of one hundred thousand people, one hundred or fewer people would be walking around with the virus inside them. A case fatality rate of 1 percent implied a terrifying pandemic. It also implied that, at the critical decision-making moment, only one person in the entire city of one hundred thousand people would have died. Might not even have died yet, but was merely lying in some ICU bed, about to die. It would take extraordinary leadership to look at that situation and say, "Shut it all down." The decision would necessarily be unpopular, and difficult to explain to the public. But that's what a leader would need to do. And on May 5, the day after the forecasters showed that the strength of the storm was still impossible to predict, the CDC let the leader off the hook:

CDC rushed to issue guidance today to recommend that schools be reopened. This revised guidance was announced at a press conference in Atlanta... Earlier that day I saw [Homeland Security] Secretary [Janet] Napolitano speaking on Fox News, apparently about swine flu, with a banner running under her on the screen saying something to the effect that "The worst is over!" Surely that was an attribution, not a point she'd made but it is clear that people have rushed to dismiss the threat. It is uncanny, like something from a bad science fiction movie ... [CDC acting director] Rich [Besser] has leaned over and unclipped the leash without knowing whether he was setting free a puppy dog or a tiger. The recklessness of the decision, given the uncertainties, was astonishing, a deep failure, to my mind, of the institution to perform its primary duty, which is to protect the public health.

From that moment, Richard and Carter had trouble getting good information from the CDC. They had imagined that the CDC would simply send everything it knew about the outbreak to the White House. The CDC seemed intent on preserving their privileged view of the outbreak. Several times Richard caught the CDC slow-walking data about the illness and deaths caused by this new flu. They had to strain to see what was going on.

I see New York City as the chief battleground right now. There's now potentially as many as 300 chains of infection in the city and it is conceivable that the virus could explode there.

On May 17, the week after Richard wrote those words, Mitchell Wiener, a fifty-five-year-old assistant principal in New York City, died of the new swine flu. But it was impossible to actually say what that meant: it was one death. The secretary of education, Arne Duncan, had said he would do what the public-health people told him to do. But one set of experts, inside the White House, thought they should close schools; and the other, at the CDC in Atlanta, thought they shouldn't. When Obama had asked Carter what he should do, Carter had told him that he ought to close schools until they knew what they were dealing with. Obama had instead listened to the CDC.

A few months later, the fog would have lifted and the war would be over. The new flu would turn out to be less lethal than it might have been. The CDC would report that somewhere between forty and eighty million Americans had been infected but only 12,469 had died. Their judgment had been vindicated, and President Obama's decision had worked out, and everyone would soon move on and forget about the pandemic that wasn't. To Richard's way of thinking, the fact that the decision happened to have worked out did not mean it was the right decision; in a funny way, it was alarming that it had worked out, as it created a false sense of confidence in the process that had rendered it. In late September he noted that others sensed this, too.

An idea that has gained currency in the White House is that we will be extraordinarily lucky if, as appears increasingly likely, we dodge the bullet. It will not have been because of the quality of the response. The prerequisites of failure were all in place.

Richard's other takeaway from his second tour of duty in the White House was just how little government was able to do quickly. "You only have whatever buttons to push that you had going into the crisis," he said. "You don't get any new buttons. You could see by September how little we had in fact gotten into place that was different from when the pandemic started." The vaccine that went into production in May 2009, weeks after the new flu was detected, wasn't ready for mass distribution until late December. Had the virus been as lethal as it first appeared, a lot of people would have died.

But in one way, Richard felt reassured. The event dramatized the importance of the work they had done three years earlier. The United States government might not have closed the schools and used other social distancing measures, as Mexico had, but these things were now real options. The country had a new button to press, and new experts who might press it. And one expert, Richard thought, stood above all others.

Carter seems to be the only guy who knows where we are in the movie: he is constantly watching, scanning, trolling, calculating, second-guessing.

*

When Carter Mecher was eleven years old, he'd had a strange experience that he'd never really removed from his mind and that, once the swine flu pandemic began, returned to the front of it. The year was 1967. The nation lived with this constant low-level anxiety about nuclear war. Some researchers had decided to study how people would actually respond during a nuclear attack. Right there in downtown Chicago, they'd built a nuclear fallout shelter and asked for volunteers. For some reason Carter's mother had thought it a good idea to raise her hand, and so without Carter's fully understanding why, he and his parents and his five siblings were taken to the shelter. "There's barely enough room for four hundred people," he recalled. "There's concrete floors with no pillows or blankets. To eat, you had crackers, plus water that tasted like bleach. There's one light that's powered by a bike, so someone has to ride the bike to keep the light on. But the bike also can power a fan, so you had to choose between the light and the fan. It's hot as hell." The only creature comfort allowed was cigarettes. So the whole place filled with smoke.

There Carter and his family remained for three days. The researchers stepped around them, taking notes. "They wanted to watch how people would behave," said Carter. "So I got to watch, too." What he realized, as he watched, was that there was no way a nuclear war would be anything like that. "My mom would be at home, and we'd be at school, and my dad would be at work," he said. "We'd all be separated. We wouldn't know how to get to the shelter, and that's not where we'd go anyway." His mind unspooled a different scenario that left him with a conviction that nuclear fallout shelters were probably a dumb idea. "Going through that experience forever changed my vision of these events."

He had a similar feeling at the end of the faux pandemic of 2009. Things went down differently than he'd ever imagined. If he had to do it all over again, he'd still have told Obama to close the schools. The lesson many had taken away from the event was how smart it was not to have closed the schools, or taken the kind of aggressive action that was necessary at the start of a deadly outbreak, to prevent its explosion. "It's like someone who looked down at their phone while driving and drifted onto the shoulder but didn't hit anything," he said. "The lessons aren't as strong and defined. Had that person hit a mailbox or ended up in a ditch and wrecked his car, he would have learned a hard lesson. Had they hit and killed a pedestrian, they probably wouldn't want to get into the driver's seat again for a long, long time. In all cases, though, the lesson is really the same."

People didn't seem to get that. There was, Carter thought, a downside to experience. "Experience is making the same mistake over and over again, only with greater confidence," he said. The line wasn't his, but he liked it.

When Carter left his home in Atlanta for the White House three years before, he'd told his wife he'd be gone six months. He assumed that now he'd finally be going home—but then something funny happened. Heidi Avery, the hard-ass boss, asked him to stay in the White House to help her think about any problems that might arise. Carter now sensed when she might have changed her mind about him. Early on, they'd been discussing the pandemic plan, and he had shared with her his thoughts about maps. They were also his thoughts about plans, as a plan is a kind of map: a map of what you plan to do. He told her a story about some troops who'd gotten lost in the Alps. "They're in a blizzard," said Carter. "A guy finds a map in his backpack. The map leads them to safety." What was cool about the story, Carter thought, was that once the soldiers were safe and able to study the map more closely, they saw that it was a map not of the Alps but of the Pyrenees. "A map has value when you are lost," he said. "It gives you a starting point." There was an analogy with his earlier life as a doctor in an intensive care unit. "The patient is fading right there in front of your eyes," he said. "You cannot run out of options. Because what do you do when you run out of options? You panic. Having something in front of you, a map, a plan, a list of treatments, even if it isn't completely right, is better than nothing."

Carter agreed to stay until the end of Obama's first term. Whenever some urgent problem arose that needed thinking through, Heidi Avery would bring it to Carter and ask him to think about it. Deepwater Horizon. Fukushima. The earthquake in Haiti. "She'd say, 'Run ahead and see what you can find, and then come back and tell me,'" recalled Carter. She gave him a nickname: Scout. As in: "Scout, tell me what no one else is seeing." She'd figured out that Carter Mecher saw things that other people didn't.

At the end of 2011, Carter finally returned to the Veterans Health Administration in Atlanta, and people there soon forgot, if they had ever known, that he'd worked in the White House. He'd never lost his power of invisibility, and there were times he was pretty sure that his superiors simply forgot he was there. He had time on his hands again and spent some of it thinking about the next pandemic. "I walked away from that one saying, 'Next time this isn't going to be easy,'" he said. "The whole thing assumed you would know how bad the pandemic was. And that was a really bad assumption. This fog, this not knowing, is such a big part of it. You almost need to be clairvoyant."

His mind groped for the right analogy, so that the next time he might lead people to a different kind of understanding. Managing a pandemic was like driving a weird car that only accelerated, or braked, fifteen seconds after you hit the pedal. "Or think of looking at a star," he said. "It's the same thing. The light you see is from years ago. When you are looking at a disease, the disease you are seeing is from last week." The CDC had lots of great people, but it was at heart a massive university. "A peacetime institution in a wartime environment," Carter called it. Its people were good at figuring out precisely what had happened, but by the time they'd done it, the fighting was over. They had no interest in or aptitude for the sort of clairvoyance that was needed at the start of a pandemic. Yet the CDC was now the home for the strategy he and Richard had created. "So the CDC is the authority, and everyone is going to be waiting for the CDC to make a decision," said Carter. "And who is going to go against the CDC—some local health official?"

*

For as long as Charity Dean could remember, she'd been a list maker. She scribbled her lists on whiteboards, inside of books, on scraps of paper, and even, in the case of her annual birthday resolutions, on the back of the portrait of her grandmother that hung beside her desk at home. A lot of her lists were mental. One of them detailed the roughly twenty things that had tried to come between her and her life purpose.

At the top of that particular list was Junction City, Oregon. She'd grown up in that farming community, in a family that was poor even by local standards. "I grew up with the shame and embarrassment of trying to hide how poor you are," she said. She never showered after gym class, because showering meant changing in front of other girls, and her underwear always had holes in it. Her clothes came from the pile collected by their church to send to Africa with the missionaries. They survived on food stamps. She found the deprivation less painful than her inability to disguise it.

The church was the second item on her mental list. The church ran her family's life, and she learned to fear its elders. "The fact that it was nondenominational was the important thing," she said, "because it floated off on its own, unlike Baptists and Catholics, and they made it clear they thought they, and they alone, were going to heaven. They didn't seek commonality with other churches. It was divisive and fear-based." At a very young age, she sensed that she was being trained, as a dog might be trained, to grow up to be a woman with no ambition other than to bear children. She learned that while there was only one road to heaven, there were a great many to hell. Secular music, for instance, which she was forbidden to listen to. Science, for another. In sixth-grade science class, when the theory of evolution came up, Charity was handed a note saying she needed to go straight to the principal's office and wait it out until those lessons were over. The other kids who went to her church all got the same note.

Which is not to say that she had not learned things in church. When she was seven years old, missionaries who'd been to Africa came and spoke of plagues they'd witnessed. That experience had triggered an obsession: from then on, she'd wanted to know everything she could about disease and the viruses that caused them. She decided to become a doctor before she grasped all the reasons why she couldn't. "I didn't know anybody who had graduated from a four-year college," she said. "That's not what people in Junction City did." Her school guidance counselor told her that kids from Junction City didn't become doctors, and that she should change her mind. Instead of changing her mind about her ambition, she guarded it. "I learned to hold that card close, because no one believed it," she said. In her senior year in high school she was thrown a lifeline, in the form of a scholarship from a foundation set up by a local lumber tycoon, for kids whose parents hadn't gone to college. The Ford Family Foundation, as it was called, offered to pay her way to Oregon State. "The elders said I was disobeying God's will because I wanted to go to a four-year college," Charity recalled.

She went to Oregon State. The first thing she learned after she got there and began taking the classes she'd need for medical school was how fantastically ill-prepared she was. There'd been no AP science classes in Junction City. No one had ever taught her how to study. Her academic adviser suggested that she drop science altogether and major in art. Instead she fell fully in love with microbiology. She learned that every creature, even the tiniest, was evolving all the time. Evolution wasn't really a matter of opinion. She tried to explain that to her parents—that it wasn't a matter of whether humans had evolved but how the entire process had started—but they didn't want to hear of it. The more science she learned, the more she drifted from family and community, and the more pressure she felt to do something to restore herself in their good graces. "When I went to college, I was ostracized," she said. "The only way back in was to marry."

She badly wanted to go to Tulane University for medical school. She got into four other schools, but Tulane wait-listed her. On its website, she saw that the university boasted of the diversity of its student body. She wrote a letter to the dean of admissions, telling him about her upbringing and asking him if the school had ever admitted anyone like her. "I was poor white trash from Oregon. That's all I had." She made a batch of chocolates shaped like the state of Oregon and sent them with the letter. "I got a phone call the day the chocolates arrived," said Charity. "It was from a woman who worked in admissions. She said, 'I'm not calling because he was swayed by what you sent, but we're offering you admission to Tulane Medical School.'"

The church elders were not happy about it, but they allowed her to go to New Orleans, on the condition that she return to Junction City afterward and marry the young man they'd approved for her. Now twenty-two years old, with a husband she did not want, she found herself in a strange and sinful city competing with medical students who had undergraduate degrees from places like Harvard and Stanford. She finished the first semester at the top of her class. Her new husband complained to the church elders that his wife was spending all her time working. "He told me I was being disobedient by working so hard," recalled Charity. "And they agreed with him. They told me I should be at the fiftieth percentile of my class. No better." After the next semester, when her grades remained high, the church elders sent her a letter instructing her to drop out of medical school and return to Junction City.

She had to think about it, actually. She was still terrified of them. "I thought I was choosing between heaven and hell," she said. But after thinking about it, she told her husband she wanted a divorce. He soon left; in his place came a letter from the church elders. "It said I was dead to them," she said. There was nothing worse in the church than being divorced, and the split was not just with the church but with her entire community. Her friends cut her off; relations with her family grew tense. "I decided I would rather go to hell and become a doctor," she said. Twice a month, she had what she thought of as "the wedding dream." In the dream, it was her wedding day. She is walking down the aisle when she realizes that it's all wrong. He's not the guy. There on the spot she announces she's out and walks away. "It's the decision I didn't have the courage to make," she said. "I always make it in the dream."

She was a twenty-three-year-old medical student living alone and cut off from pretty much every person she had known before the age of eighteen. This only brought her to the end of Part 1 of her mental list of the challenges she'd faced. Part 2 would turn out to be even more hair-raising. Yet she didn't think of her list as dark. It wasn't a list of grievances. Or at any rate, by the time she'd become the deputy chief health officer for California the story had become to her a necessary one.

David had always been her favorite character in the Bible. As a boy, David had terrifying encounters with lions and bears, but they left him with skills. Courage was one of those skills; and Charity very much considered courage a skill. She was grateful for the fears that life had forced her to face up to in the way that she thought David should have been grateful to the bears, for preparing him to fight Goliath. "That list of twenty things I've overcome is the reason I'm a good health officer," she said. "Those are my bears and lions."

On her forty-second birthday, Charity drew up her annual list of resolutions. Once again, she needed to buck herself up with the story she told herself about herself. Lots of weird and unsettling stuff had happened during her first year as the deputy public-health officer for California. The job had had no shortage of drama. By all accounts she'd excelled at it and was in line to run public health for the state of California. Governor Jerry Brown gave way to Governor Gavin Newsom, who dismissed Dr. Smith, the chief health officer who had hired her. Charity had spent the first four months running the show for

Newsom, certain that the show was hers to run for good. In the event, Newsom brought in a New York City health officer named Sonia Angell. Angell specialized in chronic conditions like obesity and diabetes but had no experience with the control of communicable disease.

Her arrival only added to Charity's sense of unease, seeded by her experience in Santa Barbara. American society had no ability to deal with what she felt was coming. "The United States doesn't really have a public-health system," she said. "It has five thousand dots, and each one of those dots serves at the will of an elected official."

She sat down in her bedroom to write her birthday resolutions and painstakingly transferred them to the back of her grandmother's photograph, which hung beside her desk in Sacramento. It was December 21, 2019. She'd spent the previous few months asking herself why she'd ever come here, but now she felt this premonition. It resembled the feeling she sometimes had at the start of an outbreak back in Santa Barbara County. "It always starts with one case and an eerie silence," she said. None of her resolutions of the previous fifteen years was anything but an expression of personal goals. "Play the piano again." "Get my sea legs in this new job." "Go to Africa." She began this year's list with one deeply personal goal. Then, on the second line, she made a prediction. "It Has Started," she wrote.

PART II

SIX

The Red Phone

He'd just been reading the news, like everyone else. He had no special access to any new disease outbreak, and no one would have expected him to intervene. All that Joe DeRisi had was his new lab at the University of California–San Francisco, and what seemed, to him, an almost magical new weapon for hunting viruses. Joe described his lab as a "a do-it-yourself Maker Faire." He talked about the weapon as just one of the cool things they'd made—and were still figuring out how and where best to deploy.

Then Joe read about the new outbreak in China. On February 10, 2003, the Beijing office of the World Health Organization received an email about a "strange contagious disease" in Guangdong Province. The flu-like disease was killing at a rate that the flu never had. It sickened children as well as adults. It infected people who knew enough to try to protect themselves from it. An Italian doctor named Carlo Urbani, detailed by

WHO to investigate the outbreak, died before he could figure out what killed him. When Joe read about the Italian doctor, he put what he was working on to one side and looked for a way into this new game. "We got in touch with the CDC," said Joe, "and we said, 'We have this new chip thing. And we might be able to help identify the pathogen.'"

By then, weeks into the outbreak, the CDC was playing a leading role in a frantic investigation. "They were initially dismissive," said Joe. They'd never heard of Joe DeRisi, or his "chip thing." It was the last time Joe or his chip thing would be a secret. The next year he'd receive a MacArthur "genius" grant, and his office phone would be ringing so often, and with such urgency, that he'd start calling it the Red Phone. But to the CDC, in March 2003, Joe DeRisi was just another young research biochemist on the make. The chip thing he'd created—well, no one outside of the DeRisi Lab knew much about it. "We literally had to beg the CDC to send us a sample of the virus," said Joe. "But they finally sent us a sample."

The sample resided in a chunk of lung, taken from a person who'd died of the new disease. To Joe's surprise, the CDC shipped the lung in an ordinary FedEx box. Weekend delivery. Until a new pathogen is formally identified, the CDC explained, it remains classified as just another benign packet of genetic material. Joe realized too late that the UCSF package reception center was closed on weekends. Some guy in a FedEx truck carrying a chunk of lung from a human being who had recently died of a deadly airborne disease would be cruising around the UCSF campus searching for a way in. The Saturday morning of delivery, Joe and his postdoctoral students staked out the streets. It was Joe who spotted the FedEx truck and stopped it. "Dude!" he shouted at the driver. "Do you have a box for the DeRisi Lab?"

The driver gave him a look. Joe was then thirty-three years

old but could have passed for twenty-three. Seemingly carefree, radically informal. Most days he dressed in the same uniform of running shoes, cargo shorts, and a t-shirt with some random thing printed on the front. He could pass more easily as a surfer or a skater or some other category of person who routinely called other people "Dude" than a guy with his own biochemistry lab and a new weapon for hunting viruses. The first impression was deceptive. Three years earlier he'd been handpicked by UCSF's faculty to skip the usual postdoc stage of formal scientific training and been given his own lab—because they didn't want to waste a moment of his mind. "It's a mind without boundaries," said Don Ganem, a UCSF microbiologist and medical doctor who had pushed for DeRisi's hire. "It's a mind that is interested in everything and afraid of nothing. It's a bandwidth that is hard for most people to fathom."

Actually, the first impression made by Joe didn't linger all that long. Something he did or said usually gave him away. As the FedEx driver retrieved the box—which he now noticed came from a place called the Centers for *Disease Control*—Joe reached into his cargo shorts and extracted a pair of thick laboratory safety gloves. Suddenly Joe did not seem like a man without a care in the world. Clearly he cared very much about not touching the FedEx box with his bare hands.

At that moment, the FedEx delivery guy could be forgiven for asking a question: If *this* dude thinks he needs gloves even to touch the box, how come I don't? Instead of asking it, he asked another. *Hey, what's in the box?*

Oh, it's nothing, said Joe.

The driver looked at him again.

I'm never coming back here, he said.

That was a very Joe moment. A twofer, like the double helix. He now had not only the chunk of human lung but a funny story about how he got it. Then he went to work on the lung.

Twenty-four hours later his lab had identified the pathogen that had killed its original owner: a new coronavirus. Back in March 2003, this was shocking news. No one had ever heard of a coronavirus causing severe illness in people. Coronaviruses could be deadly to animals, but in people they'd always manifested themselves as the common cold. The World Health Organization would eventually give the disease caused by this coronavirus its name: severe acute respiratory syndrome, or SARS. "After that I was hooked," said Joe. "I said I want to do more of this."

Joe sensed that the CDC was stunned by what the DeRisi Lab had done, and by how quickly they'd done it. It felt less like science than magic. The CDC would also eventually identify the new coronavirus. But it would take them many weeks to do what an unknown biochemist at UCSF with no training in virology had done in hours. "No one knew about our technology or what we were doing," said Joe. "It just wasn't on anyone's mind." But now it was. And so was Joe.

Not long after SARS, the ringing of the Red Phone commenced. Ditto the letters and emails with their often bizarre requests. For instance, at the end of 2003, Joe got an email from a man claiming to be a senior officer in the United States Navy. *We would like you to come to DC and talk to the Jasons*, it began. The note was short and to the point, and the point was that "the Jasons" wanted Joe to explain how this new biological threat had crept up on humanity, and how the DeRisi Lab had identified it. "My first question," said Joe, "is who the fuck are the Jasons?" Googling, he found mostly websites promoting conspiracy theories. "Whatever QAnon was back then, that's what I got," said Joe. "It was all deep state stuff." At length he stumbled upon a source that sounded at least faintly credible. The Jasons, it explained, were a shadowy group of scientists and military leaders who met in secret in Washington, DC. "I thought, Hell, I can't turn this down," said Joe.

A few months later he flew to Dulles Airport, where he found waiting for him a black SUV with the navy guy inside of it. On the drive to wherever they were going, the navy guy said next to nothing. "I think, *Whatever, this dude is just weird,*" said Joe. The car dropped them in front of a glass office building in Tysons Corner, Virginia. A man behind a glass counter handed Joe a badge. "I notice it has a color code, and my color is different than the navy guy's," said Joe. The navy guy then passed Joe to an old white guy. The old white guy escorted Joe down halls and around corners and through security checkpoints until finally they entered an elevator and descended. In the middle of a lot of awkward silence, Joe noticed the name on the old guy's security badge. Jason. Like the navy dude, he was a man of few words, but, as they descended into what felt like Middle-earth, this dude who was clearly not named Jason turned to Joe and said, "It's cool, huh?" After Joe agreed that, yes, it was indeed cool, the old guy said, "It's like going down the rabbit hole, son."

The old guy said not another word until they arrived inside a small auditorium. Maybe one hundred fifty seats, all filled by old white men, many in military uniforms. "It was generals and stuff," said Joe. The old guy handed Joe a sheet of paper with the titles of the many presentations to be given to the old men that day. Each talk was color-coded, to indicate the security clearance level required to hear it. Before Joe even asked the question, the old guy said, "We will make sure you leave the room." That's how Joe learned that the only talk that he had the security clearance to hear was his own. The talk after his own, he noticed, was called "The Night Fist." "I wanted to stay and hear that one," said Joe. "I mean, who wouldn't want to stay and find out what the Night Fist was?"

As he walked to the podium, Joe noticed that the guys in the front row weren't merely on the old side. They were ancient— and now so close that he could read their name badges, too.

Jason. Every person in the room was pretending to be named Jason; and Joe, officially, was now having the time of his life. "I'm thinking, This is real, this is cool, this is Tom Clancy shit," he said. Whoever the Jasons actually were, they'd allotted him just ten minutes to explain how he and his team at UCSF had so quickly identified the virus that had eventually killed hundreds of people in Hong Kong and mainland China. Ten minutes to describe what was less a technology than a worldview, evolved over years in Joe's mind. From the sounds of the talks to be given that day, he could see that the scientists were mostly physicists. Not his crowd. He was relieved that he'd prepared to explain his work to a lay audience, as that's what this was, in spite of all the drama.

He began by telling them about his new technology. Until now, he explained, the identification of a new virus has been a tedious, slow-moving process. The trouble with viruses is that they're so very small. You need a lot of virus before you can see it, even with an electron microscope magnifying it several million times over. Virus extracted from some infected human is seldom sufficient, and so virologists usually need to take whatever they find and then grow more. To grow virus they need first to find an animal in which virus will grow. They inject a tiny bit of live virus into a mouse, for example, and hope that it replicates. If the virus fails to replicate inside the mouse, they move on to some other animal. It's a pain in the ass just to get enough virus so you can see it. Only after you have it can you form a hypothesis about what the virus might be. Your hypothesis needs to be tested, and each test might take a day or more. If the test comes back negative—that is, if the virologist has guessed wrong—the process starts all over again. One down, dozens to go. "It's a fishing expedition," said Joe. "They're just hoping that whatever they see reminds them of something they've seen before. But what if it's something entirely new, or

something you've never seen before? Then you're in trouble."
The human mind was simply no match for nature's variety.
Nature was full of surprises that no scientist, however smart,
could predict. "You start looking only for things that you are
trained to expect," said Joe. "And you miss what's there." The
new chip created by the DeRisi Lab did not require him to grow
enough virus so that he could see it. The new chip also removed
the prediction part of the investigation, and allowed science to
proceed without hypotheses. The new chip allowed the human
mind to escape its boundaries.

The Virochip, as it was called, was actually a glass microscope slide. Its surface held genetic sequences from every known
virus. These sequences, along with the genetic information of
living creatures, were stored in a federally funded database
called GenBank, inside the National Institutes of Health. Gen-
Bank amounted to a massive gene library, updated every two
weeks by scientists from all over the world. "It's like a puzzle
store where you can walk around and look at the pictures on the
boxes," said Joe. A few of the puzzle pictures were complete, like
the picture of human beings, as the human genome had been
fully sequenced. But most of the pictures were partial, including those of many viruses. The DeRisi Lab had grabbed from
GenBank the full or partial genetic puzzle pictures of twenty-
two *thousand* viruses and transferred them onto a single glass
slide. Genetic matter from any unidentified virus would bind
to any identical genetic matter belonging to a known virus. All
you had to do was wash the unidentified genetic material across
the slide and see what stuck. "It's like you're going through the
puzzle store with a single puzzle piece trying to find the picture
it fits into," said Joe.

Joe's team took the lung sample sent by the CDC, dissolved
it, and washed the genetic material across the Virochip. Bits of
it had attached to bits of three different previously identified

viruses: a cow coronavirus, a bird coronavirus, and a human coronavirus. "It was like pieces of a jigsaw puzzle from three different puzzles," says DeRisi. "They didn't fit together. It said to us this is a novel coronavirus." The new virus's similarity to known viruses inside cows, birds, and people did not imply that it had come from a cow or a bird or a person. The so-called reservoir species—the animal harboring the virus before the virus jumped into humans—remained a mystery. The virus obviously hadn't come from humans; if it had, humans would have some immunity to it, which they clearly did not. Joe was fairly certain that the virus hadn't come from cows, either, as the viruses that threatened moneymaking animals tended to be thoroughly studied and well known. Investigators would wind up grabbing animals across China until they found the SARS virus inside one of them, reproducing without sickening the animal. To the surprise of all, the new virus's old home turned out to be the horseshoe bat. "No one had ever seen bat coronaviruses," said Joe. "They didn't exist."

To the Jasons, Joe explained how the Virochip had taken the guesswork out of the investigation. When some new pathogen infected human beings, you didn't need some expert virologist to make guesses about what it might be. You could now approach the pathogen without any knowledge or preconception, and allow its genes to tell you what it was. The biology would reveal itself, if you gave it a chance.

There was much that Joe didn't explain to the Jasons that day. He didn't explain, for instance, where the Virochip had come from. How it was an extension of a massive machine he'd built with his own hands as a Stanford graduate student, or how he'd also built the robot that placed genetic sequences of twenty-two thousand viruses onto a glass slide. He didn't explain that those sequences were, by necessity, only partial genetic pictures of each virus, as the full ones would never fit onto a single glass slide. To maximize the likelihood of detecting a new virus, he and his team had put onto the Virochip the oldest gene sequences of each known virus—those strings of genes that had been preserved even after the virus had evolved. If the virus further evolved, into something that seemed entirely new, it likely would continue to possess those old sequences. In his speech, Joe didn't go into any of that. The Jasons were busy men. They'd given him just ten minutes to say what he had to say, and they had questions.

If the unidentified virus is a new virus, why would it stick to anyplace on the Virochip?

People always asked this. All viruses on earth are genetically related, Joe explained, because they'd evolved from common ancestors. If a virus is new, and thus doesn't match up perfectly with the DNA on the chip, the chip can still lead you to its family. Its grandparents or, at least, its distant cousins. The chip, in other words, could be used not just to diagnose an existing virus but to discover a new one, as it had with SARS. And its power to diagnose grew with the addition of new viruses to the chip.

What if the virus had zero genetic connection to any virus on earth? What if it came from Mars?

Another common question. And harder to answer satisfactorily. There actually was a phrase: *the dark matter of genomic sequencing.* It referred to genetic material without any connection to known genetic material. But SARS wasn't that. And neither were any of the other likely biological threats to humans.

Why had the virus vanished? Why had it infected eight thousand people and killed eight hundred of them and then just stopped? Where had it gone?

The first SARS outbreak had ended because those infected had been isolated quickly and prevented from infecting others. Those capable of infecting others were easy to identify because they were so obviously ill. There were few, if any, asymptomatic spreaders. The virus had not vanished, however. "It's still out there," said Joe. "It didn't come from outer space. There's a very meaningful probability that it can arise again."

In other words, now was not the time to chill out on biological threats. Too little was known; even about SARS, much remained a mystery. How it had passed from person to person, for example.

In the fall after the first SARS outbreak, the World Health Organization published a report. To Joe this report was as good as any detective story. It explored what had happened after a doctor had traveled with his wife from their home in mainland China to Hong Kong to attend a wedding. The doctor had died, and sickened people in five other rooms on the same floor of Hong Kong's Metropole Hotel. The question was: How did they get it? Two months after the hotel outbreak, a team from WHO had visited the Metropole, and treated it as a crime scene. They'd searched for the virus's genetic material, in the carpets and curtains and even in dust in the air. They tested the plumbing and the ventilation. They swabbed the maids' vacuum cleaners and the janitors' closets. They discovered, for instance, that the hotel's air-conditioning pushed air ever so gently from the rooms out into the corridors. They paid special attention to the room in which the doomed Chinese doctor and his wife had stayed: 911. Inside, they could find no trace of the virus. Outside, in the hall, they hit pay dirt. Two months after the death of the Chinese doctor, his killer's genetic material was still very much there, in a big circle on the carpet near the door.

Most of the others on the ninth floor of the Metropole Hotel who had contracted the virus had one thing in common: to get from their rooms to the elevator, they'd had to walk past Room 911. The WHO team wondered if perhaps these people had walked through this very spot and later, when they removed their shoes, had infected themselves. They further surmised that the doctor had vomited on the carpet, then cleaned up the mess himself, as the hotel had no record of a call for help. But in truth they were just guessing. No one knew.

When Joe was finished speaking he was escorted from the room, so that he wasn't exposed to classified information. He realized that the Jasons had asked him a bunch of questions without ever getting to the most important one: How do we use this new technology to get a jump on the viruses of the future? Viruses had a natural edge on people. "They deliberately make errors in their genetic code," said Joe. "They evolved to make mistakes. And their mistakes give them an evolutionary flexibility that is unprecedented." We needed to be able to respond to the special power of viruses, by speeding up our ability to understand them.

*

It was after that first outbreak of a new coronavirus that Joe's phone got named the Red Phone. "We had gained some fame during the SARS thing, and we began to get cold-called," he said. "If you've tried everything else and you don't know what it is, you can pick up the phone and call us." The urgent cries for help he classified into two very broad categories. The first concerned the extinction, or at least a big die-off, of some animal species without commercial value. The snakes, for example.

In early 2009 Joe got a letter from a woman who enclosed a picture of herself wrapped in a boa constrictor. "I heard you're a virus hunter," it began, before explaining that the snake in the photograph was her service animal. His name was "Mr. Larry," she wrote. Her snake's veterinarian had heard Joe speak about this new chip he had created to identify viruses. Might he use it to investigate the mysterious illness killing snakes across the world, before it carried away Mr. Larry?

All of this came as news to Joe. He had no idea snakes could be of service, or that they were dying in large numbers from some new illness. "I thought, Wow, that's crazy," he recalled. "I let the letter sit on my desk for maybe a year. It was a weird letter."

Joe loved science. He also thought that science was in some ways misunderstood, at least as it was often taught to children. After the fact, scientific progress was often described as a cool, antiseptic affair. A lone scientist or team of scientists had formed some hypothesis, created a way to test it, and discovered some new truth, or not. Joe thought that scientists should be encouraged to look at stuff without having any idea of what they were looking for. "There's a time and a place for a hypothesis," said Joe, "and there's a time and a place to let it go." He also thought that people who looked at stuff without any preconception of what they might find were the ones who saw the things that no one had seen before. "It's science's dark secret," he said. "If you actually look at the great discoveries—okay, maybe not in astrophysics, but in medicine and biology—you don't have to go back more than a couple of steps to find a chance observation." Science was just curiosity's tool. Progress often began when someone saw something they hadn't expected to see and said, "Huh, that's weird."

And so "that's weird," when said by Joe, was less a footnote of mild interest than a prologue to an investigation. At length his curiosity got the better of him. He called "Mr. Larry"'s vet. "Is it true that snakes are dying of some mysterious disease?" he asked. "Oh yeah," said the vet, as if everyone knew this: zoos everywhere were seeing their snake populations being wiped out. "I then went on YouTube and typed in 'Hey, my snake is sick,'" said Joe. "And all these videos start popping up, from all over the world. Whatever it was made the snakes go crazy. Have you ever seen a python go crazy?"

He soon found himself trying to understand what amounted to a snake pandemic. In the five years since the DeRisi Lab had helped to identify SARS, the virus hunter's arsenal had expanded. Big, fast genomic sequencing machines had come onto the market to do what the Virochip had done, but with even more fantastic possibilities. Instead of washing genetic material across a glass slide, you now dumped that material into the magical gene machine and let the machine figure out what it was. The machine busted up the genetic material into fragments and, in effect, handed you back a million little jigsaw puzzle pieces. You could then take the puzzle pieces and see where they belonged, by comparing them to the puzzles stored in GenBank. The Virochip had allowed Joe to identify only the pieces of virus that stuck to it. The new machine allowed him to inspect *any* genetic material that didn't belong. Say, for example, he got sent genetic material from a human being with a mysterious illness. He could identify all the human genetic material in the sample and discard those puzzle pieces, as the human genome was fully known. What remained was whatever genetic puzzle pieces did not belong inside a human—not just viruses but bacteria and single-cell organisms and anything else that might have taken up residence. He could then take those pieces and compare them to everything in GenBank. "It's like you get these pieces and you go into a giant warehouse of puzzles," said Joe. "And you look for which puzzle the piece fits into."

The new technology worked great for humans, or for that matter any species whose genome was fully known. Snakes were not one of them. "Who founded the Python Genome Project?" said Joe. "No one!" And so that's what he first did. He took his team of postdocs to a San Francisco aquarium, extracted the blood of a healthy boa, and set about creating, in essence, the puzzle picture of a snake. Once they'd finished, he was able to extract genetic material from a snake that had died of the mysterious illness, dump it into the new gene machine, wait for it to spit out all the puzzle pieces, and throw out everything that belonged in the genetic picture of a snake. "The whole game is to separate everything that is snake from everything that is not snake, then see what is not snake," said Joe. Snakes that had died of the mysterious illness indeed harbored a previously unidentified virus. The DeRisi Lab could see that it belonged to the family of arenaviruses, which was odd. Arenaviruses had been found in rodents and, on truly unfortunate occasions, in people. Arenaviruses caused Lassa fever and Brazilian hemorrhagic fever and a few other death-sentence diseases. They'd never been found in snakes.

Even more strangely, this new snake arenavirus had one genetic sequence in it that was not part of the puzzle picture of any known arenavirus. But it fit into the puzzle of the Ebola virus. "What we found was actually an ancient ancestor of Ebola," said Joe. "Dinosaurs had this same virus."

There's a widely agreed-upon standard of proof in virology, collectively called Koch's postulates, for the German doctor who first developed the criteria, in the late nineteenth century. "The only way to prove that a virus causes a disease is to isolate the virus and inject it into a healthy animal," Joe explained. "If the injection causes the disease, everyone agrees that you've proved your case." To prove that the virus they'd isolated was killing boas and pythons, they'd first need to grow this ancient ancestor of Ebola in the lab, find some healthy boas and pythons, and then infect them with the virus. To inject a virus into an African python took some trouble. Snakes don't have injectable veins. They do, perhaps surprisingly, have hearts, and that's where the virus must be injected. Snake hearts don't stay put, like human hearts, but travel up and down the snake's body. To inject a snake's heart with a virus requires two postdocs and one full professor: one to hold the snake in a death grip, one to use a Doppler radar to find the snake's heart, and a third to plunge the needle into it.

It seemed exactly the sort of mission that might test the loyalty of a graduate student. The postdocs who spent time in the DeRisi Lab were, at Joe's insistence, a mixed bag: biologists, chemists, deep learning specialists, medical doctors of every sort. But they had one thing in common: they were up for anything. "I try to recruit all kinds of people," said Joe. "But the people who are attracted to us would have zero reservations about jumping onto that ship." The professor and the students injected many boa constrictors, and many pythons, with the arenavirus. The boa constrictors proceeded to sicken and die in exactly the same way as boas in zoos across the world were just then doing. The finding would turn out to be a big win for snakes—a zoo could now quarantine any new boa and test it for the virus before allowing it to socialize with the other snakes. It was also, potentially, a win for human beings, as any virus inside of snakes might one day develop the ability to jump into them, too, and, if one did, it would be good to know exactly what it was.

On top of it all, the DeRisi Lab had stumbled into a surprising discovery. When they'd injected pythons with the same virus, this ancestor of the Ebola virus that killed boas, the pythons had survived. "Pythons are an old-world snake and boas are a new-world snake," said Joe. "This thing that didn't bother old-world snakes caused havoc inside new-world snakes." He wondered: perhaps the pythons had survived their injections because they had long ago evolved a tolerance for Ebola. That is, perhaps they were the species in which Ebola was stored. "The little game of finding the reservoir species has been easy for coronaviruses," said Joe. "No one has *ever* figured it out for Ebola. People took whole zoos out of Africa and they never found the animal."

There were a couple of ways to solve this mystery. The less satisfying was to travel to Africa and gather a bunch of pythons and see if any harbored the Ebola virus. On one hand, you might find what you were looking for; on the other, if you didn't, that did not mean it did not exist. You might simply have gathered the wrong snakes. "That's the thing in science," said Joe. "Negative data doesn't mean much. You don't get much from it." A more promising approach, he thought, was to grab a python and inject it with live Ebola virus and see what happened. To see if it lived even as the Ebola replicated inside of it.

Like much of what occurred inside the DeRisi Lab, this was more easily said than done. There were tight restrictions on the use of the live Ebola virus that didn't grant an exemption for even the most curious virus hunter to inject the live virus into the heart of a python. Joe found himself in a long conversation with people inside the laboratory at Fort Detrick, in Maryland, where the United States Army Medical Research Institute of Infectious Diseases studied biological threats. It was the same lab from which, back in 2001, anthrax had escaped. It had employed the scientist who, in 2008, had committed suicide after being fingered as the likely sender of the letters containing anthrax that had killed five Americans. It was the only lab in the United States capable of doing what Joe wanted done.

They agreed that it would be useful to find the animal that harbored the Ebola virus. But they also thought that, as Joe put it, "this is a crazy-ass experiment." The conversation leading up to the event took months. "They ran us through all these decision trees, of all the bad things that might happen," said Joe. "They got to decision branch number twelve and—I shit you not—it was, 'What happens if you inject the snake with live Ebola virus, and you come back later and there is a hole in the snake's cage and the snake is gone?'" To which Joe's first response had been: "You fucking run!" In the end, the U.S. Army's scary lab agreed to take the risks. A brave U.S. Army scientist stabbed pythons in the heart with a needle carrying live Ebola virus. And the snakes lived—had not so much as the sniffles. Even domestic pythons met the first requirement of any reservoir species. Still, it was not enough for the snakes to survive; the Ebola needed to prosper. The army lab went looking for the Ebola virus inside the snakes, but before they could find it they got shut down for safety violations. Their lab workers "systematically failed to ensure implementation of biosafety and containment procedures commensurate with the risks," said the CDC's report to Congress. And so the mystery remains unsolved. "There are some regrets there that we didn't finish," said Joe. "But the safety stuff had nothing to do with my snakes."

At any rate, that was one kind of urgent call that came into the Red Phone: *Can you help us figure out what is killing all these animals?* There was a second kind of call, more urgent than the first. The voice on the other end of the line would say: *This person is dying and we don't know why.*

*

Michael Wilson was a medical student at UCSF in 2007 when he first heard Joe DeRisi lecture. The talk was about how the DeRisi Lab had helped to identify the original SARS virus. "Most medical school lectures aren't suspenseful," he said, "but his was a page-turner." Wilson went on to do his residency at Massachusetts General Hospital. His field was neurology, but he had a particular interest in brain diseases, especially those caused by infection. In the United States alone there were roughly twenty thousand cases a year of encephalitis. *Encephalitis* sounded like a diagnosis but it was merely a description, a fancy word for inflammation of the brain. Thousands of encephalitis cases a year went undiagnosed: the doctors never learned what had killed the patient. At Mass General and Brigham and Women's Hospital, Wilson sat through a great many stimulating conversations with fellow students and older doctors. "A lot of the time the discussion ended with, Well, that was a great discussion, but we still have no clue what the person has."

At some point during his residency, Wilson realized that if he were to become a neurologist who specialized in infectious disease, he'd spend a lot of time giving up hope. "There was a fascination with these patients," he said, "but there was also a certain nihilism." Toward the end he decided that Joe DeRisi, and the tool he had created that had identified the SARS virus, might be able to help. "I wrote him two emails during my residency and he didn't respond," recalled Wilson. "I couldn't get his attention." Through a mutual friend, a famous neurologist, Wilson arranged to visit Joe in his lab at UCSF. ("When you talk to Joe," the famous neurologist had said, "you'll get the feeling that lightning bolts are about to shoot out of his eyes.") Sitting in Joe's office, Wilson saw why Joe hadn't written him back. "I looked over his shoulder at his computer and his inbox had over thirteen thousand unread emails in it," recalled Wilson. But once Wilson had explained the problem to Joe, Joe agreed on the spot to take Wilson into his lab, and to help him figure out whatever was infecting people's brains. As the meeting ended, Joe also said, "By the way, other things will come up."

"What do you mean?" asked Wilson.

"You'll see," said Joe.

Joe then sat Michael Wilson with Mark Stenglein, the post-doc who had taken the lead on the DeRisi Lab's investigation of snakes. Soon Wilson realized that the DeRisi Lab was to science what Willy Wonka's Chocolate Factory was to candy. "Once a week," recalled Wilson, "Joe would come strolling into the lab and say, 'I just got a phone call.' And it was something about a snake, or a polar bear, or a parrot. Even though it was unpredictable, it was completely predictable." Like lightning bolts.

Not long after Wilson arrived, Joe had a phone call from a friend in Wisconsin. The friend, a neurologist, had a patient, a teenage boy, dying in an ICU of some mysterious brain disease. The doctor sent the DeRisi Lab a sample of the kid's spinal fluid, and the lab performed the same trick on it as it had on dead pythons. It took the scientists less than a day to discard the human genetic material and identify what remained: *Leptospira* bacteria, which, in rare cases, caused a disease in humans called leptospirosis. They later learned that the boy had traveled to Puerto Rico and had gone swimming in a warm lake; but in the Wisconsin hospital no one had realized the relevance of that event. There was a cure for leptospirosis: penicillin. There was also a law that prevented labs without formal medical certification from the CDC—labs like the DeRisi Lab—from reporting any results to physicians. By the time they appealed to the CDC, the boy would be dead. Joe had sat down with UCSF's resident bioethicist—his actual title—and, whatever he had said, it had been persuasive. Joe told his friend what he'd found, and his friend gave penicillin to the boy, and, inside of a week, the boy walked out of the hospital. He even sent them a video. *Hey, you guys, thanks for saving my life . . .*

That sort of happy thing happened every so often during the three and a half years Michael Wilson spent in the DeRisi Lab. But the Red Phone was wildly unsystematic, and the central truth about it was that by the time people rang it, it was usually too late. The calls would come only after some doctor, desperate for help, read about the DeRisi Lab. Or, more commonly, after someone who knew Joe or Michael Wilson met someone who knew someone who was in trouble. If you happened to be dying of an unknown brain disease, your chances of survival rose if you had no more than two degrees of separation from either Michael Wilson or Joe DeRisi. "Joe called it Michael Wilson's Friends and Family Plan," said Wilson, "but it was really Michael and Joe's Friends and Family Plan."

The Chinese woman was a case in point. They'd only heard

about her because she'd eventually turned up in a UCSF hospital, where she was treated by doctors who were friends of both Michael and Joe.

The story, in Joe's telling, began in July 2014, when the seventy-four-year-old woman, who spoke no English, walked into San Francisco's Chinese Hospital. She had a fever and felt shaky. The doctors suspected a urinary tract infection, gave her antibiotics, and sent her home. Three weeks later, on August 1, the woman appeared in St. Mary's Medical Center with fever and a cough and loss of vision. This time the doctors did an MRI. The picture of her brain suggested that she'd suffered many tiny strokes. They gave her anticoagulants, to reduce the risk of stroke, and sent her home. Two days later, her relatives wheeled her into one of UCSF's hospitals, comatose. The doctors ran her through the MRI machine again: suddenly her scans showed massive cell death in her brain. There was very little brain left to save. Still, UCSF's doctors did everything they could think of to save it. They gave her expensive drugs that killed fungal infections and more expensive drugs that killed parasites. In just one morning they gave her $150,000 worth of medications. None of it had the slightest effect.

On August 15 they removed a piece of her brain and found nothing unusual. A week later, on August 22, they did another biopsy and this time found that the blood vessels in the woman's brain were all dead. No one knew why.

And yet it wasn't until two days later, on August 24, forty-five days after the woman walked into a hospital and three weeks since she'd arrived at UCSF, that anyone thought to call the Red Phone. Four days later, she was dead. Her hospital bill came to $1,000,100, and why they didn't just round it to the nearest million was an open question. So, still, was her disease. Looking into the woman's brain, the UCSF pathologists had decided that the little critters that had overrun the healthy brain cells were human immune cells, doing their best to attack some unidentified infection. The cause of that infection was the mystery.

The DeRisi Lab ran the woman's spinal fluid through the gene machine. A few hours later it spat back a picture, broken up into tiny pieces. Of the 19 million genetic sequences in the fluid, all but 1,863 were human. One thousand eight hundred sixty-three puzzle pieces that did not belong inside a human brain. When compared to the existing puzzle pictures, 1,377 matched nothing at all. But the other 486 fit perfectly into known pictures of a pathogen called *Balamuthia mandrillaris.*

The puzzle picture of *Balamuthia* was incomplete; its genome had been only partially sequenced. The amoeba had been discovered in 1986 in a dead mandrill in the San Diego Wild Animal Park; hence its name. Since then it had been defined mainly by how little anyone knew about it. So little about it was known that a trained pathologist had stared at a picture of it and mistaken it for human immune cells. It had been detected only a few dozen times since its discovery—once in a dead four-year-old girl. No one knew what it ate when it wasn't eating the brains of mandrills or humans. No one knew, really, how it entered people. Asked to explain what he'd found, Joe would only say, "*Balamuthia* is an amoeba and it eats your brain, and there is no cure."

By then Michael Wilson had seen the DeRisi Lab work its magic often enough that he almost took it for granted. What struck him was what Joe did next. "He could have just left it there," said Wilson. "He could have said, 'There, we found what it was,' just like he could have said, 'We found a snake virus,' and moved on. But he didn't leave it there." Having identified and isolated *Balamuthia,* Joe wondered if the lab might also find a cure for it. After all, if the DeRisi Lab didn't find the cure for *Balamuthia*, who would? No drug company would bother. There was no money in *Balamuthia* cures. There were only a handful of cases each year.

Joe asked his team to test every drug that had been approved by either the U.S. Food and Drug Administration or the European regulators. "No weird Russian shit," as Joe put it. The postdocs subjected *Balamuthia* to the 2,177 drugs known to have done no harm to humans. Each day, they'd remove the amoeba from its place on the rack in the world's most dangerous refrigerator and see if any of the drugs might kill it. "It's scary to work with," one of the postdocs confessed, but then suddenly it wasn't. Because one of the approved drugs indeed killed the amoeba. Nitroxoline, it was called. Joe and his postdocs wrote up their findings and published the result in *mBio*, a microbiology journal, in October 2018.

There were several points to this story. One was how screwed up the incentives were inside the medical-industrial complex. It was possible to spend $1,000,100 on drugs to prevent you from dying without anyone's having any idea if any of them would work; at the same time, inside of a few weeks but too late to save you, some ill-paid postdoc was able to find a cheap cure. Another was that even when you might have thought that problem was solved, it wasn't. Two years after Joe and his postdocs published their findings on *Balamuthia*, the FDA had yet to approve Nitroxoline, long since cleared by European regulators, as a treatment. The CDC website continued to recommend an old treatment (another one of the 2,177 drugs) that the DeRisi Lab had demonstrated did nothing but create unpleasant side effects. Which is to say that American citizens could and would die of *Balamuthia* without ever knowing what they had, or that there was a cure. Unless, somehow, they'd heard about the Red Phone.

That was Joe's big takeaway from the story: what he called the last mile problem in medical science. Corporations were interested only in stuff that made money. Academics were interested in anything worthy of publication, but once they had their paper done, they tended to lose interest. The government was meant to fill in the blanks, but the United States government by now mystified Joe. He'd visited the CDC to explain the new genomic technology, only to be met with boredom and blank stares. In the Food and Drug Administration there was one woman—a single human being—trying to curate the academic literature so that doctors and patients could easily access new knowledge. She'd taken it upon herself; no one had asked her to do it. "It's often individuals who pick up the baton, and they're not even doing it as part of their day job description," said Joe. "Scattered throughout those organizations there are these people, but they aren't organized, trying to compensate for the deficiencies in the system." The Red Phone could save your life if you called it in time. The system had configured itself in such a way that, more often than not, you didn't.

*

On the first of January 2020, Joe DeRisi was passing through the airport in Guangdong on his way to Cambodia. In addition to his lab at UCSF, he now ran a peculiar new institution called the Chan Zuckerberg Biohub. Created with a $600 million gift from the Facebook founder and his wife, the pediatrician Priscilla Chan, it had set itself a preposterous goal: to eliminate all disease on earth by the end of the twenty-first century. Chan had then asked herself: Who on earth might actually be able to do that? As a medical student at the University of California–San Francisco, she'd heard Joe DeRisi lecture. She thought: *he* might be able to do that.

Just then Joe was flying to Cambodia to install a node in what he hoped would one day be a global network to detect disease. "Early-warning radar for emerging pathogens," he called it. It was an idea that had once interested the U.S. government. The original pandemic plan, conceived by the Bush White House, spawned a program called Predict, which set out to test animals around the world to determine which contained viruses that might jump into people. The Trump administration had zeroed out the program's funding and so Predict, in the end, failed to predict anything. That didn't trouble Joe so much as the thought that the Biohub, using genomic technology, had found a simpler, more practical way to achieve the same goals: by catching any new virus the moment it appeared in humans. When some child appeared in a Cambodian emergency room with a fever of unknown origin, Cambodian doctors, newly schooled by Joe in the use of genomic technology, would be able to figure out instantly what had caused it. If it had not been seen before in humans, they'd know that, too.

The natural home of such an ambitious global project was the U.S. government or the World Health Organization. The absence of pandemic prevention was another example of a deficiency in the system. Compared to its expected benefits, its costs were trivial, but no one company or person had the incentive to attack the problem. "We went to the CDC and pitched them and we were given a fairly cold reception," said Joe. "And we were like, 'We'll pay for it!' And they were like, 'Huh, that's weird.' They basically didn't care. Walking out, I kind of knew in my gut we'd have to go it alone."

In the end, the Biohub had partnered with another nonprofit, the Gates Foundation, to build, in effect, a global network of infectious-disease trip wires. Joe reckoned they'd have the system in place by 2022. It wouldn't be seamless: China would remain a black hole, as the Chinese had declined to participate. But Joe thought they could see what they needed to see inside China by creating trip wires in surrounding countries. That was one reason Cambodia was important, and why he was on his way there. It was close to China, and a draw for Chinese tourists. If a new virus ever took a trip out of China, Cambodia would likely be an early stop.

He spent ten days in and around Phnom Penh and left feeling good about his new friends' ability to work the gene machine. It was the flight home, on January 10, 2020, that he found unsettling. He changed planes again in Guangdong—the province from which the Chinese doctor, the superspreader of SARS, had come. The airport was transformed. There were now lots of security people wearing masks. Passengers were required to step, one by one, inside an acrylic stall and be scanned for fever. "They weren't fooling around," said Joe. "I thought, What the hell is going on?" He'd never seen a fever box and, as he stepped inside, he had a feeling in the pit of his stomach. "I thought, These people know something we don't."

SEVEN

The Redneck Epidemiologist

I t had been more than a decade since they'd served together in the White House, but whenever Richard Hatchett wanted to noodle over some problem, his first impulse was to write to Carter Mecher. Richard had moved to London back in 2017 to run a curious new organization called the Coalition for Epidemic Preparedness Innovations. CEPI, as it was simply and thankfully known, had been funded by European governments, the Gates Foundation, and others with deep pockets to develop new vaccines, and faster ways to make them. On January 8, 2020, Richard had been going back and forth with Carter on something or other when Carter changed the subject. Carter's mind had drifted from the assigned task to a new and more interesting one. "On a different note," he wrote, "I saw that a novel coronavirus was isolated in the China outbreak."

Carter had been back in Atlanta for nine years. He'd left the White House at the end of President Obama's first term and returned to the Veterans Health Administration in Atlanta. The people around him either never knew, or soon forgot, where he'd been for the previous six years, and what he'd done there. No one ever brought up the White House, or pandemics. As he'd given up his position running hospitals, the VA just called him "senior medical adviser," which meant that he could do pretty much anything he wanted to do, wherever he wanted to do it. "They just sort of forgot Carter existed," said Richard.

Every now and then someone gave Carter a task, but mostly he found problems on his own inside the VA and worked on them. He became curious how the VA's hospital staff used their sick leave, for instance, and figured out that the number of sick days taken by nurses correlated strongly with flu activity—so that you could use flu activity to predict nurse shortages. For a long stretch he worked on making the hospitals more efficient. The Veterans Health Administration, soon after Carter returned to it, had gotten into hot water after veterans complained about long wait times: one guy who had waited six months to see a cardiologist had died of a heart attack before his first appointment. "So the question is, Why is that occurring?" asked Carter. "Is it because the doctors are so busy and overworked and understaffed that patients are backed up, or is it because the practice is inefficient?" He found a woman named Eileen Moran, who'd been working on how to measure the performance of the VA's doctors. She was not popular with the VA's top brass. "They wanted to shut her down," said Carter, "but I looked into it and I said, 'This is really good!'" Carter teamed up with Moran to create a system that allowed the VA to see, when veterans weren't being cared for, whether the problem in any given case was a shortage of doctors or a deficiency in the way those doctors practiced medicine.

All of which was part of a bigger problem that he wanted to

tackle: how any big government agency allocates its resources. Each year, Congress would hand more than a hundred billion dollars to Veterans Affairs, and various people inside the VA would bay for more than they'd gotten the year before. The top brass had no way to figure out who was actually busting their ass and needed more help and who was loafing. "It wound up being who has whose ear," said Carter. "I saw all that and I hated it." He hated in particular the way some people were able to use their own inefficiency to create a seeming need for more funding; and other people, people with a gift for making do with less, were, as a result, given even less. "It drove out the entrepreneurial spirit," said Carter. "It made me wish I had a system to figure out what the hell was going on."

At any rate, he was never idle. At the end of each year he was able to find stuff to fill in the four or five pages of his self-assessment report. But he was, in effect, managing himself. "I think they totally lost track of me," he said. "It gave me so much freedom to play."

Outside the VA, at least a few people from his White House days had not lost track of Carter Mecher. Tom Bossert, for example. As deputy homeland security adviser to George W. Bush, Bossert had watched Carter and Richard reinvent pandemic planning, reinterpret the greatest pandemic in human history, resurrect the idea that a society could control a new disease by using social distancing in its various forms, and then somehow lead the CDC to the conclusion that the whole thing had been their idea. Donald Trump had shunned most anyone associated with any former president but had made an exception of Bossert, whom he'd named his first homeland security adviser. "The job I had was chief risk officer for the country," said Bossert. "And it should have been named that." After his appointment, Bossert built a team of people to deal with biological risks, and instantly called Richard Hatchett and Carter Mecher. *I just want you to know that if the shit ever hits the fan, the first phone call I'm making is to you,* he'd said. He considered clearing Carter and Richard into the White House in the first days of the Trump administration so that in the event of some disease outbreak, they could fly in and get right to work.

But then, on April 9, 2018, Trump hired John Bolton as his national security adviser, and the next day, Bolton fired Tom Bossert, and demoted or fired everyone on the biological threat team. From that moment on, the Trump White House lived by the tacit rule last observed by the Reagan administration: the only serious threat to the American way of life came from other nation-states. The Bush and Obama administrations' concern with other kinds of threats was banished to the basement. Bolton redesigned the White House to focus on hostile foreign countries rather than, say, natural disasters or disease. Bad people, rather than bad events. "In a world of limited resources, you have to pick and choose," an anonymous Trump White House person told the *Washington Post*.

And so, on January 8, 2020, as Carter typed his email to Richard, in which he noted this new coronavirus in China, he was sitting not in the White House, nor even inside Veterans Affairs, but at the Ethan Allen cherry top desk just off his bedroom. He may not have been in his underpants but then he might have been, too.

Carter and Richard had never really stopped working together. Around them a small group had formed. Seven men, all doctors. All were younger, some a generation younger, than Carter, who was about to turn sixty-five. Most had seen combat in Iraq, and all, at one point or another, had worked with Carter in the White House. All except Rajeev Venkayya, who had brought Carter and Richard into the White House in the first place and now ran vaccine development for one of Asia's biggest drug companies, had served in the military. Duane Caneva and James Lawler had come from the U.S. Navy, Matt Hepburn and Dave Marcozzi from the U.S. Army. And all had a role to play in the event of any pandemic. Lawler ran the Global Center for Health Security at the University of Nebraska, for instance. That was the federally funded facility to which any American infected with some deadly new pathogen was likely to be sent to be studied and cared for. They'd treated some of the Ebola patients.

For more than a decade the seven doctors had come together each time a biological threat presented itself. MERS, Ebola, Zika: they'd all been involved in each of those outbreaks, one way or another, behind the scenes. In flurries of phone calls and emails, they'd seek to figure out what was going on, and what each might do to influence the situation and save lives. They might be mistaken for a secret society—if the person at the center were not so insistently happy to share his thoughts with anyone who asked. They'd even been given a name: *Wolverines.* A former Bush White House colleague had come up with that, and somehow it had stuck.*

Carter mentioned the novel coronavirus in his email to Richard—on which he copied the other five doctors. Then he vanished; and they were mystified. Carter hadn't bothered to mention that he was setting out with his wife on a long, quiet

---

* A reference to the 1980s dystopian Cold War film *Red Dawn*. The Soviets have successfully invaded the United States. Some American high school classmates operating from the mountains outside of Denver create the resistance. They call themselves Wolverines, after their high school mascot. Carter was never exactly sure how much he resembled a guerrilla fighter—and who were the Soviets in the analogy?—but he thought it was kind of fun that the group had a name.

drive to the remote place that their son had chosen for his wedding. The others quickly noted his absence. Carter was always the first to leap into any new disease outbreak and make original sense of it, in much the same way he had made sense of the 1918 pandemic. He had no formal training in epidemiology or virology or any other relevant field. He simply had a nose for data, and an ability to squeeze the meaning from it. At the start of any outbreak, Carter was back in the ICU again. He had a gift, in a crisis, for figuring out what was going on while there was still time to do something about it. "Most of our calls start off with, 'Carter, what are you thinking?,'" said Duane Caneva, who was, in January 2020, the chief medical officer of the Department of Homeland Security. "He's like a savant on all this stuff."

Nine days into Carter's silence, on January 18, the world was still paying little attention to what appeared to be a small local outbreak. The World Health Organization was saying that there was "no sustained human-to-human transmission" of the virus, and the Chinese government was allowing forty thousand families in Wuhan to gather for an annual celebration, complete with a buffet. And still no sign of Carter; and so James Lawler finally stepped in. "Saw unconfirmed reports today of 17 more cases in Wuhan," he wrote to the others. "So I got to thinking and pulled a Carter. Is it likely that this thing is much larger than what we are seeing?"

That day was the first in more than a week since the Chinese had announced new cases. The total number of infected people had risen from forty-five to sixty-two, most of them in Wuhan. Outside of China, two cases had already been identified in people who had traveled from Wuhan—one in Thailand, the other in Japan. Lawler pointed to those two cases and asked: What were the odds that there were fewer than one hundred cases in all of China if there were already two infected international travelers from Wuhan? Then he launched into a Carter-like back-of-the-envelope calculation, which is to say that it was both academically laughable and fantastically insightful. Redneck epidemiology.

Lawler began by noting that Chinese travelers had made 131 million foreign trips in 2017, the most recent year for which he could find the data. Wuhan contained eleven million people, slightly less than 1 percent of the country's population. Its citizens were perhaps more cosmopolitan than the average Chinese, and more likely to travel abroad, and so Lawler granted that they might do more than their share of foreign travel. He did some math and estimated that, in any given two-week period, the people of Wuhan made fifteen thousand trips abroad. He then proposed that those people who had remained in Wuhan, where the coronavirus was at large, were at least as likely to be infected as those who had made trips outside the country. "My estimate is that during the first two weeks in the month, there were at least 3000 cases in Wuhan," he wrote. "And that assumes that all infected travelers are being identified, which is obviously not true."

It was a funny way to approach a problem: by first imaging how Carter Mecher might approach it. If you were going to approach a problem pretending to be Carter, you didn't worry about finding the perfect answer. There might never be a perfect answer. *To this day* no one knows how many people in Wuhan were infected on January 18, 2020, but everyone now agrees it was a lot more than sixty-two. (In March 2020, a mathematical epidemiologist in Hong Kong published a paper estimating that by January 23, there were between a thousand and five thousand infected Wuhanese.) But once you got past the necessary imprecision, you arrived at a better place—a place where the critically ill patient might not just be studied but treated. That was the place the Wolverines needed to be. A place where you could say to yourself that you were more or less right, even if you were a little bit wrong. But a place that you had gotten to fast, so that you might act.

The next day, the first American tested positive for the new virus. He was a man in his thirties who had traveled a week before from Wuhan to Seattle. Still the United States government was showing no sign of alarm; the only action the CDC had taken was to issue a travel alert, and to screen travelers entering the United States from China for fever. "It's one person coming in from China, and we have it under control," said President Trump. "It's going to be just fine." When he uttered those words he was at the World Economic Forum in Davos, Switzerland. So too, as it happened, were Rajeev Venkayya and Richard Hatchett. "Rajeev and I had breakfast this morning," Richard wrote to the others, "and were imagining someone going to get Carter in a forest or cave or on a remote windswept plain kind of like Rey going to find Luke . . ."*

That's when Carter finally materialized. "You and Rajeev must have ESP about me being in a remote place," he wrote to Richard. "Caught up on the ride home . . . Agree with your rough estimate. About 1% of Americans travel outside the US each month for comparison. Maybe disease outbreaks need a warning like the one on your car mirror—things are much larger than they appear."

Back at his desk, Carter collected the official statistics from China: cases, hospitalizations, deaths. He compared them to whatever he could find in Chinese blogs and newspapers. It was slow going, as much of the information he found was in Chinese. "I had no idea what the stuff was," he said. "It was all gobbledygook to me. My computer kept lighting up: 'This site is Unsafe!' "

---

* Another movie reference. *Star Wars: Episode VIII, The Last Jedi.*

He'd cut and paste what he found into Google Translate just to see what it was. Some were death notices. He saw that the dates on deaths reported by the authorities every day at midnight were later than the dates in the local reports—that is, the thirty-seven people in Wuhan who had reportedly died by January 23 had died earlier than the official stats suggested. The timing was important. "I was trying to get a sense of how old the starlight was," said Carter. The average time from infection to death was maybe two weeks, and so the deaths gave you a sense of how widespread the disease had been maybe two weeks earlier. If, on top of that, the Chinese were slow to report the deaths, the lag, and the multiple, was even greater. He noticed that, while the Chinese government had been reporting only a handful of cases two weeks earlier, they were now behaving as if there had been many more. "Reading tea leaves," he wrote to his fellow Wolverines. "I see that China is building a 1,000 bed quarantine hospital in Wuhan—in 5 days. They also called in the military to assist . . . Reminds me of the military called in to Chernobyl."

He wasn't working alone, at least as he saw it. All the Wolverines chipped in. Richard Hatchett was in constant touch with his friend Neil Ferguson, a leading modeler at Imperial College in London. Ferguson had guessed the R naught at 3— which is to say that, at the start of the outbreak, each infected person was infecting three others. That was shocking: in the fastest-moving flu on record, the flu that created the 1918 pandemic, the initial reproductive rate had been 1.8. The reproductive cycle was roughly a week. If you had three hundred cases a week ago, you would have nine hundred cases today. If those three hundred cases had actually been identified a month ago, you would have 24,300 today. At some point it became math, but to do the math you needed to make some guesses about exactly how fast the virus was moving.

Carter accepted that no one would have a full, clear picture of

the speed of the virus until it was too late, and he set out to generate as many partial fuzzy ones as he could. His approach was
a peculiar combination of analysis and analogies. "You rely on
patterns," he said. "That is exactly what analogies provide. But
you need to temper that, because you can see patterns that aren't
really there. The analogies are shortcuts—really the equivalent
of deductive wormholes that take me very quickly from A to B."
In effect, he was asking: *What other virus does this virus most
closely resemble?* The obvious first answer was the new virus's
closest known genetic relative, the original SARS of 2003.

Carter stayed up all that first night creating a spreadsheet
that listed, side by side, the reported cases and the deaths in
the first forty-four days of both SARS outbreaks. They were so
similar—the same number of identified cases and deaths on the
same days—that at first it was impossible to tell them apart.
The original SARS had infected only eight thousand people,
killing eight hundred, before it was contained. This new SARS
had similar official stats, but he saw signs that the stats were
misleading. The new SARS was spreading much more quickly
from country to country than the original, for example. It was
also eliciting very different behavior from the Chinese government. On January 23, the authorities closed Wuhan and forbade anyone from entering or leaving the city. "It underscores
the point that Richard has made many times about how hard
it is to get a feel for how bad or mild an outbreak is while it is
happening around you," Carter wrote. "I could be wrong, but
this just doesn't feel mild." Then he nodded in the direction of
the 1918 pandemic. "Wuhan = Philadelphia. Hopefully, we are
watching and learning like St Louis . . . We are soon going to be
running uphill from a brush fire."

On January 24, the CDC announced the second case in the
United States. The woman had traveled from Wuhan. The next
day, January 25, the Chinese reported 2,298 cases, up from 446

four days earlier. "Epidemics don't behave like this," Carter
wrote. The newly infected did not quintuple in five days. He
suspected that the Chinese were catching up on their reporting;
still, the sudden leap in case numbers was shocking. He noted
that the Chinese government started building yet another giant
hospital in Wuhan, this one with 1,300 beds. Back in 1918 government officials had thrown up new hospitals in Philadelphia,
too. He also read the news that a prominent ear, nose, and throat
doctor in Wuhan had died of the new virus. That put paid to the
idea, still at large, that all the infections were being caused by
humans coming into contact with animals. It also suggested the
virus's stealth: even people who knew enough to wear protective
gear could be infected. "It just flashes warning lights," said Carter. "It could have been sloppy infection control, or it could mean
something more concerning." He found yet another article, about
a Chinese man identified as the source of the infection in several
others who had himself experienced no symptoms. If true, cases
were going not just unreported but entirely undetected.

Taken together, the stories he dug out of public sources helped
to explain why the Chinese government was behaving as if the
virus was spreading much faster than the reported numbers, and
also faster than the original SARS. What Carter couldn't understand was why the United States government lacked the same
urgency. "I suspect that a significant number of infected individuals made it past the CDC entry screen and have likely already
infected others," he wrote in an email to the Wolverines. "We
are already far behind the curve and fire is racing up the hill but
we haven't gone far enough down the valley to see it. . . ."

He had fire on the brain. Fire was his favorite metaphor to
convey how hard it was for people to wake up to a threat that
grew exponentially. One fire in particular had captivated his
and Richard's imagination when they'd read of it years earlier. It was known as the Mann Gulch fire, after the area in

Montana that had burned back in 1949. A decade earlier the U.S. Forest Service had created an elite team of smokejumpers who parachuted into fires. One August afternoon, fifteen young men, most between the ages of seventeen and twenty-three, parachuted into what they thought was a small and simple fire. They landed by 4:10 p.m. and began to hike down into Mann Gulch, with their heavy packs and Pulaski axes on their backs. They didn't know each other and, as they hiked, split into smaller groups. To their right was a steep ridge, to their left a creek. The fire they'd been sent to fight burned safely on the other side of that creek, or so they imagined. There weren't many trees, just tall grass, but they were unable to see much ahead of them. A mile or so down the gulch, the creek drained into the Missouri River. Their plan was to walk to the river, cross over the creek, and fight the fire with the river at their backs. The river at their backs was their escape route.

But as they neared the river, there came a shocking sight: fire. It had jumped across the creek and now blocked them from the river. Worse, it was moving across the grass toward them. One moment the fire had been invisible, the next a terrifying wall of flames thirty feet high. It was now 5:45.

They turned to flee, but the only escape route was up and over the steep ridge. Investigators later measured the ridge's 76 percent slope. The fire had a tailwind of 30 or maybe even 40 miles an hour and was growing exponentially. Grass fires moved faster than forest fires. The investigators later estimated that the grass fire had been moving at 1.2 miles per hour when the young men first spotted it. Ten minutes later, at 5:55, the fire was traveling at 7 miles per hour. One minute later, at 5:56, the hands on the wristwatch of one of the young men melted in place: that's how the investigators determined exactly when ten of the fifteen had burned to death, some still carrying their heavy packs and Pulaski axes.

The other five had escaped. Three had dropped their Pulaskis and made it over the top of the ridge—though one died the next day of his burns. The fourth was also dead within a day. The fifth, their thirty-three-year-old leader, the beautifully named Wag Dodge, survived.

His was the most interesting story, at least to Carter. At 5:55 p.m., with the fire just a minute away and rushing toward him at ever greater speed, he'd lit a second fire, up the hill he needed to climb. As his fire burned the grass in front of him, he walked into it and threw himself onto the hot ashes. He'd called for his men first to abandon their packs and Pulaskis, and then to follow him into the fire he'd set. Either they didn't hear him or thought he'd lost his mind; at any rate, they didn't really know Wag Dodge or have any reason to trust him. Dodge alone heard and felt the main fire passing by on either side of him, leaving him unscathed.

Until that moment there was no history of a firefighter having done such a thing, but it became an accepted strategy in the fighting of grass fires. "Escape fire," was what they'd call it. The event so captivated the writer Norman Maclean, best known for his only other book, *A River Runs Through It*, that he wrote a book about it, called *Young Men and Fire*. It so interested a doctor named Don Berwick, maybe best known for running Medicaid and Medicare during part of the Obama administration, that he'd given a talk about it. Carter had heard the talk and thought: the Mann Gulch fire isn't about fire, or at least not only about fire. It's also about pandemics. In fire you could see lessons for fighting a raging disease. He jotted them down:

> *You cannot wait for the smoke to clear: once you can see things clearly it is already too late.*

> *You can't outrun an epidemic: by the time you start to run it is already upon you.*

Identify what is important and drop everything that is not.

Figure out the equivalent of an escape fire.

The Mann Gulch fire captured the difficulty people had imagining exponential growth, even when their lives depended on it. "We are reactive and tend to only intervene when things are getting bad," wrote Carter. "And what we underestimate is the speed that what's bad moves."

At midnight on January 26, the Chinese authorities announced 2,700 new cases and 80 new deaths. "I thought back to 2009 H1N1," wrote Carter at six the next morning, "and remembered how we used the 1918 Pandemic as the model in our heads (the movie) and a lesson I learned would be to be careful the next time to not cling to a single model (movie in my head) but use a range. I almost fell into the same trap this time by focusing on SARS. I did pull the 2009 H1N1 data but didn't look at that data as closely as I should have. I finally did last night." What he saw in that data was that, while the number of deaths looked a lot like the number in the early stage of the SARS outbreak, the speed at which the disease moved did not. It was moving much, much faster, and very like the swine flu had moved. "The movie isn't SARS. And the case ascertainment isn't SARS—it is more like H1N1."

It was as if he'd taken the virus to a clothing store and tried trousers on it until he found the best fit. H1NI fit this new virus in the speed at which it was traveling. There was good news and bad news here. The good news was that it meant that a lot more people were surviving the virus than anyone knew. The bad news was that the virus would infect, and kill, vastly more people than the original SARS. Carter found a study that the CDC had made, after the fact, of the cases of swine flu that had gone undetected, or at least unrecorded, back in 2009. The numbers were incredible. For every case that had been recorded, somewhere between

eighteen and forty cases had been missed. He then asked: What
if right now health authorities around the world were detecting
only between one in eighteen and one in forty cases? "Yesterday
we had 2700 cases and 80 deaths," wrote Carter. "Let's assume the
real number of cases is 18–40 times greater, or 48,600–108,000."
The 80 deaths were the result of some lower number of infections
that had occurred roughly two weeks earlier; to figure out the
fatality rate of the virus, you needed to know how many cases
there had been. Carter did some rough math, using a reproductive
rate of 2, on the low side, and 3, on the high side—that is, each
week, the number of cases was either doubling or tripling. "The
case count 2 weeks ago would be 1/4 or 1/9 of 48,600–108,000 or
5,400–27,000," he wrote, and was likely doing the math in his
head as he did. "So 80 deaths with a denominator of 5400–27000
projected cases 2 weeks ago, gives us a case fatality rate of .3%–
1.5%. But these are very crude estimates."

He was under no illusion that he was engaged in anything
resembling scholarship. He was simply trying to learn enough
about the virus to make decisions about it. For instance, he
might help the leader of the Veterans Health Administration
prepare the nation's largest hospital system for the onslaught.
The other Wolverines all had decisions to make, too, and the
faster they made them, the more lives would be saved. Matt
Hepburn, for instance, had spent much of the previous decade
inside DARPA, the Department of Defense's elite research unit,
working on rapid vaccine development.* He needed to know
whether to throw the weight of that massive agency behind the
chase for a coronavirus vaccine. In making that judgment, he,
like the other Wolverines, was now more or less entirely depen-

---

* Hepburn would eventually be in charge of vaccine development for
Operation Warp Speed.

dent on the group's collective wisdom, and the curious talents of
Carter Mecher. "We knew none of this stuff could ever be published anywhere," said Carter. "What we were trying to do was
a quick reckoning of what the hell was going on. So we could
take action. We weren't doing this for the federal government.
We were doing it for *each other.*"

Still, they could hardly ignore the federal government. They
watched the U.S. government repatriate Americans from Wuhan
on January 29. The first group went to March Air Reserve Base,
in Riverside County, California; the second, in early February,
to four different places, one of them a National Guard base just
outside Omaha, where they remained quarantined for fourteen days. The Omaha National Guard base was a short drive
from the Global Center for Health Security, the place charged
with treating Americans infected with mysterious new pathogens, and run by James Lawler. Lawler discovered—and could
not quite believe—that the CDC didn't plan to test any of the
new arrivals unless they had a fever. All of the foreigners being
shipped home from Wuhan were being tested before they got
on the plane, and the CDC felt that was adequate. The Germans
and the Australians and the Japanese had tested all of their citizens after they'd flown home from Wuhan and discovered that
1 to 2 percent of them were infected, and that many of those
had no symptoms: the tests in Wuhan hadn't identified any of
them. Lawler called the CDC to ask if he might test the Americans now quarantined down the road from his hospital—if for
no reason other than to make sure they didn't let them loose
while they were still shedding the virus. "There was very little
data to support the fourteen-day quarantine," he said. "There
are clearly people who have incubation periods of twenty-one
days. I thought we needed to know if they were infected when
they got here, or shedding when they leave." He and his staff

had already created their own test, based on the test created by the World Health Organization, and so they didn't require the CDC's help, merely its approval.

The CDC sent one of its epidemiologists to visit James Lawler. At the end of the meeting, the guy said he needed to check with Atlanta. "The next day I get this panicked call from him," said Lawler. "It's gone all the way up to [CDC director Robert] Redfield. He said, 'You can't do it!' I said, 'Why?' He said I would be 'doing research on imprisoned persons.'" Never mind that every single one of the fifty-seven Americans in quarantine *wanted* to be tested: the CDC forbade it. And Lawler never understood the real reason for the CDC's objections. Did they want to avoid finding cases to avoid displeasing Donald Trump? Were they concerned that, if they tested people without symptoms and they found the virus, they'd make a mockery of their current requirement that only people with symptoms be tested? Were they embarrassed or concerned that someone other than the CDC was doing the testing? If so, then why didn't they just perform the tests themselves? Whatever the reason, fifty-seven Americans spent fourteen days quarantined in Omaha, then left without having any idea of whether they'd been infected, or might still infect others. "There is no way that fifty-seven people from Wuhan were not shedding virus," said Lawler.

At that moment, Carter guessed that the case fatality rate of the new virus—the percentage of people who got it that would die—fell somewhere between 0.5 percent and 1.1 percent. He further guessed that, if left unchecked by the government, it would infect between 20 and 40 percent of the U.S. population. The plan that he and Richard had created and passed off to the CDC back in 2006 classified pandemics, in a way that made them sound like hurricanes, by how many Americans they were projected to kill if left unchecked. A disease projected to kill fewer than 90,000 Americans was a "Category 1" and called for nothing more than home confinement of the obviously ill. A Cat 5 (more than 1.8 million Americans) or a Cat 4 (900,000 or more dead Americans) required the CDC to call for all available measures: isolate the ill, cancel all public gatherings, encourage telework, enforce social distancing, and close schools for up to twelve weeks. After his back-of-the-envelope calculation, Carter concluded that, if the society failed to intervene, the virus would kill between 900,000 and 1.8 million Americans. "The projected size of the outbreak is hard to believe," he wrote.

According to the pandemic plan, the federal government should at least have been preparing the country for the full suite of interventions. It wasn't. So far as Carter could tell, it wasn't even working all that hard to keep track of the virus. "Last thought before I go to bed," he wrote on the evening of January 27. "We have confirmed 5 cases in the US. We would estimate that the true number of cases might be 18–40 times that number (say 100–200 already in the US and we only know about 5 of them)." At that moment, the CDC said it had one hundred so-called PUIs, or persons under investigation. Thus far, one out of seven people tested by the CDC had been infected by the virus.

To find the one hundred to two hundred that Carter imagined were already roaming around the United States, the CDC would need to be testing seven times that many people, or between seven hundred and fourteen hundred. "Right now we are in containment," wrote Carter. "Think of the cases that popped up across the US like embers that are capable of starting a fire. As part of the containment strategy, we find these embers as quickly as possible and then stamp them out. This strategy only works for cases coming from the outside or for very short chains of transmission . . . It also requires incredible vigilance that is exhausting. Because the territory where embers could fall is so vast, it is easy to miss an ember. And where the ember falls matters—does it fall into a pond or on an asphalt/concrete parking lot or a green lawn or on some very dry leaves or pine straw. It is just a matter of chance where that ember falls and whether or not anything ignites and a fire starts and begins to spread."

The next day, Richard wrote to Carter with a question. As the head of CEPI, Richard had the power to direct hundreds of millions of dollars to companies with new ideas about how to make vaccines more quickly than they had ever been made. It was interesting to note, and Richard noted it, that the free market had no interest in funding these companies in their early stages. Matt Hepburn's unit inside the Department of Defense had provided funding for most of them back when they were a glint in the founder's eye. Now CEPI was in a position to help them speed their vaccines through trials.

They'd identified a Boston-area outfit called Moderna, an oddly named British-Swedish one called AstraZeneca, and several others as promising candidates that might develop a vaccine. The sooner CEPI's money went out the door, the sooner people would be vaccinated, and the sooner any pandemic would end. Four days earlier, just after Carter generated his first view of the virus, CEPI had made a grant to Moderna to cover costs of the first two stages of clinical trials. "I was getting a hell of a lot of heat inside CEPI that I had my hair on fire and had gone over the edge," recalled Richard. If the novel coronavirus turned out to be a reprisal of the 2009 flu—if nature had merely shot humans with anther BB gun—the money would have been wasted and his donors would rebel. CEPI was at risk. And it had a chance to play a huge role in future pandemics, Richard felt. "Grappling with both horns of the dilemma here," he wrote to Carter. "Would welcome you wrapping your brain around how to proceed in the most prudent way."

Carter already had a view about these kinds of decisions. He thought that they should be approached the way an ICU doctor treated a patient clinging to life. Play forward whatever you are thinking about doing, or not doing, and ask yourself: Which decision, if you are wrong, will cause you the greatest regret? Richard agreed, and never looked back. CEPI wound up handing out more than a billion dollars to various manufacturers to speed the development of a vaccine. But hardly anyone else in positions of authority seemed to be thinking this way. "I'm seeing comments from people asking why WHO and CDC seem to be downplaying this," wrote Carter. "I'm certainly no public health expert . . . but no matter how I look at this, it looks bad."

On January 31, the United States government finally acted, sort of. It restricted travel by foreigners into the country and required any Americans returning from China to quarantine for fourteen days. "We pretty much shut it down from coming in from China," said President Trump. By then, thought Carter, the virus was likely already so widespread inside the United States that the focus on foreign travelers was a pointless distraction. "It's a waste of time," he wrote after Trump's announcement. "You're protecting your front door from intruders and they're taking your stuff out the back door."

Four days later, on February 4, an infectious-disease doctor within Veterans Affairs named Michael Gelman wrote to Carter. Gelman belonged to a small group of doctors scattered around the VA who, starting out, had bumped into Carter by accident and come to realize that when they had an impossible problem they should throw it to him. They'd all discovered that Carter wouldn't intrude unless they asked him to, but once they'd asked for his help his mind would sort of overrun whatever they were doing. The first time Gelman had written to Carter, it was to ask if Carter might help him with some complicated problem about hospital management. "Thirty-seven minutes after I wrote to him, he responded with this long, perfectly thought-out answer," said Gelman. "He's the vampire at the door, waiting patiently to be invited in."

Gelman wanted to know just then what Carter was making of the novel coronavirus. As it happened, Carter had already written to his superiors in the VA to suggest that they should imagine waves of illness in the population of elderly veterans in six cities with the most inbound flights from China: New York, Los Angeles, Chicago, Atlanta, San Francisco, Seattle, and Atlanta. (He'd checked flight schedules going back to early December.) Carter thought that hospitals were likely to amplify the virus, as they wouldn't be prepared for it to walk in the front door. "Here is the scenario I would prepare for and why," Carter wrote to the young VA doctor, in a message he also shared with the Wolverines. Then he went on:

> It is very likely that we have undetected community transmission in the United States and in many of the other 26 countries with confirmed cases in travelers. Except for the evacuees from Wuhan, nobody was screening asymptomatics. Some have likely slipped thru our screening and our ongoing surveillance. It will take time for those numbers to increase to a level or signal that we will recognize. For the current time we are going to be chasing after symptomatic patients who have traveled to China and monitor close contacts and find sporadic transmission among close contacts—primarily household contacts like the cases in CA and IL [both husband-and-wife transmission]. But this is like the misdirection of a magician— we aren't seeing what we cannot see because we aren't looking for it. Sooner or later, the transmission that is now smoldering out of view is going to lead to someone presenting with pneumonia in an ER somewhere in the

US. Staff in that ER will take a travel history and find no recent travel and treat the patient as a community acquired pneumonia.

He then explained how doctors' not looking for the virus and therefore not finding it till it was too late would lead to a dramatic moment further into the future, when the American people woke up to the realization that they'd been overrun.

It will feel like when the magician tells you to look over here! And we'll feel like we were thrown an unexpected curveball and will be scrambling at that point to respond and to hurriedly reissue new guidance for screening and suspect case definitions. There will be urgency in implementing NPIs [non-pharmaceutical interventions, such as school closures and social distancing] and as we do we will realize that just like in China, disease in the community is much greater than we realized. And we realize that we are now at the equivalent of 5:45 for the Mann Gulch Fire.

*

What does one do, in the Mann Gulch fire, at 5:45? How does one respond to the sight of a thirty-foot-high wall of flame racing in one's direction? State and local health officers still had no ability to test, as they were waiting for a test being created by the CDC. The CDC itself was testing only sparingly. With so little testing capability, Carter argued, you had to be smart about how you tested. He hit upon an idea: hospitals in the five biggest American cities should test anyone who showed up with flu-like symptoms. "I thought, Let's go on a fishing expedition," he said. "I thought, Why don't we focus on where we think it is." He began to track hospital reports of such cases and map them against numbers from previous years—and soon saw odd blips in Seattle and New York City. Those blips, he suspected, were cases being misdiagnosed as flu. The blip in Seattle would prove misleading; but the blip in New York, it became clear later, would have uncovered cases, likely a lot of them, had anyone bothered to test the patients.

Carter was still regularly in touch with Tom Bossert, Trump's first homeland security adviser, and thought Bossert might offer a way to deliver messages to the White House. Bossert had cultivated a relationship with Trump and, even after John Bolton eliminated his position, felt Trump had once actually trusted him, as much as Trump could trust anyone. But Bossert had come out publicly and refuted an idea being peddled by the White House during the first impeachment hearings—that the Ukrainians, not the Russians, had interfered in the 2016 election. From that moment he was dead to the White House. Bossert had been reading the collected writings of Carter Mecher. He'd tried over and over again to get through to people near Trump, but, as he put it, "I kept getting blocked and blocked." Whatever was happening in the White House was happening without the benefit of the people Bossert felt qualified to advise the president. "The chains had been broken," he said. "None of the people who had been involved in the last fifteen years of thinking about pandemics were in the conversation. They were deep state."

Carter vented his swelling frustration in an email to the Wolverines. "I am still having issues in VA with leaders avoiding the use of the term pandemic and then not wanting to implement key portions of the VA pandemic plan because this is not a pandemic," he wrote. "They will not say that word or use that word . . . They expect to see the term pandemic used by CDC and WHO. CDC continues to say this is not a pandemic . . . My response is that a pandemic is not defined by what is happening in the US—it is defined by what is happening across the world (pan = all, demic = people, all people) . . . I know that this is not CDC's intent but it is creating problems for bureaucrats who suffer from malignant obedience."

He and Richard and others had spent years creating and selling the ideas that would, if quickly seized upon, prevent a lot of Americans from dying. Those ideas were useful, and yet no one in authority seemed willing to use them. "We were going nuts," said Carter. Each of the Wolverines went into their contact lists to look for what Carter called "high-value nodes." People they knew who might influence American policy. Rajeev Venkayya had been at medical school with Amy Acton, director of the Ohio Department of Health and a direct path to Ohio's governor, Mike DeWine. Dave Marcozzi, now at the University of Maryland School of Medicine, was just a couple steps away from Maryland's governor, Larry Hogan. James Lawler knew the governor of Nebraska, Pete Ricketts. Matt Hepburn had the attention of people at the top of the Department of Defense. Lisa Koonin had retired from the Centers for Disease Control, but she could help Carter worm his way back into the place— maybe even get a meeting with the director. And they all knew Bob Kadlec, the head of an abstruse but possibly powerful division inside the Department of Health and Human Services called the Office of the Assistant Secretary for Preparedness and Response, or ASPR. It had been Kadlec who, way back at the end of the Bush administration, had dubbed Carter and the others "Wolverines."

The goal was to find at least one state to take the lead and roll out an aggressive response to the virus, introduce the social interventions outlined in the pandemic plan, and create a dom-

ino effect. "We had to create an epidemic for an idea," said
Carter. At some point Duane Caneva realized that he had something to add. He'd been in the shock trauma unit that deployed
with marines on the battlefield in Falluja, and not much rattled
him, but he also knew what he didn't know. He'd worked with
Carter Mecher and James Lawler in the Obama White House,
but he didn't regard himself as really even being in the same
field. "These were the guys I considered our national pandemic
experts," he said. "Not me." Duane was on his second president
as the DHS's chief medical officer. His White House unit was
meant to detect and prevent biological, chemical, and nuclear
threats to Americans and assist the states in various medical
emergencies. When he joined the Obama administration, the
unit had employed nearly two hundred people. The Trump
administration had busted it up and sent pieces of it to other
places, and entirely neglected other pieces. By the middle of
2019, Duane found himself more or less on his own, grappling
with such problems as how to deliver health care to the growing
numbers of Central Americans and Mexicans detained by U.S.
Immigration and Customs Enforcement—ICE—on the border.

In late January and early February, Duane had been invited
to the White House for National Security Council meetings
to discuss what, if anything, to do about this new outbreak in
Wuhan. He was disturbed by the lack of understanding, or even
information, in those meetings. It was at once shocking and
unsurprising to Duane that Carter Mecher, sitting at a desk in
his bedroom in Atlanta, was creating a clearer view of a virus
in China than anyone in the United States government. "The
CDC kept saying the response would be data-driven, but they
weren't getting any data," said Duane. "And any data they got
was going to be a lagging indicator. They were calling the shots,
and we needed someone else to call the shots." If the United

States government wasn't even going to try to save the American people from the virus, the states would need to do it.

In his two years inside Trump's Department of Homeland Security, Duane had had various dealings, many acrimonious, with various public officials in states that shared a border with Mexico. One struck him as just the type to grab hold of an entire state and turn it into an example that might lead the nation. "Just got off the phone with Dr. Charity Dean," Duane wrote on February 6, 2020, to his fellow Wolverines, before explaining who Charity Dean was, and why he'd sent her all of their emails from the previous month. "She agrees that we're in Mann Gulch."

EIGHT

In Mann Gulch

It is easy for us to assume that as the result of modern science "we have conquered nature," that nature is now confined to beaches for children and to national parks where the few remaining grizzly bears have been shot with tranquilizers and removed to above the timberline, supposedly for their safety and our own. But we should be prepared for the possibility, even if we are going to accompany modern firefighters into Mann Gulch, that the terror of the universe has not yet fossilized and the universe has not run out of blowups.

—NORMAN MACLEAN, *Young Men and Fire*

It has started. Charity was a doctor and thought herself, if not a scientist, at least scientifically minded. She didn't believe that she or anyone else had some mystical power to predict the future. She knew that the human mind played tricks on itself. She'd heard about the anchoring effect and confirmation bias and the rest. At the same time, she could not deny that these inchoate feelings that she sometimes had were as persuasive to her as data. Her initial tingle inside Thomashefsky's clinic had been like that. So had her first response to the UCSB student who might, or might not, have signaled a meningitis outbreak. If on December 21, 2019, you had asked her what it was that had started, she couldn't have told you, but she'd had the feeling before. A picture formed in her mind: a giant wave. A tsunami. "It's a foreboding," she said. "A knowing that something is looming around the corner. Like how when the seasons change you can smell fall in the air right before the leaves change and the wind turns cold. I know things before they happen sometimes, although I can't put my finger on the details."

Still, when Duane Caneva called her she was taken completely by surprise. They were hardly friends: if anything, the opposite. Their antagonism dated from her first days on the new job back in late 2018, as the number two public-health officer for California. She'd driven from Santa Barbara to an Airbnb in Sacramento and, that same day, been asked by then governor Jerry Brown to turn around and go back down south to the U.S.-Mexico border and, in effect, go to war with the Trump administration. A report had arrived on the governor's desk, of a big caravan of would-be immigrants moving through Mexico in the general direction of San Diego. The local health officer in San Diego had declared it a federal problem; but the U.S. government at that moment seemed more keen to inflame the problem than to solve it. Charity had heard that the Trump administration might be using new arrivals from Mexico as weapons in a public relations war. When space in the migrant shelters ran out, ICE workers would drive these people into cities in the dead of night and just leave them there. "I'd heard that Trump was trying to create a crisis," said Charity. "Trying to turn people against immigrants. It was just a rumor. But when I get there I find this is all true. They're just dumping families on street corners at two in the morning. They were trying to create a disaster."

Her assignment was to mitigate the health risks posed by the new arrivals. It was flu season. Drug-resistant tuberculosis could almost be counted as an export of several Mexican states. She never stopped worrying about chicken pox and measles. Measles had a spectacular R naught of somewhere between 12 and 18—which is to say that each person who got it on average gave it to between a dozen and eighteen others. In San Diego, volunteer workers had been picking migrants off the streets where United States immigration officers had dumped them and bringing them to Our Lady of Guadalupe Church, which had offered shelter. Inside the church, Charity found hundreds of tired, scared, and obviously unhealthy refugees. Each night, the church volunteers told her, she should expect between twenty-five and one hundred twenty-five new arrivals. "It felt like chaos," said Charity. "The hallways are lined with families sitting on the floor. These are like mothers and babies, who, by the way, have been kept in cages." She noticed how quiet and still the smaller children were. "Three-year-olds don't behave like that," she said. "They all looked shell-shocked."

At first she wasn't as concerned by what she saw as by what she smelled. Just by the odor, or lack of it, she was pretty sure that there was no gangrene, and that there were no bacterial infections. "You can't smell viruses," she said "But there's a smell when people are ill—you know how when your kid is sick and the smell of their breath changes. It's like that." She needed to set up a health care delivery system, fast, without the usual sources of help. The only medical supplies on hand had been brought by church volunteers from home medicine cabinets. The U.S. government under Donald Trump obviously would be of no use. San Diego County wanted nothing to do with it. She called the Red Cross, only to find that the Red Cross has no interest in helping, either. (She learned later that they didn't want to offend their Republican donors.) The problem now belonged to the state of California, and *she* was now the state of California.

At length she reached a friend, an executive at Direct Relief, the massive Santa Barbara–based philanthropy dedicated to disaster aid. Caring for the ill and the hungry who had been detained while crossing the U.S.-Mexico border was no part of their mission, but she had come to know the executive—and thought of him as a kindred spirit. "I asked him, Would you be willing to send supplies and money and oh, by the way, you won't be able to take credit for it?"

He was. Then she found a clinic in San Ysidro that was willing to accept the seriously ill. Then Jewish Family Service stepped in to help—and she was struck by how private American forces of mercy were straining to offset America's public agents of cruelty. She herself became a force of mercy. Technically, she was not supposed to see patients. She had her stethoscope with her, however, so she began to examine children. "You just write a sign that says MEDICAL CLINIC and stick it on the door and it becomes one," she said. The first thing to do, she knew from her training with Dr. Hosea, was to learn her patients' social history. "Where are you from?" was here the money question. Her patients' answers enabled her to check the vaccination rates in their home states and determine the communicable diseases to which they were most vulnerable.

Her new migrant health care system spun up into a success. (It would still be operational two years after she created it.) She didn't know it at the time, but the feds who had created the problem that she had resolved noticed what she'd done. A few months later she had an email from the Department of Homeland Security asking her to join their weekly call on border issues. After the death of some Mexican children in ICE's supposed care, Congress was pressuring the Trump administration to explain the health care system on the U.S.-Mexico border. There wasn't one, at least none that anyone cared to describe in a congressional hearing. The Department of Homeland Security had tracked down Charity Dean, in a panic, to ask her how she'd done what she had done—because they wanted to reproduce it elsewhere. "They went from wanting a crisis to 'Oh shit, we need to keep kids from dying,'" said Charity.

By then she knew that the Trump administration had been *flying* migrants in transport planes from Texas to California, so that they might create more stress on the system she had built and, at the same time, take advantage of it. She got on the phone with this Duane guy and another colleague, a tough, bullying type from Texas who began by mansplaining to her how to manage an outbreak and then tried to deny the existence of the flights. "At which point I was like, *Fuck you. I was there. I saw it.*" A few days later the flights stopped. Charity never learned why.

When Duane Caneva got back in touch with her, she didn't think of him as an ally. "I saw him as a storm trooper for Trump," she said. She surely was not prepared for what he had to say. "His voice was different than all the other times I'd talked to him," said Charity. "It was kind of low and quivering. I thought, *Oh my God. He's doing something illegal!*" Suddenly there was this other Duane. This Duane who was telling her that he belonged to this small, informal, almost secret group of doctors who had once worked in the White House under Bush or Obama and were now scattered to the four winds but not without influence. This Duane was now working, *without the White House's permission,* to coordinate some kind of national pandemic response. "It was clear that he was doing something he knew could possibly get him into trouble and get *me* into trouble," she said. He needed her help, he explained, in getting what this secret group of doctors had to say to the governor of the nation's most populous state so that it might take the lead for the country, as the White House clearly was not going to. "I was like, Wait a second," said Charity, "there's a group of people—a break glass group—who meet during pandemics?"

Thinking it over, she decided that whatever Duane was doing probably wasn't actually illegal. It was just wildly insubordinate. Plus it was an admission that she might actually be useful to him. "Just to call me he had to humble himself, which said to me this must be important," she said. At any rate, this new Duane Caneva wasn't a storm trooper for Donald Trump. He was part of the resistance. If discovered, he'd likely be fired. She loved it when people were brave; bravery always had her at hello. "That he had that in him, I didn't know," said Charity. After the call she read the massive strings of emails Duane had forwarded—pages and pages of insight into the virus that, whatever the CDC might say, she suspected was already spreading inside the United States. "I went through all their old email chains," she said. "I devoured them like a starving person."

At that moment, the world felt as upside down to her as it ever had. She had sold a house she loved and left Santa Barbara with her three young sons, only to have her ex-husband decide that, no, he'd rather have the children remain in Santa Barbara. She was prepared to give up a lot for the new job but not them. And then the job wasn't what she had expected it to be. Working for the state of California wasn't like working for the county of Santa Barbara, only bigger and better. There had been very few occasions that required her to rise to them. The border crisis in San Diego had been an exception. Most days she felt trapped at a desk inside a massive faceless bureaucracy. Often the work felt mundane. Impersonal. Low-stakes. Did she really want to spend her days sorting out tedious inefficiencies in the licensing and certification of California's hospitals? Plus, no one inside the 4,500-person operation that was the California Department of Public Health knew what anyone else did. People thought it weird that she tried to learn. She'd been installed in an office on the seventh floor on a hall with the rest of the department's leadership. The first few weeks in Sacramento, she'd stepped off the elevator at random floors and walked around introducing herself, to figure out who did what, and to invite them to the seventh floor for coffee whenever they wanted. Her little walk-abouts ended when a friendly colleague took her aside and said, *I think you're making people uncomfortable.* Seventh-floor people didn't just walk around the other floors. After that she stopped getting off at other floors.

The most disorienting aspect of the job by far was her new boss. Charity had assumed that she herself would replace her old boss, Dr. Karen Smith, whenever Dr. Smith stepped down. That's why Dr. Smith had brought her in in the first place. Dr. Smith had left in June 2019, and for the next few months Charity had filled her shoes—but then, in October, she was returned to her original position. The new governor, Gavin Newsom, broke with the tradition of naming a former local California health officer to run the state when he instead brought in Sonia Angell, a for-mer CDC employee in the agency's Noncommunicable Disease Unit. Angell had experience in neither California nor communi-cable disease. Her most recent job had been working on heart dis-ease in New York City's health department. Only later, in August 2020, at the press conference where he announced Angell's abrupt resignation—without going into why she was resigning so abruptly—would Newsom explain why, in part, she'd been recruited by his administration: her work in righting racial injus-tice in health care. Charity was later told that she herself had never been a serious candidate. "It was an optics problem," says a senior official in the Department of Health and Human Services. "Charity was too young, too blond, too Barbie. They wanted a person of color." Sonia Angell identified as Latina.

The first thing Karen Smith had asked Charity to do was to resolve a crisis on the U.S.-Mexico border. The first thing Sonia Angell asked her to do was to figure out how to set the time on the clock on her desk phone. Charity never used her desk phone; she had no idea how the clock on the thing worked; but her new boss said that without it she would not be able to tell the time and so the clock must be fixed. As Charity fiddled with the phone, she thought to herself, *This isn't my job*, and finally arranged to have someone who actually knew how the desk phones worked set the phone's clock. She also found her new boss a tailor, a hairdresser, and a dry cleaner, and—well, at first it seemed to Charity that her new boss was asking her to do things as a way of becoming friends. She worked to dismiss the thought that her new boss was asking her to do these things to remind her of her place. Charity wasn't particularly well suited to being reminded of her place, and was further unsettled when rank-and-file staff began to turn up in her office to complain about the new boss. "After a while it just felt like *Mean Girls*," said Charity. "I decided to suck it up and pretend everything was fine."

Suck it up she did, during the days. The nights were not so simple. For the past year, she'd told herself a story: she'd left behind all these things she'd loved in Santa Barbara, but for a purpose. Something was coming, and she was rising into a position to confront it. That story no longer rang true. "I had given up everything to come here and take this job," she said. "I was like, Holy shit, why did I do this?"

Then came the virus. Charity had started to follow the events in Wuhan in early January, about the same time that Carter Mecher pointed the virus out to his fellow Wolverines. Like Carter, she had set out to learn what she could about it, and also, like Carter, she was surprised by how little there was to find. "I'm the number two health person in the biggest state in the country," she said. "I'm expert in communicable diseases and trained to control them. And there is nowhere for me to look." There was no place where she could get a reliable take on the things she needed to know to make any sort of prediction about how the virus might play out in California: its R naught, its infection fatality rate, the rate at which it sent people to the hospital. She wanted to know how much time passed from the moment people were infected to the moment they became infectious (the incubation period), and how much, if any, time passed between the moment they became infectious and the onset of symptoms, when they would know to isolate them- selves. "The perfect pathogen has a very long infectious period and a very long incubation period—because the longer it takes for the pathogen to declare itself, the harder it is to track," she said. One reason measles was so wildly transmissible was that a person with it was infectious for four days before he knew he had it. This new thing felt to her a bit like that, just watching how the Chinese were reacting to it. "China was behaving like this was the perfect pathogen," she said.

Like Carter, she started googling and reading Chinese news- papers. "I knew that I needed to get as close to the source as I could get," she said. Twitter was a great resource: by mid- January, someone had posted video of the Chinese authori- ties *welding* the doors on homes in Wuhan, to keep the people infected with the virus inside. "It looked pretty real, but I didn't know if I could believe it," she said. Many months before, she had subbed at the last minute for Governor Newsom, at his request, as host to a delegation of fancy Chinese doctors. She and the Chinese doctors had discussed, among other things, pandemics, and how to respond to them. "I said, 'Hold on, what would cause that group of doctors to, say, solder the doors shut on apartment buildings with suspect cases?'" said Charity. "I mean, locking people in buildings to die was not part of their ops plan." She read the *Journal of the American Medical Association* and *The Lancet* and every other publication generating quick takes out from Wuhan. She found data in bits and pieces, all the while knowing that she'd never have the data she'd need to act—or, rather, that by the time she had that data, it would be too late to act. "The data was super-sketchy, but that's the job: using scattered information from unreliable sources to make decisions," she said. "And I wasn't just looking for data. I was looking for all those little clues that something is wrong."

Soon she had a rough idea of the virus's behavior in Wuhan—the R naught, the hospitalization rate, and the fatality rates. Using these, she played out its spread in California. Assuming that the first case of transmission inside the state had occurred by early January, and using a reproductive rate of 2.5, she drew on her office whiteboard a so-called epi curve. It described the next five months, with infections on the y-axis and time on the x-axis. When she'd finished, she saw that the curve resembled a giant wave. A tsunami. By June, if the government did nothing to mitigate the virus's spread, twenty million or so Californians would have been infected, two million would have required hospitalization, and one hundred thousand of them would have died. And that didn't count the people who died of other illnesses they might have survived, had there been an open bed in the hospital.

She erased the whiteboard and did the math all over again, with the most optimistic assumptions that were still plausible. "The numbers seemed nuts to me," she said. "What I was really doing at that whiteboard was coming to terms with exponential growth." Fairly certain that her boss wouldn't want to hear about the numbers, she waited for a week to mention them. A week later, her boss was still not ready for the news. "I started to say that this could be a big deal and we should put a plan together, but Sonia didn't let me finish," recalled Charity. "She cut me off and said, 'If this is a real thing, the CDC will tell us.'" The CDC, Charity knew, already had its mantra: "the risk to the American people is very low." Nancy Messonnier, a senior CDC official, had been saying that, and Sonia Angell often repeated it, right up until the end of February. "She was looking for the CDC to pull the fire alarm," said Charity. "The CDC does not know how to pull the fire alarm. In fact, there is no fire alarm in this country."

By the third week of January, Charity Dean, like Carter Mecher, did not believe that the risk to the American people was low. She thought that the virus was already spreading exponentially inside the United States.* It was as if she, and she alone, had spotted the fire in Mann Gulch, and no one else was willing to turn and run. She sent out a survey to California's hospitals to get a sense of how many beds they could create in rooms with negative air pressure—that is, rooms that did not allow whatever might be exhaled by a patient to escape. She looked into the capacity of the morgues. "Everyone forgets about the morgues," she said. "It's the part of the health care system that's never included in disaster response preparations." She went to bed at night thinking about the need to establish sites for mass graves. "A switch flipped in me mid-January," she said. "My whole being came alive."

---

* The first death caused by COVID-19 recorded in the United States occurred in Seattle on February 28. In late April, Santa Clara County reclassified two earlier deaths after figuring out that they, too, had been caused by COVID-19. The first had occurred on February 6, the second on February 17. Both patients would have been infected by the virus roughly a month before death. As neither victim had traveled outside the area, the virus had clearly been circulating in the Bay Area by early January.

She found the old pandemic plan and dusted it off. It had come from the CDC, and, like all the CDC papers, it was well done. "They really should just change the name," she said. "It shouldn't be the Centers for Disease *Control*. It should be the Centers for Disease *Observation and Reporting*. That's what they do well." She had no idea who exactly had written the plan for a flu pandemic, or what had prompted it, but it was hugely useful, as a starting point, for anyone hoping to mitigate the damage caused by any disease without the help of antivirals or vaccines. "It was really useful because it basically said, 'We're in 1918. There are no medical countermeasures. What do we do? Here are the tools.'" No one was asking her to write a battle plan for the state of California, but she wanted to be ready in case they did.

On January 20, the virus made the television news. Charity seized upon that as an excuse to bring the subject up more bluntly with her boss. "I knew it was going to be a delicate balance," she said. "Of not seeming to know something she didn't know, or not raising an alarm that she didn't raise." It wasn't long into the meeting before Charity realized she'd failed to achieve the balance. Afterward, Angell banned her from using the word "pandemic" and told her to erase the math and the tsunami curve on her whiteboard. "She told me I was scaring people," said Charity. "I said 'Shit, they *should* be scared.'"

From that moment Charity found herself left off email chains and not informed of meetings. "The way you do it in government is not explicit," she said. "It has to be subtle. She just left me out of everything. It was just leaving me completely out and saying, 'This isn't your area.'" The first few weeks of January she had not slept well or eaten properly. "I'd be lying in bed trying to imagine how it was going to play out. Which cities would be cordoned off first? Which people would we let die?" On January 22, her heart began to beat strangely and she visited a cardiologist, who confirmed she'd developed an arrhythmia, fitted her for a heart monitor, and told her to take it easy. "It's like Noah building the ark," said Charity. "Everyone thinks you are totally crazy."

For maybe both better and worse she was just then reading, or rather rereading, over and over again, a section in the second volume of William Manchester's biography of Winston Churchill. The book described the years 1932–1940, when Churchill was out of power and watching with mounting frustration and anger as British prime minister Neville Chamberlain minimized the rise of Adolf Hitler. *Alone,* the book was subtitled. Charity was less interested in World War II than in the events leading up to it. The book had sat on her bedside table for the past eighteen months. She remained fixated on the run-up to the agreement made by Chamberlain with Hitler in Munich on September 30, 1938. To avoid war with Germany, Chamberlain had caved to Hitler's demand for a chunk of what was then Czechoslovakia. He'd then returned home to a temporarily grateful British public and, to a cheering crowd, had delivered remarks in which he said that Great Britain had achieved "peace with honour." Churchill had issued his own statement in response, to less fanfare. "You were given the choice between war and dishonour," he said. "You chose dishonour and you will have war." Churchill had no data, either. But he was able to see the threat Hitler presented when others did not, because he was not blinded by a desire for peace.

A history Charity had started for pleasure had become something else. She didn't so much read it as investigate it, the way she might an outbreak of tuberculosis. By late January she'd underscored half the lines on the pages leading up to Great Britain's declaration of war, and scribbled comments in every margin. *"Chamberlain publicly accused Churchill of lacking JUDGEMENT!"* she wrote. *"The leaders with the worse judgement smugly claim they have the best."* A bit farther on: *"Don't prepare a white paper when you need to be bombing the shit out of Germany!"* (Chamberlain had spent the final few days before the war writing a white paper that defended his strategy of appeasement.) After that: *"There will be no standing ovation when you are proven right."* And, finally, *"Churchill was a dragon too."*

Occasionally she wondered if the tendency to remain forever on red alert—to *always* be straining to look around the corner to see what might be coming—might be classified as a neurosis. "My whole life I've been preparing for a war," she said. Now she saw very clearly that the enemy was attacking, and no one but she herself felt the urgency of the situation. Everywhere she turned in government she saw this distinction, in leaders, between Churchills and Chamberlains. The people who presided in times of peace tended to have a gift for avoiding or at least disguising conflict. People made for battlefield command did not find their way into positions of authority, at least not until the general public sensed existential risk. By then—by the time people knew enough about a communicable disease to be terrified—the war's most critical phase was over. She had spent her life preparing for just this moment: now, when you attacked the virus and contained it before it overran California. And yet she was now less relevant than at any time since she'd gone into public service as the deputy health officer in Santa Barbara County. "I was feeling worthless and useless," said Charity. "It didn't appear that me being here for the state meant anything."

Everyone has a story they tell themselves about themselves. Even if they don't explicitly acknowledge it, their minds are at work retelling or editing or updating a narrative that explains or excuses why they have spent their time on earth as they have.

A decade earlier, in the story that played on the loop inside the mind of Charity Dean, she'd cast herself as the victim. She had every reason to do so. Every terrible thing that a man can do to a woman, short of killing her, some man had done to her. After the difficult birth of her third child, she had stopped consuming alcohol in a normal way and started to use it. A drink could make the story she was telling herself feel more satisfying. *It's like scratching an itch until it bleeds, it feels so good.* That thought had crossed her mind, even as she scratched. There had come a moment when she realized that if she did not stop scratching the itch she would claw herself to death. Something very, very bad had happened to her: the details did not matter. In that moment she had seen the fire, growing exponentially, coming straight for her. In response she'd created an escape fire. Her escape fire was a story.

In this new story she told herself about herself, she was never simply a victim. For whatever had happened she bore some responsibility. Whether she did, or did not, was beside the point: the new story had the very practical effect of shifting the focus from others onto herself, and from things she could not control to things that she could. In this story, she was put on earth for some purpose, and it was her job not just to figure out what that purpose might be but to make sure she did not allow herself to become distracted from its fulfillment. The new story had gained focus after she'd taken the job as a local public-health officer. Its theme was bravery, and it compelled her to recognize those moments when she was doing, or failing to do, a thing out of fear. Coupled with her natural interests and abilities, it had turned her into an action hero. She believed that, in the bargain, her narrative had saved her life.

Soon Charity's purpose was clear, and not only to her but to anyone who watched her in action: she was put on earth to fight battles, and wars, against disease. To save lives and perhaps even an entire country. She'd quit her job as a county health officer and moved to the state because she sensed something big coming that she needed to be there for. Just before she left, she had confided to a friend that she had this feeling she was going to wind up in the White House one day; and when that newly bewildered friend asked why on earth she thought that, she said, "because I have to fix this."

Something big had come, just as she'd imagined in her story. But her office was fifteen yards down a hall from where she needed to be, to play the role that she assumed she would play. The feeling of powerlessness had knocked her back hard. She was now reduced to scribbling math on her whiteboard at home at night. By the end of January, when she walked into the building and took the elevator to the seventh floor, she was asking the universe a question: "Why won't you let me do my job?" A bitterness she thought she'd banished had returned. She felt a despair she had not felt in a decade. "I was the lone person in state public health who was saying this is a pandemic," she said. "I wasn't talking to anyone else. I had no validation that I wasn't a crazy person."

*

Then, out of the blue, on February 6, Duane Caneva called her and asked her to have a look at a bunch of old emails. For some reason Charity couldn't fathom, he'd labeled the entire chain "Red Dawn." (Duane's first working title had been "Avengers.") However preposterous that sounded, the characters immediately jumped out at her, one more than the others. "This guy Carter," she said. "The way they interacted with him. They clearly thought he was the guru." With help from the others, which consisted mostly of just prodding and teasing, Carter had written these long and curious missives. She read in them an echo of her own thoughts, and then some. They were just incredibly smart and insightful and . . . never-ending. "I wondered how he had time to write all this," recalled Charity. "The question I was asking myself reading the emails was: Doesn't this guy have a job? It was like two thousand words on the difference between South Korea's response and Japan's. He's in the VA. In Atlanta. But he's clearly, like, the guy. The guy with the answers."

She looked at the names of the other six people on the Red Dawn emails. All men. She'd never heard of any of them, and so the first thing she'd done was to google them. All doctors, at least two of whom worked inside the Trump administration. Then the names of Carter Mecher and Richard Hatchett finally registered. "I said, Holy shit, these are the guys who wrote the paper!"* She'd been energized by Carter and Richard's reinterpretation of the events of 1918. The takeaway resonated with her experience in Santa Barbara. Social interventions, if done early, could have huge effects on disease transmission; in the extreme they could contain it. Weeks before, she'd printed out their paper and stuck it in a fat three-ring binder she'd created for herself. Her nerd bible. Everything in her nerd bible was ammunition for the argument she was being forbidden by her boss from making: that the virus had already arrived in the United States, and that it might well lead to a 1918-like pandemic, and that if you wanted to prevent a lot of people from dying you had better start working at it now.

---

* One of their two papers on the 1918 pandemic, as distinct from the pandemic plan. Charity wouldn't learn that Carter and Richard had written the original pandemic plan for the country until many months later, when someone else told her. Carter and Richard never mentioned it.

Three days later, a Sunday, Duane asked her to join them on a conference call. She hadn't responded to the emails. Anything she wrote from her state email account might as well be made public, and she worried what might happen if anyone suspected that she had entered some back-channel conversation with the Trump administration. She'd learned, from other battles, that there was a fair chance that anything she said, even in private, would end up in the *Los Angeles Times*. She told Duane that she'd come onto his conference call but only to listen, not to speak. "I was nervous about being fired for even being on the call," she said.

That first call—all these calls, she'd soon learn—started with Duane Caneva asking Carter Mecher to share his most recent thoughts. "The emails were intriguing," said Charity, "but as soon as Carter started talking, I knew I had found my person." His idea of that moment was something she'd not heard from anyone else: not health care experts, not the CDC, not the armchair epidemiologists on Twitter and cable television, who reminded her of gentleman farmers who had never actually plowed a field or milked a cow. Carter proposed using the patients with flu-like symptoms who turned up in emergency rooms across the United States as a quick and dirty tool to figure out where the virus was. Take those numbers and compare them to the seasonal averages and they might lead you to outbreaks, where you could test for the virus. "So far we have only identified two examples where disease spread from a traveler (and in both circumstances it was very close contact in the household—a spouse)," he later wrote, then continued:

Opening up wider surveillance would seem impractical and unnecessary. This conclusion is correct until it is wrong. The problem I see with this approach is the only way we will recognize community transmission is if a contact tracing of a known case (derived from travel screening) finds an extended chain of transmission. But assuming all is well denies the possibility of disease already in the community, just hidden from sight or diagnosis because of a bit of a Catch-22. We are in the middle of an active flu season. These cases could look similar to and be confused with flu. Even if a patient presented with fever and lower resp tract symptoms and flu tests were negative, CDC will not test these patients for nCoV. So how exactly do you find something that you refuse to look for because you believe it can't be there?

To show the feasibility of his idea, he'd run all these numbers—there were roughly five thousand hospitals in the United States, and 23,000 people a day showing up to them with flu-like symptoms, and so each hospital need only test five people each day. If that sounded like too much trouble you could take a shortcut, by looking for hospitals where the number of people who showed up with flu-like symptoms was rising, while the number of people testing positive for flu was falling. (Exactly that was about to occur in New York City, though no one would notice before it was too late.) "He sounded like an auto mechanic," said Charity. "Everything he said was really simple, but I kept thinking, *Oh my God, that's incredibly insightful.* He didn't seem to want the spotlight, but his thoughts belonged in the spotlight."

At the same time, she didn't understand why she'd been asked to listen in. Two-thirds of the way into the call she figured it out, when Duane, ignoring their understanding, called on her to speak. From the way Duane spoke of her, she realized that he, and they, had somehow gotten it into their heads that she was running California's pandemic response. They also seemed to think that if she made the right moves in California, the state might be used to steer the entire country's response. "They knew the CDC had no legal authority to run a pandemic response, but they thought the states had it," she said. "And they thought I personally ran the whole front lines of public health in the state."

She had planned to keep quiet but now didn't want to. "I couldn't stand it," she said. "Here was a group of people who, forty minutes in, clearly thought like I did. And clearly wanted to hear what I had to say." Duane Caneva wasn't some nobody. He was chief medical officer of the Department of Homeland Security. He was putting his job at risk: why shouldn't she? Almost in spite of herself, she began to lay out for the men how, in her view, the world worked. She began by explaining that the local health officers in California, as in certain American states, had real autonomy. She couldn't just make them do whatever she wanted them to do but had to lead them. "We know what the virus will do," she liked to say. "We don't know what the humans will do." What the humans would do, she felt certain, is what they were led to do, if only they were well led.

As she explained the critical role of the local public-health office, and the need for the state and the federal government to stand behind health officers in their dealings with their communities, her audience on the phone call pushed back against her. "They didn't want to accept it," she said. "Anyone at the federal level is so removed from the shitstorm that is the CDC that they have no clue. They wanted to believe that the CDC, or the state, could just make local health officers do what they wanted to do. You know why I think they didn't want to accept it? It's too terrifying. Too chaotic. Too WTF. Too much of a shake to federal officials' foundation to digest the truth that local nobodies are really in charge."

In effect, she was telling them what she had figured out when she was herself a local public-health officer. There was no *system* of public health in the United States, just a patchwork of state and local health officers, beholden to a greater or lesser degree to local elected officials. Three thousand five hundred separate entities that had been starved of resources for the past forty years. Yes, these local nobodies might allow themselves to be led by a health officer they respected—say, somebody from the Centers for Disease Control, or a state health officer who knew what she was doing. But the CDC had demonstrated time and again to her that, once the shooting started, it didn't know what to do.

Just then the CDC was supervising the return of Americans from China, and that offered her a case in point. Many of the returning Americans had passed through airports in California, and Charity had seen the ineptitude with which they'd been handled. The CDC hadn't bothered to test them—not even the people returning from Wuhan. When local health officers, her friends and former colleagues, set out to find these possibly infected Americans, and make sure that they were following orders to quarantine, they discovered that the CDC officials who had met them upon arrival had not bothered to take down their home addresses. When local health officers called the CDC to say how hard it was to track down John Smith when the CDC had listed his residence as "Los Angeles International Airport," the CDC said, "Just don't follow up on them." What was the point of having these travel restrictions from Wuhan if the federal government was going to just let people loose upon their return?

The CDC was now holding conference calls with the health officers in the cities whose airports had received the returning Americans. Charity's boss tried to block her from speaking with the CDC, but she had gotten herself onto the first of these calls. She'd posed a rude question to the senior CDC official on the call: *How can you keep saying that Americans are at low risk from the virus if you aren't even testing for the virus?* She'd been answered with silence, and then the official moved on to the next topic. "The single most important question is how many undetected cases are out there in our community," said Charity, "and we don't know."

Charity thought that the virus was already spreading fast, and unseen. Her attempts to sound an alarm in California had gotten her banned by her new boss from participating in discussions about it. There was, in effect, no leadership, either from the state or the federal government. She knew that the weaker-spined local health officers around the country would defer to the CDC, as it got them off the hook for making their own hard decisions, but the better local health officers would not. At least a few local health officers in California, she thought, would summon the nerve to go it on their own. "The peasants will revolt," she said to the Wolverines. Sooner or later, some local health officer would devise her own test and go hunting for the virus—and shock everyone, and make a mockery of the state of California, the CDC, and the federal government, by finding lots of it. That, in any case, is what she would have done, were she still a local public-health officer.

Here was the only place in her little speech where the men had seriously interrupted her. They simply could not or did not want to believe that in a crisis any local health officer would not defer to the CDC or, if the CDC was asleep at the switch, the state of California. "You don't know who you are talking to," she said. "I *was* that local health officer." After that they just let her speak, and when she'd finished speaking, she realized that she had just sort of let rip, in a way she'd never intended.

She hadn't told them what she thought of her new boss, or the CDC. She'd tried simply to describe the CDC's actions without offering her editorial opinion. Still, she had let them know that, however bad they might imagine the situation on the ground to be, it was worse. She wondered how long it would take before word got out about what she'd said and she got in serious trouble with her superiors for ignoring the chain of command and working behind their backs. "I thought, That was really intense," she said.

Soon after that first call, James Lawler was asked by the Department of Health and Human Services to fly to Japan, extract the 430 American citizens who were on the *Diamond Princess*, load them onto cargo planes, and fly with them back home. Though he didn't work for the Department of Health and Human Services, he didn't give it a second thought. Lawler called his friend and honorary Wolverine Michael Callahan and asked him to join him, and after stuffing a giant pile of negative-pressure helmets into seven giant duffel bags, the two set off for Japan the next morning. Seeing this made the decision about whether to throw in with this preposterously named group of men much easier for Charity. "It made me like them," she said. "It was action, not white papers." She still wasn't entirely sure what to make of the men, or what the men made of her or what she'd said. But soon one of them sent her a message: "Where did you *come from*???" Another began to refer to her as "Wolverette." "We liked her right away," Carter said. "She's spitfire."

NINE

The L6

The names at the top of the Red Dawn emails grew in both number and importance. Charity thought of it as "the Carter show" and noticed that, even though Carter Mecher supplied almost all of the interesting material, he demanded none of the attention. It was never "look at me!" but always "look at this!" The audience for Carter's analysis would come to include the health officers of a bunch of states and a pack of current and former Trump administration officials, including Tom Bossert; the surgeon general, Jerome Adams; and Trump's White House doctor turned presidential adviser Ronny Jackson. A small crowd inside the Department of Health and Human Services also joined, among them Bob Kadlec, who ran ASPR, the office responsible for responding to medical emergencies. Charity watched as important men took insights and data generated by Carter at his bedroom desk and repeated them on television and Twitter as their own. "Everyone is cheating off Carter," she said, but Carter did not seem at all to mind. Just the reverse: he told everyone to take what they wanted and insisted that he had no special claim on anything he wrote.

Then there were the phone calls. The emails were where people turned to listen to Carter's mind at work; during the conference calls, held on weekends, people felt safe to voice their own private thoughts that might get them into public trouble. Charity found this a bit odd, as it was not at all clear who was on these calls, or how safe it was to say anything. "There were always fourteen people lurking who never identified themselves," she said. "I was never sure who was listening." On the line at various times, she later learned, were Tony Fauci, White House staffers, and members of the president's coronavirus task force.

By some mechanism Charity never fully understood, the things she said on these calls could have real effects. During one call in mid-February, she railed about the idiocy of the CDC's requirement that to qualify for a COVID-19 test an American needed to be in an ICU, with a history of travel to China. The disease was clearly already spreading inside the United States; there were almost surely people walking around with it who had not traveled to China and had no symptoms; how on earth would it ever be controlled if local health officers couldn't test, at the very least, people with flu-like symptoms? A week or so after she'd vented, the CDC changed its definition of a person under investigation to include severely ill people with no travel history. "They did it in like a footnote in eight-point type," said Charity. "It felt passive-aggressive." "Good job Charity," Carter wrote that very day, at the end of one of his long emails to the group. "They just added your footnote."

What Charity couldn't figure out was how, or even if, what she said on the calls found its way into the ears of the decision makers—and who those people were. At one point she put the question to James Lawler. "James," she asked, "who exactly is in charge of this pandemic?" "Nobody," he replied. "But if you want to know who is sort of in charge, it's sort of us."

*

To the new and growing group of people sort of in charge of the pandemic, Carter found himself explaining all over again the truths that he and Richard and Lisa and Bob and Laura Glass had discovered fourteen years earlier. "I want to pass along some slides that help explain what we mean by early targeted and layered interventions . . . ," he began, in an email in early February, then explained the effects of school closures and social distancing and the rest. He walked the crowd through the different outcomes in Philadelphia and St. Louis and how they should think of Wuhan as Philly and the United States as having a shot at becoming St. Louis.

He went right away to his favorite analogy. "One could think of the interventions like a fire extinguisher," he wrote. "It will be effective if the fire is caught early (say only a grease fire on the top of a stove). But once the fire has spread and half the house is ablaze, you can empty the fire extinguisher, but it won't do much (probably as effective as just throwing it through a window). The problem with implementing (the social interventions) too late is you get all the downsides and little benefit, so speed is critical. The challenge is that they need to be implemented before things get bad." By the time people realized that their house was on fire, they needed more than a fire extinguisher. The trick was to learn how to smell smoke.

To Carter, that was the beauty of the *Diamond Princess*. The American authorities were either unable or unwilling to smell the smoke. A lot of people seemed to be viewing events in Wuhan as just one of those bizarre things that happened in China. *Isn't it odd how they throw up an entire 1,000-bed hospital over a week-*

end? Chinese data was sketchy and possibly unreliable: that was true. But the view of the fire on board the *Diamond Princess* could not be clearer. "The 2666 passengers are similar in age (and likely in co-morbidities) to the population we see in a nursing home or residential care facility," wrote Carter. "The 1045 crew are a proxy for a young healthy population."

He pulled the ship's itinerary and reconstructed what had happened on board, day by day. The *Diamond Princess* had left Yokohama on January 20. Five days later it docked in Hong Kong, where an eighty-year-old passenger disembarked. On February 1, the passenger, still in Hong Kong, tested positive for the new coronavirus. The ports for which the cruise ship was headed canceled its certificates of landing. On February 3, the *Diamond Princess* chugged back into Tokyo Bay and its port of origin. Two days later the first passenger tested positive; two days after that the number of confirmed positives reached sixty-one people. "Think about this," Carter wrote on February 9. "If that 80 year old man had instead flown to the US, stayed for 5 days and then flew home and was found to have nCoV do you think we would have identified the 61 cases through our usual approach? Look at the details. This 80 year old wasn't even from China. He wouldn't have even qualified under our definition for a PUI to be tested. We would have missed the entire cluster."

At that moment there was essentially no COVID-19 testing inside the United States. The Food and Drug Administration was still insisting that state and local health officers wait for the test kits supplied by the CDC. And the CDC was still saying that the risk to Americans from the virus was very low. The entire country was dismissing what the redneck epidemiologist had glimpsed in Wuhan. The Japanese weren't dismissing it, though. The Japanese were alert. They had their own labs and planned to use them to test everyone on board the cruise ship.

Until then, Carter had felt a bit like a man searching a dark cave with a match; the Japanese were about to wheel in floodlights. The cave was the cruise ship—but not only the cruise ship. The cave, thought Carter, was his own mind. The picture that he had created in his head about Wuhan, pieced together from news reports, was not reality but some version of it, distorted by forces beyond his control. "We were constantly triangulating and we were constantly reminding ourselves that the models in our heads could be wrong—reminding ourselves to not make the same mistake," he said. "There were so many parallels to patient safety and error." The strategy of layered and partially overlapping defenses that he'd used to reduce deadly mistakes inside American hospitals he now applied to his own thoughts.

Of course he knew that a cruise ship stuck in Tokyo Bay with 3,711 people aboard, confined to their cabins, was an artificial social environment. A virus on board a ship would spread differently than it would, say, in an American city. But it could still say a lot about what the virus might do inside an American city—most importantly, how likely it was to kill. For the first and perhaps only time, in the calculation of the percentage of infected who died, they'd be able to see not just the numerator but also the real denominator. They'd know exactly how many had been infected.

Over the next three days, the case count on board the ship rose from 61 to 135. The numbers shocked even Carter. "This is unbelievable," he wrote. "We are so far behind the curve." He laid out side by side the first ten days of the 2009 swine flu outbreak against what had already happened on the cruise ship. Swine flu had been so frightening because it spread so fast; this new virus was spreading much faster. Over the next ten days, the numbers grew exponentially. On February 16, when Lawler and Callahan evacuated 329 Americans from the ship, the count reached 355. By February 19, when the first two passengers died, 621 people were infected. Two days after that, Carter found, on the website of Japan's National Institute of Infectious Diseases, a field report filled with data from the cruise ship. "I can't understand why no one is paying attention to this," he said. "It's a gold mine."

The level of detail in the report about the spread of the virus was new. It described not only how many had been infected but their ages, when they had first exhibited symptoms, and the number of people with whom they shared a cabin. It gave the dates they first exhibited symptoms. It revealed that 51 percent of those who tested positive were asymptomatic. Carter took that number with a large grain of salt, as the infection in many was new, and they might still develop symptoms. Still, it was an astonishing number: up to that point there had been no study of asymptomatic spread.

The cruise ship was dramatizing just how stealthy the virus might be, and also helping to explain what appeared, in Wuhan, to be a truly fantastic rate of transmission. "The only way I make sense of things is through stories that I tell myself," Carter had written to his new audience of total strangers a few days earlier, as an excuse to tell them all over again about the Mann Gulch fire. "What has me worried is that what happened on the cruise ship is a preview of what will happen when the virus makes its way to the US healthcare system (not to mention institutionalized high risk populations in the US, like nursing homes). I'm not sure that folks understand what is just over the horizon. Remember the story about Mann-Gulch? We are at the equivalent of about 5:44. I anticipate that when we reach 5:45 there is going to be chaos and panic to get anything in place. I doubt that what we would then hurriedly put in place will be any better than what they did on that cruise ship."

The report gave Carter a more complete real-time picture of the virus inside a community than anything he'd seen or was ever likely to see. That new data served as a check against the model in his head—the narrative that he'd been constructing since he first started poking around the internet in China. The attack rate on the *Diamond Princess* was 20 percent. Within a month, one in five of the people confined to their rooms had been infected. That would be on the extreme low end of the likely attack rate over a longer period of time in a more natural setting. But it lined up with his mental model. All that remained was the calculation of the death rate.

In Wuhan that was tricky, as it was impossible to know just how many people had been infected. Now it was tricky because most of the people who were going to die on the cruise ship hadn't done it yet. It could take as long as three weeks for the end to come, and Carter didn't think he had three weeks. He resorted again to redneck epidemiology. The seriously ill pretty quickly landed in intensive care units, he reasoned, either in Japan or in the home countries to which they had returned. Carter followed the news reports about them and tracked their progress. It was a strange and quixotic hunt, but in the end he made an accurate count of the number of passengers on the *Diamond Princess* who had wound up in ICUs. He also knew the mortality rates for patients in ICUs with all causes of respiratory failure: between a quarter and half of them died. By assuming that the passengers on the *Diamond Princess* in ICUs would die at the same rates as the others, he got a rough idea of the lethality of the new disease, before the deaths had actually occurred.

The infection fatality rate on the ship, Carter reckoned, fell somewhere between 1 and a half and 2 percent. Its population skewed older than the American population, but you could, and he did, take those numbers and adjust them, by assigning different mortality rates to different age groups in the United States. Once he'd finished, he had an infection fatality rate of between half of 1 percent and 1 percent.

The redneck epidemiology he'd done in Wuhan would have predicted the outcomes on the *Diamond Princess*. "I think this data is close enough to convince people that this is going to be bad and we will need to pull the full array of NPIs [social interventions]," wrote Carter on February 28. "All that is left is when (timing)." Back in 1918, St. Louis had introduced social interventions one week after the first local cases, he pointed out. Philadelphia had waited three weeks. Already there were cities in the United States behind St. Louis, and maybe even behind Philadelphia. "We should be treating this like we treat strokes and acute coronary syndromes where time = tissue," wrote Carter. "In this case time = transmission."

He had the right mental model for the virus. The glitch was in his mental model of his own country, and its leadership. Every day brought him more evidence of their unwillingness to act on what he'd seen. On February 26, President Trump announced at a press conference that only fifteen Americans had been infected with the virus, and that "when you have fifteen people, and the fifteen within a couple of days is going to be down close to zero, that's a pretty good job we've done." The next evening, taking questions after a White House meeting with African American leaders, Trump had simply declared, "It's going to disappear. One day—it's like a miracle—it will disappear." The CDC, for its part, lagged about five steps behind where it should be. On March 1, it announced that the United States would screen people arriving from other countries for symptoms of the virus. "I wouldn't waste a moment of time on travel restrictions or travel screening," Carter wrote. "We have nearly as much disease here in the US as the countries in Europe."

Every passing moment could be measured in lives lost; and yet, a week after Carter had all the confirmation he needed for his mental model of the threat, nothing had changed. "I sense confusion among very smart people," he wrote in early March.

"[They] hear that more than 80% of those who are infected have mild disease and that overall case fatality rates are on the order of .5%. And then they equate these states to a mild outbreak." To "help people get their head around what is perceived to be a mild outbreak," he ran some numbers. Using the most conservative assumptions suggested by the cruise ship—an attack rate of 20 percent and a fatality rate of half of 1 percent—you wound up with 330,000 dead Americans.

Carter was by nature conciliatory—the sort of person who, after his car is rear-ended, wonders if perhaps he hadn't hit his brakes too suddenly. He was forever looking at any problem or dispute from the other person's point of view. It wasn't easy to get him into the state of mind in which he found himself by mid-March. "I notice a lot of HHS [Department of Health and Human Services] addresses on this email and group," he wrote on the eleventh. "You all have been quiet for most of the discussion over the past several weeks. I would urge you to read the article I just sent out and upbrief your boss . . . History will long remember what we do and what we don't do at this critical moment. It is time to act and it is past the time to remain silent. This outbreak isn't going to magically disappear on its own."

He liked to imagine himself two weeks into the future, looking back on the moment and asking himself: Knowing what I know now, what do I wish I had done back then? In the early stages of a pandemic, the question was especially pointed. At least once the reproductive rate of the virus is known, it isn't that hard to see what you might know two weeks from today: some multiple of today's infections. But if you lacked the will or the ability to test for the virus, those numbers could be truly shocking. Italy was just then illustrating the point. Back on February 20, a grand total of three COVID-19 cases had been discovered in the whole of the country. None of the infected was seriously ill. By March 13, the Italian case count had gone to 17,660, with 1,328 people in intensive care and 1,266 dead. "What would CDC guidance have advised Italy to do on Feb 21?" Carter wrote. "How would CDC have described what was going on in Italy? Would this have met their definition of wide-spread community transmission? I doubt it. CDC and the CDC modeler would have recommended sitting tight."

He sent emails to people inside the CDC, "but they were all tight-lipped. It was a black box." On March 15, after the CDC suggested both that gatherings of more than fifty people should be avoided for the next eight weeks and that schools should remain open, Carter went off. "That CDC would not want 50 people being together for even an hour while hundreds of thousands of kids could be together for 8 hours defies common sense," he wrote. "Imagine CDC getting on TV and trying to explain. Good luck with that."

He'd now awakened to the possibility that at least one of his mental models badly distorted reality: his model of American government. People who might be led to prepare for what was coming were being led not to. One morning in early March, Carter and his wife, Debra, went shopping in the Atlanta exurbs. A few months before, they would have been shopping for groceries; now they were hunting for the supplies that Carter suspected would soon be scarce. As Debra shopped, Carter watched. "I said, 'Look how carefree everyone is. In a week or two everything is going to change. And these people have no idea what is about to happen.' Debbie is looking at me. And she said, 'Maybe that's a good thing—not to know what's about to happen.'"

*

Charity Dean had been living for years with a mental model that fit exactly with the facts on the ground. Her model started with two assumptions. One, something was coming. Two, the CDC wouldn't deal with it. The CDC reminded Charity of a person who allows a false but flattering story about himself to circulate. If everyone has somehow come to believe that you speak French fluently, why contradict them? What does it matter that people keep saying that you played wide receiver on your high school football team when really you only caught a few passes in gym class? The CDC had allowed people to believe that they were battlefield commanders—that, in a pandemic, they'd actually run the show. How that rumor got started Charity neither knew nor cared.

What she cared about, suddenly, was this rogue group of patriots who were working behind the scenes to save the country. They captured her imagination, and lifted her spirits. "When I met Carter, it was a game changer," she said. "I was no longer a crazy person. I got more of a spring in my step. More of a fuck-it attitude." That new attitude found its highest expression in her interactions with the boss who was acting like a shill for the CDC. One day as she dressed for work, she swapped her usual battle armor of dark suit and grandma heels for sneakers and a t-shirt that read NOT TODAY SATAN. "I was obnoxious," she said. "I'd walk into her office and put Carter's graphs on her desk."

She used the word "pandemic"; she left her math on her whiteboard and encouraged others to stop by and see it. She further ignored her boss's order to never put thoughts or recommendations into an email. "Email created a record," explained Charity. She began to put her thoughts in emails—for instance, after the state of Washington, on February 28, reported its first COVID-19 case that could not be explained either by travel from China or contact with some person known to have been infected by the virus. With the virus openly spreading in greater Seattle, Charity wrote an email to her boss suggesting that the western states—California, Oregon, and Washington—seize the moment to form a coalition. They would stop waiting for the CDC to create a test for COVID-19 that actually worked and create their own test, using their own laboratories. The three states together would have a credibility that no state on its own could generate. "She called me at nine at night and started screaming at me about having put it in an email," recalled Charity.

Her nerd bible grew fatter by the day: it became a kind of weapon. In addition to the greatest hits from American medical journals, it held one of Carter and Richard's two papers about the 1918 pandemic, plus the papers that Bob Glass had written with his daughter, about the use of models to study the effectiveness of various social interventions. She'd crash meetings that her boss didn't want her to attend and announce her arrival by dropping this huge binder on the table: *Boom!* Charity was struck by how little interest people had in some of its contents. The analyses of the events of 1918, for instance. She could get her colleagues' attention with Neil Ferguson's latest analysis out of Imperial College, which looked, to Charity, like an academically respectable version of what Carter had been doing in emails. But when she tried to show what the country might learn from the last time it was overrun by a disease, people listened with the wary indulgence of the sane in the presence of a fanatic. "I realized there was this arrogance, or unwillingness, to even fathom that America in 1918 might know more about this than we do right now," said Charity. "That 1918 had nothing to teach us. But it did."

She was now going back and forth privately with maybe twenty of the fifty-eight local California health officers. She knew them all, in one way or another, and thought of herself more as one of them than anything else. They supplied her with a steady flow of on-the-ground intelligence, and she, in return, told them what she thought they might do to compensate for the lack of action by the federal and state governments. She thought they should use their labs to create their own COVID-19 tests, for instance, and make their own decisions about how to use them. "I was basically encouraging them to go rogue, because the state's chief health officer is team CDC," she said. "And they all asked the same question: 'How bad is it going to be?' I said, 'Doomsday.' And they'd say, 'The state's not saying that.'"

Charity knew or thought she knew what needed to be done for the state to have any shot at containing the new virus. In her head, up until the end of February, was a plan not just to limit the damage caused by the virus but to contain the virus. Containment, not mitigation, had always been what interested her. "I didn't want to manage it," she said. "I wanted to beat it." Her ambition to contain was not simply strategy but an expression of a deep character trait. It was why each flu season she lost interest the moment it became clear that there were no dangerous mutations to monitor. It was why, in the biography of Winston Churchill she was reading, she'd never gotten past the Munich Agreement. That was the moment Germany ceased to be a problem of containment and became one of mitigation.

A number of countries had set out to contain the new virus. Charity admired them for that. She thought that the United States should have had the good sense to emulate them. The state of California should close its borders with other states, she believed, until it figured out exactly how much virus was circulating, and where. It should blow open testing and allow every microbiology lab to develop its own test. It should test anyone turning up at any hospital with flu-like symptoms. She'd borrow for California the smartest strategies being used by Asian countries. Thailand required anyone entering the country to wear a GPS wristband: that ensured that people obeyed the quarantine rules and also told you, if they didn't, whom they might have infected. Singapore was using law enforcement to escort people to their place of quarantine and ensure that they remain there for fourteen days; those requiring isolation included every new arrival to the country. "That's what you do in TB control," Charity said. "The nurses take them to a hotel room and the sheriff watches them. If you think you have a shot at containing it, that's what you do. You have to do it by health officer authority. People say you can't do it, but we do it every day for TB."

Japan was doing something clever with their contact tracing. Perhaps from their close view of the *Diamond Princess*, public-health authorities had figured out early that superspreaders played a far bigger role in the explosion of COVID-19 than in, say, the spread of flu. It wasn't clear why, but never mind why; *why* you could worry about later; *why* the CDC could write a paper about. The practical effect was that a relative handful of people played an outsized role in the spread of the disease. Most people gave it to no one; a handful gave it to twenty other people. When the Japanese health authorities found a new case, they did not waste their energy asking the infected person for a list of contacts over the previous few days, to determine whom the person might have infected in turn. Again, most people with COVID-19 infected no one. Instead they asked for a list of people with whom the infected person had interacted further back in time. Find the person who had infected the newly infected person and you might have found a superspreader. Find a superspreader and you could track down the next superspreader before she really got going. You could stamp out embers before they turned into big fires.

Charity thought that the governor should hold a daily video press conference in which he took questions from the public and explained, in the event that the virus proved impossible to contain, exactly when and why he would impose various social interventions—school closures, a ban on mass gatherings, and so on. "The trigger points go right back to the 2007 pandemic plan," said Charity. "I thought that people could handle the bad news so long as you're straight with them. What they don't like is uncertainty. Say 'here's where we are and everyone needs to understand that this is going to get really bad.' You tell them what is going to happen. So they can emotionally prepare for it." One evening, in a cold sweat, she marched into Sonia Angell's office and told her all this—and what she, the chief health officer of the state of California, should say to the governor. "You need to say, 'Stand up a plan or fire me now,'" she told her boss. "And if it doesn't work, you can fire me then." But then Charity took an odd view of the state health officer's job. "The role of the state health officer in California is to have someone to fire," she said.

She now watched what happened when the health officer declined to accept that role. On February 19, the UC Davis Medical Center admitted a patient who had symptoms and no history of travel—and so did not meet the CDC's criteria for testing. In any case, the hospital did not have the ability to test; for that matter, no one in Sacramento County had the ability to test. "By then Zimbabwe could test but California could not, because of the CDC," said Charity. "Zimbabwe!" The hospital sent a sample to the CDC in Atlanta on February 23, and the CDC returned a positive diagnosis—but not until February 26. Even then they failed to flag it as community transmission but lumped it in, unremarked upon, with the test results of people who had returned to California from China, or some cruise ship. It was the director of the California state lab, Deb Wadford, who caught the oversight. In the seven days between February 19 and February 26, hospital workers had been exposed to the new virus without knowing it. In those seven days it was possible to have known that the virus was not just a threat from the outside but was already traveling from person to person, inside the United States.

February 23 was a Sunday. The following morning, Sonia

Angell held a conference call with the health officers from California's fifty-eight counties. "This is among friends," recalled one of those health officers. "No one else here but us health officers. Sonia got on the call and took a very distant approach. She said, *I'm not at liberty to share the details of the case.* We were like, *What???!!*" There were no rules preventing the state health officer from sharing the details of a case with other public-health officers; the medical privacy laws did not apply. The patient by then had been moved to the ICU at UC Davis Medical Center and was on a ventilator. The health officers needed to know her symptoms and how they'd progressed. They needed to know who she was, so they might trace her contacts. They needed to know all kinds of details so they might keep people from dying, while they gathered the resources to fight the new pathogen. The patient had come from Solano County, and the health officers from the surrounding counties grew apoplectic. "To me it sort of betrayed a complete lack of understanding of what was meant to happen between state and local health officers," said one. Speaking of Angell, she added, "She botched it right out of the gate. From that moment no one trusted her."

Donald Trump had said that it was every state for itself. In that one phone call, the Newsom administration had signaled to the local health officers that it was every county for itself, too. They would learn the lesson Charity had been forced to learn during her time as a local health officer: *No one's coming to save you.*

Charity had been excluded by Angell from any calls with the local health officers, so she only knew what happened when they began to call her and holler into the phone. But she noticed when the CDC made a curious pivot, from downplaying the virus to behaving as if it never could have been contained. For the better part of two months, they'd repeated the same mantra: the risk to Americans is low, and there is no evidence of transmission inside the country. That fiction ended on February 25, when the CDC's lab in Atlanta identified as positive for COVID-19 the patient inside the UC Davis Medical Center with no history of foreign travel. That day, the CDC's Nancy Messonnier held a press conference to say that the spread of the disease was inevitable. "It's not so much a question of if this will happen anymore," she said, "but rather more a question of exactly when this will happen and how many people in this country will have severe illness." The stock market dropped 1,100 points, and Trump ranted and raved, thus frightening everyone else in the CDC into silence and turning Messonnier into a martyr. An order came from Vice President Mike Pence's office saying that henceforth no one in the Department of Health and Human Services was allowed to say anything that might alarm the public. People were soon saying how brave Messonnier had been to say that the virus could not be stopped. To Charity, her words sounded like the CDC letting itself off the hook for failing even to try. To Charity, it looked as if Sonia Angell had declined to discuss the case of local transmission to give the CDC time to appear to be on top of the situation by announcing it first.

By then she and her boss weren't speaking to each other unless speech could not be avoided. Then, suddenly that didn't matter so much. Charity had found another, more important audience. On a Red Dawn phone call in early March, she was laying out her ideas about what California and every state in the country should do when a new voice came on the line. "This is Ken," it said. Ken Cuccinelli, the acting deputy secretary of homeland security and a member of Trump's coronavirus task force. "He said, 'Charity, you need to push these things through. You're the only one who can do this.'" She was taken aback by his insistence. "He wasn't pleading with me to do the right thing. He was yelling at me. He was basically implying that the White House is not going to do the right thing. The White House is not going to protect the country. So California needs to take the lead." That was the moment she learned that the White House was listening in on the calls—and also the moment when she realized just how lost and desperate the people at the top were. "He's the deputy director of homeland security. He can just go talk to the president. And he's relying on some random blond girl to save the country. Really?"

A system was groping toward a solution, but the solution required someone in it to be brave, and the system didn't reward bravery. It was stuck in an infinite loop of first realizing that it was in need of courage and then remembering that courage didn't pay. Charity didn't think of it this way, but it was striking how often the system returned to her and very nearly sought her leadership, without ever formally acknowledging its need. On March 6, Gavin Newsom convened a hundred of the state's top officials to discuss the new coronavirus. Sonia Angell had told Charity that she, Angell, would give the briefing to the governor, and that it was better if Charity did not attend the meeting. *You have no role*, Angell explained, *so you should not be there*. Charity didn't believe Angell had the ability to get up in front of the audience and explain what was going on. "I just had a feeling that something would happen and she wouldn't be able to make it," she recalled. Sure enough, the morning of the event, the phone call came. Angell couldn't make the meeting. Might Charity step in at the last minute to replace her?

She spoke for twenty minutes. What she said would have been completely familiar to anyone who had read the collected works of Carter Mecher. "It was, 'This is what is coming, and these are the options.' It was just math. But the reason I was willing to speak up so loudly was because of Carter." Governor Newsom and others asked questions of her for forty-five minutes. Afterward, maybe twenty people came up to talk to her.

Oh my gosh, one had said to her, *someone actually knows the answers.* Days later she received a call from Mark Ghilarducci, who ran all of California's emergency services. He asked her to fly down to Oakland to supervise the unloading of the *Grand Princess*, another cruise ship overrun by COVID-19. "I'm the one who rescued you from the attic," he'd tell her later. And later, to Charity, that sounded about right.

In Oakland she found herself in a room inside a FEMA tent, with a whiteboard and a gaggle of Newsom's most important advisers. She offered to show them the math of epidemics, and they accepted. She proceeded to lay out the deceptions of any disease that is spreading exponentially, especially when large numbers of people with it have no symptoms and you have no ability to test. The only clear signal you get from the virus is death. In the beginning you have just one death, the first death, and, really, that seems like not such a big deal. But once you realize that only half of 1 percent of the people who get the disease die, you can surmise that for every death, there are 199 people already walking around with it. That first death—which California already had experienced—was telling you that you had two hundred cases a month earlier. And so you had to ask how rapidly those two hundred cases had been multiplying. The world's best redneck epidemiologist—Charity didn't mention Carter Mecher, but he was now a voice in her head—had figured out that each person who got the virus was infecting two to three others. Out of caution, you had to assume a reproductive rate of 3. Every week, the number of infections triples. Do the math and play it out across a California population with zero immunity, and seven weeks from today you'd have 11,809,800 cases. As much as 10 percent or so of those people, more than a million Californians, would need a hospital bed. Half of 1 percent, or a bit more than fifty-nine thousand people, would die.

All that from one death. Yes, it was just one death, but if you looked closely, you could see that it did not look like a simple event. It looked like the fire coming up the hill in Mann Gulch. "This isn't theoretical," she told the group. "This is exactly what is going to happen. It's what happened back in 1918."

Of course, she continued, that was only true if the state did nothing to stop the virus. Carter liked to say that there was no such thing as an unmitigated pandemic. Even if the government did nothing, people would adapt their social behavior to the virus. But whatever people did, Charity explained, the story ended only with a vaccine or herd immunity. There was no vaccine in sight; and the number of infections required to achieve herd immunity could be calculated, as it was a simple function of the reproductive rate. (The formula was $1 - 1/R_0$, where R_0 was the reproduction number.) The simple truth that the formula captured: the more transmissible the disease, the more people needed to be infected before the herd was theoretically safe. Measles' reproductive rate of 18, on the high end, implies that ninety-five percent of the population needs to be immune to measles before measles stops spreading. That's why we have as our goal to vaccinate 95 percent of the population against measles. Before COVID-19 stopped spreading, two-thirds of Californians would need to become infected.

It was just a bunch of numbers on a whiteboard, but Charity sensed that, at the very least, she'd held the attention of the governor's senior advisers. A few days later, the secretary of California's Health and Human Services Agency, Mark Ghaly, called her. Ghaly had hired Sonia Angell to run the California Department of Public Health. Several times in January and February, he'd told Charity that she needed to obey the chain of command and convey anything she had to say through her immediate boss. Going forward, he now said, Charity should report directly to him.

*

In mid-March, a technology entrepreneur named Todd Park
sent a note to a friend who served as Governor Newsom's economic adviser, and told him to call if he needed anything.
Without a lot of noise or publicity, Park had created three different billion-dollar health care technology companies, and then
gone on to serve for three years under President Obama as the
country's chief technology officer. He had a reputation for fixing
other people's messes without drawing attention to himself, and
so had made himself popular with public figures without ever
really becoming one himself.

Newsom's economic adviser called Park immediately and
asked him if he could help the state figure out what to do about
the coronavirus. Park recruited a pair of former Obama administration officials: Bob Kocher, a doctor turned venture capitalist
who had advised Obama about health care, and DJ Patil,* who
had served as the country's first chief data scientist. Patil pulled
together a team of some of the best programmers in Silicon Valley, and the team instantly began to collect data that would help
them to project and predict. In a couple of days, they had everything from the number of beds in intensive care units to data
from toll booths and cell phone companies that gave them a feel
for how people moved around inside the state. "No one cares
about data when everything is going well," said Josh Wills, the
former chief data engineer at Slack, who agreed to help. "People only care about data when the shit hits the fan. 'Oh my God,
what's going on??? We need data!' "

The people who had managed data and technology for the

* I wrote about DJ Patil in *The Fifth Risk*. Working with a friend at
LinkedIn, and needing a description for a new kind of job in the economy,
DJ had coined the phrase "data scientist."

entire United States government became volunteer workers for the state of California. Park and Patil and Kocher drove to Sacramento, where they were met by Newsom's technology adviser, Mike Wilkening—who had been among those to watch Charity Dean at a whiteboard doing the math that showed how and when the new coronavirus would explode in California. Park and Patil knew how to build models to analyze data, but they knew nothing about communicable disease. None of the state's data was of any use to a decision maker without some assumptions about the virus—its reproductive rate, its hospitalization rate, its infection fatality rate, and so on. "The only data points we had were China, two cruise ships, and some early stuff from Italy," said Patil. They'd need to make lots of educated guesses not just about the virus but about the effect, on its transmission, of different policies—closing schools, say, or banning large gatherings. "We told Wilkening that we need the most kick-ass public-health guru, and he said, 'I know the person,' " said Park. "And it turned out to be Charity."

They found her in a conference room inside a dull state office building. "She had this incredibly thick binder," said Park. "And she said, 'I've been keeping this binder since early January.' " Charity walked them through what had happened back in 1918 and what was happening again, in only slightly different form. She explained how, six weeks earlier, she had arrived at a fairly good estimate of all the important traits of the virus, and she said that once you knew these things about the virus, you could predict its future. She did not tell them that she had spent the previous six weeks in conversations with maybe the world's greatest redneck epidemiologist. Park and Patil mostly just listened to her and asked questions. At some point Park turned to Patil and said, "She's the L6."

In Park's time with the federal government, he'd dealt with one technology crisis after another. He'd noticed a pattern that he'd first identified in the private sector: in any large organization, the solution to any crisis was usually found not in the officially important people at the top but in some obscure employee far down the organization's chart. A case in point was the day the software used by the State Department to process visa applications stopped working. That day the U.S. government simply lost its ability to issue visas. Park sent in a team to figure out why. "They called me and said, 'Six layers down from the people in charge we found two contractors who actually understand what is broken.'" The L6. The person buried under six layers of organization whose muzzled voice suddenly, urgently needed to be heard. "I got the feeling that she hadn't been at the table," said Park of Charity. "It was clear that this was the moment that she had been preparing for her entire life, and that she was finding it incredibly frustrating that she wasn't being allowed to help."

After a couple of hours with Charity, Park and Patil decided that the most useful thing they could do for the state of California was to deliver the contents of her mind onto Gavin Newsom's desk. "Our only job was to make it possible for Charity to talk through a model," recalled Park. "Our job was to take everything in her brain and get it to the governor." To Charity, at the time, he said, "I want you to understand. I think we were sent here to find *you*."

On the one hand, it made sense to Charity. She actually *was* an L6. Four layers of bureaucracy separated her from Governor Newsom, the L1. On the other hand, she was no one's idea of a timid soul, waiting for someone to discover that she knew how to contain and control a communicable disease better than anyone else in California's state government. She wasn't some shrinking violet; she was a massive bouquet of red roses delivered with a singing telegram. She *popped.* It told you something about big organizations, and the L6s buried inside them, that they were able to turn Charity Dean into a person in need of excavation.

Charity actually didn't trust computers, and was uneasy with models, beyond the math on her whiteboard. She watched Park and Patil bring a team together to rewrite the code of a disease forecasting model created at Johns Hopkins so that it ran much faster and incorporated lots of data about California—and how they did this she had not the faintest clue. She was strangely relieved to see that once you plugged in what she (and Carter) knew, or thought they knew, about the virus, the new computer model regurgitated the coming disaster they imagined. That view happened to be radically different from the official position of the CDC, the White House, and, for that matter, the state of California.

Before Park had traveled to Sacramento, Governor Newsom's advisers had sent him an Excel spreadsheet with some calculations made by someone inside their public-health department. These showed the virus never generating so much illness that the state's seventy-five thousand hospital beds couldn't handle. "I don't know who did it," said Park. "But it was all wrong." The new model suggested that, if no action were taken to minimize the virus's spread, the state would need *seven hundred thousand* hospital beds by the middle of May. "It gave us a very fast answer, and we can see that we're fucked," said Patil. "We're going to blow through the hospital beds." However, if the state acted as, say, St. Louis had acted back in 1918, hospitalizations would peak at around seventy thousand. That is, various social interventions would reduce infections, hospitalizations, and deaths to a tenth of what they otherwise would have been.

On March 18, Park and Patil presented the model's output to Governor Newsom's senior advisers. "When we showed them what the model was saying, it sucked the air out of the room," said Park. The next day, Governor Newsom issued the country's first statewide stay-at-home order. At his press conference, he said that the decision was "based upon some new information."

"It was pretty cool," said Josh Wills, who wrote the software. "I got to see Governor Newsom tweet out some charts I made." If you googled Charity Dean at that moment, the way she had googled the men on the Red Dawn emails, you'd have found not much more than a couple of grainy pictures of her at a reunion of her Tulane medical school class. You might have found a few old columns she wrote for the *Santa Barbara Independent*, and some videos of her testifying in front of the Santa Barbara Board of Supervisors, and some vicious attacks on her by the local anti-vaxxers. Yet here she was, with her assumptions, driving the policy of California. The computer model gave the governor little choice but to shut down the entire state, and take responsibility for what should have been a national decision, because neither the Centers for Disease Control nor the president of the United States had the nerve to make it. "Carter's emails should be framed as a national monument," said Charity. "They drove decisions in California."*

The question was what to do next. You could keep people from moving around for only so long before they'd resume moving around. Park turned to Charity and said: *Go lock yourself in a room and write a plan for California.* And she did.

But there was a new problem. As late as mid-February, it might have made sense to write a plan for California. Indeed, though no one had asked her to do it, she'd as good as written one, in her head. She would have reverse-cordoned the entire state, the way Singapore had done. She'd have tried to sell the governor on holding the line until April, when other states would be burning up with virus, and everyone would see the wisdom of California's actions. She had her list of things she

* And not just in California. The two other states that moved most quickly to shut down, Ohio and Maryland, had also paid close attention to Carter's analysis.

would have done to contain the virus, but those only worked before the virus was widespread. "I wrote a plan for California," she said, when she emerged from the room. "But I can't write a plan for California. It has to be for the whole country. It doesn't matter what California does if other states don't do it, too." To which Todd Park replied, *Okay, write a plan for the entire country. We can just call all the other governors.*

And so she returned to the room and, with some help from Bob Kocher, wrote a plan for the entire country and handed it to Todd Park, with the understanding that they keep her authorship a secret; if her bosses found out she'd written it, she'd be fired. The national plan ran to several pages and had three big features. The first was for the president to announce a stay-at-home order for the entire country until it was able to test as much as was needed. As he did this, he would explain the second feature, the rules for reopening. Each community would receive one of three designations—hot, warm, cool—based on a few simple metrics: the number of cases per capita, the percentage of its COVID-19 tests that came in positive, the percentage of its hospital beds that were occupied. A community that was cool and more or less virus-free could live with few restrictions. A community that was hot with virus lived under a stay-at-home order. A community that was warm—it had virus circulating, but reproducing at slower rates—could relax some of its rules. It could have weddings and funerals, for instance, and open public transport. "These restrictions could be scaled up or down based on the heat of the community at any given time," she wrote.

She realized that all this would need to be displayed on a dashboard, so that people could check the status of their zip code every day. She picked red, yellow, and green to represent hot, warm, and cold, then had second thoughts. *That looks dumb. It's just the colors of a stoplight.* But the modeling team thought it was great: the simpler and more familiar the better. Later she changed it from three color codes to eight, each with its own menu of social interventions, all inspired by the plan written years ago by Richard Hatchett and Carter Mecher. But the basic idea remained the same. As scientists learned more about the virus, the government would update the social interventions so that they remained as potent and as targeted as possible. If it emerged, for example, that children could not be made seriously ill by the virus, or spread the virus to others, there might never be a reason to close schools.

Her most curious idea, given how she had gone about her job as a local public-health officer, was how she hoped for the plan to be enforced. She didn't want it to depend upon the bravery of some local public-health officer. "What I really wanted was for it not to be enforced," said Charity. "I wanted it to say, 'We're not going to come rescue you. You are going to rescue your-selves.' " The local dashboards would allow everyone to see who in their neighborhood had been infected, who had gone to the hospital for it, and who had died. "It's radical accountability," said Charity. "Government has a role, but its role is to empower the grass roots by giving them data."

If clusters of illness occurred, genomic sequencing would reveal how that had happened and who was responsible; as Charity sometimes put it, "You know who farted in the crowded room." The president would need to issue an executive order to make an exception for medical privacy laws, but that seemed a small price to pay for a million American lives. Highly specific personal data would leave no room for people in any neighbor-hood to retreat into a private reality in which they could imag-ine that the virus either didn't exist or was overblown. "You have to bring the carnage in front of people's faces for them to see it," said Charity. "If some areas of the country need to hit bottom, so be it."

The virus would enforce the plan. If the citizens in certain zip codes still insisted on some fiction, the virus would expose the lie, and they would soon find themselves isolated and unwelcome in other parts of the country, where businesses had reopened and a semblance of ordinary daily life had resumed. It wasn't just the effects of the virus that needed to be mitigated. The effects of the culture did, too.

For the plan to work, Charity thought, it needed to be locally controlled. Each zip code would be able to see what it needed to do if it wanted to relax restrictions. And each zip code would have its own leaders, who would know the best ways to encourage good behavior. The one shot America had at behaving well, and thus saving itself, was to remove the feeling that "the government" was imposing restrictions on people and re-instill the idea that people were imposing order on themselves, to fight a common enemy. "This is a call for all Americans to rise collectively in the spirit of patriotism with the same vigor and stubborn resolve that our grandparents' generation rose to meet the moment of WW2," she wrote, toward the end of the plan. But the spirit of the thing could be found right at the top, in the title she'd first scribbled on it: *The Churchill Plan.* "Then Todd was like, 'You can't name it that,'" she said. She wound up giving it a wonky title: "Everyone Owns Their Own R Naught." Everyone is responsible for the rate at which the virus reproduces in their own community.

A few days after Charity handed over the plan, Todd Park and DJ Patil seemed to have gotten it into the hands of people who might actually take action. First she had a call from a senior executive at Google, who said that Google could create the dashboards for every zip code in the country. Then a member of Todd's team approached her. "He said, 'Andy Slavitt is interested in your plan,'" recalled Charity. "I said, 'Who is Andy Slavitt?'" Andy Slavitt turned out to be a former banker and consultant who ran Medicare and Medicaid under Obama a few years after Don Berwick left. Andy Slavitt was also, oddly enough, speaking every so often to Jared Kushner, the son-in-law of the president and a member of the new COVID supply chain group within the coronavirus task force.

Andy Slavitt himself emailed Charity, asking if she wanted to edit her plan, which he had typed up, simplified a bit, and added some stuff to, about who in government might be assigned to perform its various tasks. What he'd done struck Charity as mostly inconsequential and inoffensive, until she got to the place where Slavitt had taken it upon himself to write the CDC into the plan, to "define standards by which a community is designated hot, warm or cold."

"No," wrote Charity in a comment. "The single most important part of this plan is IT IS NOT RUN BY THE CDC. It is run and overseen by an entity with actual experience in front line warfare in outbreaks." She stressed her feelings in the email she sent back to Slavitt, along with her edits. "Very important point," she wrote. "Who is operationalizing/leading this plan? The entity/agency/figurehead leading this must be a Churchill, not a Chamberlain." Then she thought, what the hell, and sat down and wrote talking points for the president of the United States and sent them along, too. After that there was nothing to do but wait and see if her bosses fired her for insubordination. After all, she worked for the state of California and its Democratic governor, and she was moonlighting as a policy adviser to the Republican president of the United States.

She never heard from Andy Slavitt again.* But a few days later, the Google executive called her to say, "Jared loved your

---

* Slavitt renamed the plan "Victory over COVID-19" and presented it to Kushner as his own.

plan and is briefing POTUS on it." "What freaked us out," recalled DJ Patil, "was when this memo came out of the White House with the same language that was in the plan." He sent it to Charity with a note: *now you know you made a differ-ence*. But she didn't; not really. It was just a leaked memo, not a commitment from the president to a new national strategy. And so she waited. If you had asked her just then what she was waiting for, she would have told you that, in the best case, she was waiting to hear her plan for the country rolled out by the president—which is to say that as late as the end of March 2020, she still had hope. And as she waited, her governor, in whom she still had faith, did the sort of thing that might have given her even more of it. He called the Red Phone.

PART III

TEN

The Bug in the System

The Red Phone had always been a less than perfectly efficient tool for saving lives. Joe DeRisi was the first to admit
that. Most people whose lives needed saving never knew of its
existence, and even those lucky enough to find out about it often
called it too late. They wound up like the Chinese woman with
Balamuthia, whose doctors hadn't thought to look for a brain-
eating amoeba until they'd spent $1,000,100 on ineffective treat-
ments and the amoeba had consumed most of her brain. The
Red Phone could leave both its callers and its owner upset. And
yet, even at its most frustrating, it enlightened. It showed you
what you had missed, so that you were less likely to miss it the
next time. It could also reveal big, systemic problems. After all,
if you were calling the Red Phone it was usually because some
system had failed you.

One evening in March, Joe looked down, saw an unfamiliar
number, and very nearly didn't answer it. The area code was

Sacramento, his hometown, and so he gave the caller the benefit of the doubt. "I thought it was a telemarketer, but I picked it up and it was Gavin Newsom." The California governor explained that he had a problem but was still unsure of its dimensions. He asked Joe to make two lists: one, of the three best things the governor of California might do to respond to the new coronavirus; the other, of the three worst. "I said number one was testing," recalled Joe. "Because if there is no testing, there isn't even the possibility of a solution." Testing was the only way to find the virus and to predict its movements. Testing was so important, Joe told Newsom, that there wasn't much point in worrying about the other items on either list.

The public-health system was failing California's governor, as it was failing the governor of every other state. The CDC's second attempt to create a test for COVID-19 that might be mass-produced and distributed to public-health officers across the country hadn't turned out any better than its first. The absence of federal leadership, combined with the fragmented nature of the American health care system, meant that tests for the virus either weren't available or were being processed too slowly to be of any use. Joe read stories of people waiting ten *days* for test results from Labcorp and Quest Diagnostics, two of the country's biggest private labs. "Sending tests even to the CDC was taking days, not hours," said Joe.

A test that took ten days to process was a pointless test. Absent fast tests, hospitals were being forced to treat everyone who rolled into the parking lot with coronavirus-like symptoms as if they had the virus, when more often than not they did not. Beds in the coronavirus wing were being taken by people who didn't need them. Nurses and doctors were running through scarce protective gear they needed for actual coronavirus patients. But the biggest problem of having no tests was not knowing where the virus was and where it was not. Without fast tests, you could not isolate the people who needed to be isolated, or liberate the people who didn't. Gavin Newsom had no plan to create a lot of testing in California: Why would he? Like everyone else, the governor had assumed the federal government would make sure that the country had enough testing to track any new virus.

Joe could see that the CDC wasn't going to solve the problem. But there was a solution: the United States was by far the world's leader in microbiology research. It contained thousands of microbiology labs, run by private companies and universities and nonprofits, like the one he presided over at the Chan Zuckerberg Biohub. The thing to do, Joe decided, was to transform the Biohub into a COVID-19 testing center as quickly as possible—and publish a paper to show others how to do it. Governor Newsom agreed to issue an executive order to allow people to work in a clinical lab who were not certified to do it. ("We were afraid we were going to get our asses sued," said Joe.) And the Biohub put out an APB for volunteers.

What happened next would have astonished lots of people, but not Joe. A small army of graduate students and postdocs, mostly from UCSF, rushed to help. "They came in droves," said Joe. "And it was always, *How can I help? How do I do this?* No one asked to be paid." They'd been born and raised basically everywhere: China, Taiwan, Colorado, Tanzania, Lithuania, Florida, Canada, Phoenix, Belgium . . . the Americans answered with a city or state and the non-Americans with a country, when you asked them where they came from. All were research scientists, many with PhDs. Precisely zero ever had done the jobs they were about to do. Yet within days they were trained and ready. They organized themselves into squads to be kept separate from each other—so that if one person contracted the virus it would incapacitate only one squad and not the entire army. Each squad had its hierarchy, and each person learned the job of the person immediately above him, so that he could replace him if necessary. "We built in battlefield promotions," said Joe. "It was different from a regular research lab, where people just do what they want and come and go as they please. It was more like a factory. A production line." The line was organized into stations, each staffed by someone willing to work long hours without pay. "I used to have these terror dreams that we'd have a hundred people need a cocktail at the same time for happy hour," said one of the postdocs, who had once worked as a bartender. "Now I have the same dream about thousands of people needing test results at once."

In a single room the size of a basketball court, a COVID testing lab took shape. Setting it up gave Joe his first real view of the medical-industrial complex. It wasn't designed for a crisis; if it was designed for anything, it was to maximize the profits of companies that enjoyed monopoly power. Labcorp and Quest, which were charging the state one hundred sixty dollars for every COVID test and returning the results so slowly that they were useless, were just one example. The companies that made the testing machines were another. The fancy so-called sample-to-answer machines had one big advantage: they were idiot-proof. Any low-paid lab technician could insert a patient's test tube into a slot, push a button, and wait for the machine to spit out a result: yes, you had some virus, or no, you did not. The machines minimized the risk of error, and lawsuits, but were ill-suited to a crisis. If anything went wrong inside them, you needed the manufacturer to sort it out, as you couldn't just open them and fiddle with them. To run at all, they required expensive chemicals made only by their manufacturers, and so shared the same infuriating quality as razors and office printers. Worse, the chemicals required to identify any one pathogen were specific to the pathogen. If you wanted to test for HIV, you needed to buy the chemicals capable of identifying HIV; to test for hepatitis C, you needed the hepatitis C brew. If you wanted to hunt willy-nilly for a virus you could spend a fortune, just on razor blades.

In March 2020 there were still no chemicals to test for the coronavirus. The UCSF labs were littered with these sample-to-answer machines that couldn't be used. One machine was called the Panther, which Joe loved. "They all have these really cool names," he said. "The Panther!! The Panther right now is asleep." The Panther would remain in hibernation right through the first months of the pandemic as the company that made it scrambled to make the materials required to run it. A weird black market would arise in the stuff you needed to wake the Panther up: Joe had a photo of a guy selling Panther equipment out of the back of his car. "Here is the frightening aspect of the global supply chain," said Joe. "When there is a surge in demand, inventory goes to zero. Just-in-time manufacturing. Great concept! Horrible in a pandemic."

Microbiology labs across America all had the same frustration: fancy razors with no razor blades. Joe knew enough about the sample-to-answer testing machines to know they'd be a constraint. He needed a bunch of stuff fast and called UCSF's chancellor, Sam Hawgood, to discuss how to get it. "Every time I talk to Joe he's got some new idea," said Hawgood, an Australian who had made a career managing Americans. "Coming from someone else, I'd say, 'Gee, I need to check that out.' But because it's Joe, I don't." With Hawgood's blessing, Joe and his team ransacked the university's labs for chemicals and liquid handling robots, and testing machines that were far less idiot-proof but capable of detecting COVID-19. They grabbed spare parts and built machines themselves. On a rainy evening in mid-March Joe could be found alone on the streets of San Francisco wheeling some cart bearing a purloined machine. These machines also needed special chemicals to analyze samples, and the market for these chemicals had tightened, but, as with the machines themselves, the market for them was more resilient in a crisis.

Here Joe learned, or perhaps relearned, another lesson about the private sector. As a Stanford graduate student, he had seen previously open and collaborative colleagues clam up the moment some venture capitalist threw money at them. "One day you come to work and their office shades would be down," he said. Over and over again he saw the wild inefficiency of the private sector as a creator of knowledge. Far more often than not, some promising avenue of research would die as a failed company. He hated that; he hated the way financial ambition interfered with science and progress. As a pathogen threatened to overrun the United States and shut down its economy, he detected an odor he distinctly did not like coming off the private sector. One company was the biggest supplier of an enzyme they needed to run tests. "We called and told them what we were doing and that we wanted to buy a million dollars' worth of the stuff," said Joe. "When you buy that quantity you always get a discount. But they said nope, you're paying full price." He was so pissed off that he looked around and found a smaller company, New England Biolabs, that sold the same enzyme. "Completely different spirit," said Joe. "They said, 'This is amazing! Forty percent discount right now!' That's how companies should behave."

It went that way with much of what they needed to buy: some companies sought to exploit the moment; others sought to help. "We quickly figured out that some companies actually have a moral compass and some of them don't," said Joe.

On March 18, just eight days after the idea was born, the Chan Zuckerberg Biohub's new COVID lab opened for business. It had taken Joe's new team two days less to build an entire lab than it was then taking Quest Diagnostics and Labcorp to process a single test. The new lab's two hundred or so overqualified young research scientists were able to process 2,666 tests a day, as accurately as any lab in the country. (They'd demonstrated their accuracy by taking samples that had already been processed in a smaller but highly accurate lab at UCSF and retesting them.) They'd be able to return results to people within a day; in a pinch, they could get you an answer in three hours. And—here was the kicker—they worked for *free*. There was no bill. You just handed over your test tubes with the nasal swab inside and the Biohub told you who had COVID-19 and who did not.

Joe assumed, not unreasonably, that his new team of volunteers would soon be overrun by hordes of customers delighted by the freebie. The previous week, the entire state of California had received fewer than two thousand COVID-19 test results. Test tubes holding nasal swabs from more than 55,000 Californians were lying around in labs waiting to be evaluated. By redirecting 2,666 a day from the big corporate labs, the state of California could save itself $426,560 every day and get results back in time to make a difference.

But they were not overrun by customers. The first few weeks, samples trickled in almost painfully at a rate of a couple of hundred a day. And so Joe started calling around. To local hospitals, for example. The private chain of hospitals run by Kaiser Permanente said they wanted to set up their own, not-free testing lab at some point—and, in the meantime, they'd continue to ship their samples to the big, slow, expensive private testing companies. Joe soon learned that private U.S. hospitals were either contractually obliged or habitually inclined to send tests to the for-profit labs, and that the for-profit labs had no incentive to move any faster than they were moving, as they got paid either way.

The public health care centers—the clinics run by local departments of public health—presented a different problem: they were too busy to answer their phones. A team at the Biohub sent letters to local health officers in each of California's fifty-eight counties: *Free COVID testing! Inside of 24 hours!* Still no response. Priscilla Chan herself hosted a call with the health directors of every California county and asked point-blank: "Why are you not sending samples? It's free!" A few more samples turned up, but nothing like as many as they could process. Joe couldn't figure it out. "We were asking ourselves: Is it a trust issue? Is it the Zuckerberg name? But it turned out that no one cared about any of that."

It took a month or so for them to understand why a country so desperate for tests was so slow to accept an offer of free ones. One clue came during a phone call between the Chan Zuckerberg Biohub and the recently renamed *Zuckerberg* San Francisco General Hospital. If there was a place where the Zuckerberg name would help rather than hurt, this was it.

"How much is it going to cost?" asked the woman at Zuckerberg General, after the team at Chan Zuckerberg had explained their new COVID-19 testing lab.

"It's free," said the Chan Zuckerberg person.

"There was this *super*-long pause," said Joe, who was on the line.

"We don't know how to do no-cost," said Zuckerberg.

"What do you mean?" asked Chan Zuckerberg.

"It shows up as an error in the hospital computer if we put zero cost," said Zuckerberg. "It won't accept zero."

"Can't you put like one-tenth of a cent?" asked Joe.

They couldn't. The system wouldn't allow it. It was *Balamuthia* all over again. The cure meant nothing if the patient never received it. Standing between the cure and the patient, in this case, was a U.S. medical-industrial complex that lurched between lethargy and avarice.

Joe had never really had to understand its inner workings. Now he began to see that the incentives of virtually everyone in it were screwed up. To do something as simple as accept an offer of free coronavirus testing required either unusual effort or real courage.

In San Quentin they'd needed both. Early on, Joe had called officials at the famous prison to say, *You are a sitting duck. If the virus gets in there, people are going to die.* The San Quentin officials sent in one batch of samples, in April, but asked the Biohub to keep mum about it because they were worried that the private testing company that serviced California prisons would be upset. *If Quest finds out, they are going to kill our contract,* they'd said. That first batch contained no positives for COVID-19, but San Quentin sent no further samples. Later they explained that they didn't have the time to do the paperwork. ("I was stunned," said Joe.) In late May a busload of prisoners was moved to San Quentin from a prison in Chino where a COVID outbreak had occurred and the warden had decided to thin the population. The Chino prisoners were tested a few days before they left but not when they arrived in San Quentin. At least one of them showed up carrying the virus, and it proceeded to sweep through San Quentin and infect more than a thousand men. Twenty-eight of them died.

But the biggest reason that the Biohub's free testing service went underused was the scarcity of test kits. Actually, that's not quite right. If at any point in the first few months of the pandemic you rolled into a hospital parking lot with a dry cough and a fever and asked to be tested and the nurses said, "Sorry, we have no testing kits," what they likely meant was: "We have no nasal swabs." The long translucent sticks that could be inserted deep into the nasal passage, and which offered the only reliable method to sample the virus at the start of the pandemic, were nowhere to be found. The Biohub looked into it and found that, outside of China, anyway, just two factories made them. One was in Maine, the other in northern Italy. Neither had any for sale.

That was the only time they turned to the federal government for help. The Department of Health and Human Services managed something called the Strategic National Stockpile. The precise contents of the $7 billion stash of medicines and supplies were meant to be a secret. People who had seen it (Carter Mecher, for instance) thought it looked like the giant warehouse in the final scene of *Raiders of the Lost Ark*. The stockpile offered the solution to the stress in supply chains that was bound to occur when every country on earth suddenly wanted to buy the same medical supplies. It was the government's attempt to compensate for the limits and weaknesses of private markets.

On March 13, a Biohub epidemiologist named Patrick Ayscue wrote to the HHS guy responsible for California and explained that he was sitting in what was now the fastest big COVID testing lab in California and maybe even, at that moment, the entire country. But they needed test kits, and especially nasal swabs. He asked for forty thousand swabs, which he reckoned was a two-week supply. The HHS guy, Lucas Simpson,* was totally helpful. He called his superiors in Washington, who called the people in the White House who were meant to be managing medical supplies. "I will have to ask about the extraction kits,"

---

*   Not his real name.

he wrote to the Biohub on March 15, referring to another scarce item. "But the swabs are a definite YES."

The excitement in and around the Biohub was palpable. The replies to Lucas Simpson flooded in:

Fantastic Lucas!

Lucas, You are my new best friend. You literally saved hundreds of lives.

Lucas wrote back to ask for a delivery address. The truck was leaving a warehouse a two-day drive away. And it contained not forty thousand but one hundred thousand swabs.

Thanks Lucas! You are literally a life saver.

Lucas, If you have kids tell them their daddy is a fucking hero.

The next day, at a White House press conference, President Trump delivered a message to America's governors. "Respirators, ventilators—all of the equipment, try getting it yourselves," he said, before setting out on Twitter to badger individual governors who had complained about the lack of federal leadership. Even then the truck with the nasal swabs was rolling toward Sacramento! The mood in the Biohub was Christmas Eve: never in the unwritten history of nasal swabs had nasal swabs been awaited with such anticipation. On March 18, the day the truck was scheduled to arrive, the mood changed. "Suddenly no one knew where the truck had gone," said Joe. It wasn't until three days later that Lucas Simpson called to say that the truck had been located in West Sacramento, but without swabs. What he didn't say, because he was too embarrassed to say it, was that inside the truck they'd discovered not medical swabs but Q-tips. So far as he could tell, there had never been any swabs in the Strategic National Stockpile.

The pattern continued right through the pandemic: the Trump administration would claim with fanfare that supplies were on their way to the states and leave it to the career civil servants whose job was to interact with state officials to reap the humiliation when those supplies failed to arrive. It would happen again with ventilators, with the drug Remdesivir, and, finally, with vaccines. Among other consequences of the White House's strategy was that it gutted the credibility of the career federal officials.

After that, Joe became cynical about the federal government and started to say things like "You're not actually supposed to know what's in the Strategic National Stockpile, probably because it doesn't have the shit you need." By early April, he was telling any reporter who called, and any plausible-looking person he met, about his need for nasal swabs. "It's the one thing if I could go back in time and change I would," he said. "I wish I had bought one hundred thousand swabs. It was not on my radar. It was not a thing I thought would be the limiting factor in life."

All sorts of people tried to help. A big-shot venture capitalist, for instance, called Joe one day and said he had solved the problem. *I know a guy who has some swabs,* he said. Joe was dubious. "I said, 'Really, you *know* a guy? Prove it.'" The VC said that his friend would overnight five thousand swabs directly to Joe, and so the next day, Joe went to a UPS facility and indeed found waiting for him a large box labeled as medical supplies. "I pop open the box and there's five thousand of *something* in there," said Joe. "They clearly didn't just fall off the back of a truck. And they kind of *looked* like swabs." But they weren't sterile, or even packaged, so right there he knew they weren't medical supplies of any kind. Joe studied them until the penny dropped: eyelash brushes. Some crafty soul had bought eyelash brushes, relabeled them as medical swabs, and sold them to the VC at a profit.

The absence of federal leadership had triggered a wild free-for-all in the market for pandemic supplies. In this market, Americans vied with Americans for stuff made mainly by the

Chinese. Marc Benioff, the CEO of Salesforce, flew in a plane-load of materials from China to the UCSF medical center with boxes of functional, though less than ideal, nasal swabs on board. The owner of a Bay Area chemical company, Chris Kawaja, found another off-brand Chinese nasal swab supplier and messaged them. "I said, 'Hey, do you have these things?'" Kawaja recalled, "and this woman came right back and said, 'Yeah I have two hundred fifty thousand.'" These swabs were the real deal, but before Kawaja could nab them, the woman at the Chinese supplier sent another message to say, "Some guy in Houston just took two hundred thousand of them." Kawaja charged the rest to his credit card—at 70 cents a pop, triple the old market price—and had them shipped to the Chan Zucker-berg Biohub in small batches, to bypass Chinese customs offi-cials. "It did occur to me: Why did I need to find this stuff?" said Kawaja. "Why did some random dude in Marin need to read some random newspaper article about how Joe DeRisi needed swabs, and go and find the swabs?"

In the end they found what they needed. By early April, the Biohub was able not only to run 2,666 coronavirus tests a day but to supply test kits to anyone who needed them. Late each night, lines of PhDs formed on the basketball court to assemble the kits for the resource-starved departments of public health.

Joe had never seen the U.S. public-health system from the inside. He knew there were these people called local public-health officers, but he didn't really know what they did or have any sense of the conditions in which they worked. Once his team began to deliver free test kits to them, he understood why they'd been slow to take up the Biohub's offer of free testing. Many local health offices were so understaffed and underequipped that they had trouble using the test kits. Most were unable to receive the results electronically; they needed the results faxed to them.

Some had fax machines so old that they couldn't receive more than six pages at a time. A few didn't even have functioning fax machines, and so the Biohub got into the business of buying and delivering fax machines along with test kits.

The members of the four-person team Joe assembled at the Biohub to help local public-health officers hunt the new virus didn't know any more than Joe did about the U.S. public-health system. They were just creative people who had wound up in a curious situation and were learning how America functioned, or didn't, as they went along. Josh Batson was a case in point. He'd done his PhD in mathematics at MIT without really knowing what he wanted to use math for and never imagined that he'd wind up using it in biology, or health care. But then a close friend of his from college dropped dead suddenly from a mysterious encephalitis, and, not long after that, Josh was introduced to Joe—who knew all about solving encephalitis mysteries. "It was right when the Biohub was founded," recalled Josh, "and I was like, 'That's what I want to do.'"

Joe wanted Josh to use his math skills to create a kind of search engine, to scour the Biohub's new global virus detection network for viruses engineered in labs as bioweapons. The pandemic intervened, and Josh instead found himself trying to save Americans from their public-health system. At the start, he had imagined that U.S. public health would be ready and waiting for the sophisticated tools he'd helped to create. He'd analyze genomic data, show health officers how the virus was moving in their communities, and, with the health officers in the lead, they'd go to battle. Instead no one seemed to want to hear what he had to say; by late April 2020 he felt as if he had run into a battle that lacked any commanders at all. "You rush in and you're like, 'Okay, what can I do?'" he said. "And there's no one to tell you what to do because everyone is up to their eyeballs. We had to become shadow public-health officers."

Another member of Joe's small public-health team, David Dynerman, also a mathematician, arrived with a different perspective. He'd been born in Poland and moved to the United States as a child. He had memories of Poland as a communist regime, and of the total breakdown of the government's ability to be useful to its citizens. What he saw in the local U.S. public-health offices remined him of public services in Poland, but before the collapse of communism. "Poland *now* is not like this," said David, after seeing the inside of a U.S. public-health office. "Poland now is more functional. Eastern Europeans are tough and kind of not shocked by a failed state. But these are the symptoms of a failed state."

*

The drama began, as it often did, with a call from a public-health nurse. She wanted to let Charity Dean know that a young man in Santa Maria, at the poor end of Santa Barbara County, had been discovered with four-plus tuberculosis in his lungs. The county health lab assigned a grade to each case based on how many tuberculosis bacteria they could count on the slide. Four-plus meant that the slide was so thick with bugs that they'd stopped counting them. To get to four-plus, you went first through all the other stages, and so the man likely had been infectious for months. He lived in a tiny house in a poor neighborhood occupied by an ever-changing number of migrants from the Mexican state of Oaxaca. At that moment, in early 2013, when Charity was just a year or so into her new career as a public-health officer, the house contained eighteen members of an extended family named Zeferino. Six adults and twelve children.

Then she heard the young man's name: Agustin Zeferino. She was floored. His TB had been identified nine months earlier by nurses at the Santa Maria Health Care Center. His case stuck in Charity's mind in part because it had been one of her first, but also because his TB was of a type resistant to one of the drugs, and so he'd required an extra pill. She'd confined him to a motel room for a couple of months until tests showed that he was no longer infectious, and then set him free.

By now Charity had made herself expert in the treatment of run-of-the-mill tuberculosis. She had seen cases where patients tested positive for the TB bacteria a few months into their treatment. But that happened rarely, and the bugs they found were usually dead. Agustin had been in treatment for *nine months.* Charity had never heard of someone completing the treatment and remaining not just infected but wildly infectious. "I said, 'No way it's his sputum. Someone else spit in the cup.'" Why Agustin would hand the nurse someone else's spit she couldn't imagine. He'd been caught and jailed for selling drugs, was himself an addict, and so, in her mind, capable of anything. She did that sometimes—solved the crime without pausing to identify the motive.

She called the nurse in Santa Maria and asked her to visit the Zeferino home and make all eighteen of the people inside spit in a cup—and watch them as they did it. "I thought, 'Someone else in that household is four-plus,'" said Charity. When the results came back, her heart dropped: Agustin Zeferino himself indeed had four-plus TB. She had no idea what strange microbiological event had occurred inside the man, and only the faintest clue what to do about it. She had two options: to send Agustin's spit to the CDC and wait two months for the bacteria's genome to be fully sequenced, or to send it to the California state lab, which did not have the capacity to sequence the entire genome but did have a machine capable of searching for specific mutations. Two months was too long, and so she sent the sample to the California state lab.

Two days later, they called to say that Agustin Zeferino's TB had mutated in a way never before seen in the United States. The specific mutation, previously discovered only in the state of Oaxaca, had two terrifying traits: it was resistant to more than just one of the TB drugs; and it didn't reveal itself until the infected person was in the middle of treatment for ordinary TB. At some point in the nine months of Zeferino's treatment, the bacteria inside him had made an error in its genetic code that allowed it to escape the drugs meant to kill it. "The worst thing that you can do is treat with an inadequate regimen," said Charity. "And that's exactly what I had been doing."

The expression "what doesn't kill you makes you stronger" actually isn't usually true for human beings. It is for bacteria, however. Inside Agustin Zeferino, the TB bacteria had evolved a greater resistance to any drugs used to treat it. Charity had to assume that anyone who lived or worked with Agustin had been infected with this same new deadly pathogen. She needed to track and test any number of Oaxacans who did not particularly want to be tracked or tested. One day a public-health nurse would turn up and find eighteen members of the Zeferino family in residence in their tiny house; the next they'd all have vanished.

Charity asked the public-health nurses to keep an eye out for cases—and to alert her if any children with the last name of Zeferino turned up in the county clinic. Then one morning she got a phone call from the public-health clinic in Santa Maria. A baby boy with the last name Zeferino had just been diagnosed with "failure to thrive." Failure to thrive was more a description than an understanding. Malnutrition could cause it, but other things could, too, and TB was one of them.

That day happened to be busy for Charity, too busy. She knew that babies manifested TB in particular ways, and that one of them was a failure to thrive. She didn't personally investigate, however. She asked the pediatrician to take an X-ray of the baby's chest and to call disease control if it showed abnormalities. The pediatrician had never followed up. And she hadn't pursued him. She didn't want to come across as pushy. She was, after all, a new face in the public-health office. She wanted people to like her.

A month later she had another call, about a baby boy in the ICU in a Santa Maria hospital. The nurses wanted to test the baby for TB. Charity realized instantly that it must be the same baby they'd mentioned to her a month earlier. The baby's TB test came back positive.

She scrambled to figure out what had happened. She called the pediatrician and learned that, after he'd sent the baby for a chest X-ray, but before the pictures had arrived, he'd taken a month-long vacation. His nurse had left the X-ray out for him to inspect upon his return. Charity ordered the images and now saw the TB. For most of the month, the X-ray had sat in a pile on the pediatrician's desk, and the baby had declined rapidly. When his parents finally appeared with him in the public-health emergency room, he was inert. The final horror of the situation revealed itself when the hospital called the parents to inform them that their baby was brain-dead. "We don't have a son," they said. The Oaxacan community, at least that part of it encountered by the public-health nurses in Santa Barbara County, rejected children with serious defects. They pretended that the child had never been born. Charity was informed that the little boy would live out his days in a medical orphanage.

The event had knocked her sideways. Scarred her. It taught her what it meant to be a public-health officer. It meant that you never just let things slide. "I had thought that as a health officer, my reputation was supposed to be as the good cop," said Charity. "Not after that. After that I was all about never, never letting that happen again."

She confined Agustin to a room in the Villa Motel. In her office with the TB ventilation grates, she hung photographs of the children he'd infected. She notified the pediatricians of Santa Maria, instructing them to give skin tests and chest X-rays to any child who turned up with flu-like symptoms and whose parents were Mixtec speakers. She issued an order that every case of TB in Santa Barbara had to have its genome searched for the mutant gene. It popped up inside Agustin's brother, and in Agustin's nieces and nephews. It popped up in people in the Oaxacan community who claimed they'd never heard of Agustin. The public-health nurses would investigate and discover that not only had they heard of him, but they had spent time with him—and that Agustin had broken out of quarantine. The genomic information revealed social relationships. "There were *always* surprises," said Charity. "You think you know how the disease is traveling, but you don't."

Charity had never heard of anyone using the genetic fingerprints of a pathogen to track its movement through a community. Now she saw what a powerful disease-fighting tool genomics might be, in the right hands.

Still, for the moment, it was being used mainly to reveal the many ways Agustin Zeferino was violating her order to quarantine. The number of his room at the Villa Motel in Santa Maria, 240, remained stuck years later in the heads of the public-health nurses. They kept lists of what they'd found inside when they brought Agustin his meals and medicine. One day it was a pair of high heels; another, the hooker to whom they belonged; another, the garbage from what had obviously been a huge party. Some days they'd turn up and find that the patient had simply vanished. His mutation turned up in the prostitute, in his friends, and in more children named Zeferino. At one point, a single public-health nurse in Santa Barbara County named Sandy Isaacs was treating twenty-six TB cases associated with Agustin Zeferino. Charity signed an order to have Agustin arrested and jailed. The jail kept him for a short spell but then released him without explanation—though Charity guessed that the prison officials were frightened. "I could put him in jail but I couldn't keep him there," she said.

After trying and failing to confine Agustin Zeferino to a hospital handcuffed to a bed, she secured from a judge permission to strap a GPS monitor to his ankle—which was why, of an evening, she was able to track Agustin as he left his motel room and strolled down the street to a strip club named the Spearmint Rhino. "Note to self," said Charity. "Don't put the isolation motel next to a strip club."

On August 11, 2014, a public-health nurse arrived at the Villa Motel to give Agustin his medicine and found his room empty and his GPS band in the trash can. Charity issued a warrant for his arrest, then told the sheriff that he was easily the most dangerous person in Santa Barbara County. She issued a press release with Agustin's photo and, ignoring warnings from state officials that she was courting a lawsuit for violating medical privacy laws, included information about his illness.

The ensuing manhunt was unsuccessful; as they said in the disease control business, the patient was lost to follow-up. Where Agustin wound up, likely in Mexico, was obviously important; where he had stopped along the way was equally so. He had TB in his lungs, with a mutation never found inside the United States. Charity thought that the state needed to sequence the genome of the bacteria in every TB case they found. Tuberculosis had a gift for hiding. If you breathed it in, one of two things happened: it gave you active TB, or it went dormant.

If it goes dormant, you might never know you had it. But you'll also be walking around with a ticking bomb inside you, as there is a 10 percent chance that at some point in your life it will reactivate. It might take two years, or ten, but the multi-drug-resistant mutation would reappear. And the surest way to prevent it from killing people was by hunting the genes. "You are going to find crumb trails all the way down to Mexico," Charity told people inside California's Department of Public Health. But the state health department didn't have the money to spare. "It's bonkers," said Charity. "I guarantee you that we will have cases out there that will be a perfect match. And we won't find them because 'we don't have the resources.'"

*

One measure of poverty is how little you have. Another is how difficult you find it to take advantage of what others try to give you. Only a tiny handful of local public-health offices had the interest in or the ability to exploit the most powerful tool that the Chan Zuckerberg Biohub was trying to give them for free. "They didn't know how to ask for things," said Priscilla Chan, "because they'd never gotten anything." Right from the start, the nonprofit Biohub was able to do more for local public-health offices than any for-profit lab did. The commercial labs were set up to take in test tubes containing human genetic material and spit out a simple answer: positive or negative. They weren't set up to sequence the genome of the virus in the positive speci-mens. And the genomics was the critical game within the game.

Viruses mutate, which is to say that they make errors in their genetic code when they replicate. Different viruses make errors at different rates. A perfectly stable virus—that is, a virus that does not mutate—would be impossible to track. The virus in every infected person would have precisely the same genetic code. Just by inspecting those codes, you would not be able to say who gave the virus to whom. For instance, herpes mutates so slowly it's hard to divine how it has traveled from the genetic code alone. At the other extreme, when a virus mutates too quickly, its movements are equally impossible to follow. The viruses that cause the common cold, for example. They mutate so rapidly that, inside of a single human being, they replace their entire genome, and escape the defenses created by any vaccine. A fast-mutating virus is as untraceable as a burglar who leaves behind billions of different fingerprints.

From the point of view of a virus hunter, COVID-19 sits in a sweet spot. It mutates, very reliably, every one or two times it transmits from person to person. If I catch the bug from you, the genomes of our viruses will either be exactly the same or they will differ by a single mutation. Just by watching these changes, you can track the virus's journey through a community. By 2020 it was not just possible but practical to analyze huge numbers of viral genomes. Back in 2003, Joe had spent a small fortune to sequence a piece of the original SARS virus's genome. But the cost of genomic sequencing had fallen exponentially. "What cost me ten thousand dollars to do in 2001 now costs a penny," said Joe.

In late April 2020, the underemployed Biohub COVID lab teamed with UCSF researchers to test everyone who either lived or worked in a four-square-block area of San Francisco's Mission District. The area formed a tract in the U.S. Census, number 022901, of special interest to a virus hunter, as it was less a typical American community than aspects of many different American communities. It had charming Victorian houses, less charming housing developments, and densely packed brutalist apartment buildings. It had people living on the streets. It had upper-middle-class people and really poor people. It had teleworkers and construction workers. It had four churches, a street of retail shops, and a park. It held a big working-class Latino population, and among them, like chips in a cookie, were lots of hipsters and tech bros. It was as if someone had thrown the pieces to seven different puzzles into one box. It wasn't clear that the pieces were happy about this. The lower-floor windows of almost every building were barred. Signs everywhere told strangers to keep out, and murals and graffiti had unkind words for the ICE police. Men without masks walked dogs without collars or leashes, and both eyed you a bit as you passed them on the street. Just banging on the doors had been an eye-opener. One three-bedroom apartment that was meant to be housing five people contained forty who were sleeping in shifts, around the clock.

In the end, roughly three thousand of the 4,087 official residents showed up to be tested over four days in late April 2020. A bit more than 6 percent of the Latino residents turned out to be infected by COVID, most with high loads of the virus, though many had no symptoms. There were patterns in the test results—for example, the richer the person, the less likely he was to be infected. Latinos were only 44 percent of the study but 95 percent of the positives. Of the 981 white people tested, *zero* were positive. The big takeaways seemed to be what everyone was just then figuring out: the virus was disproportionately attacking poor people of color unable to work from home; and lots of infectious people were walking around without a clue about their condition. To Joe DeRisi, however, none of those was the biggest takeaway. The biggest takeaway was the chart on page 264.

The chart was a simplified snapshot of the genetic relationships of all the virus found in the four-square-block area of San Francisco in late April 2020. You had to stare at it a bit to see the implications, and even then you sort of needed Joe's help. But look hard enough and you'd see, from the virus's point of view, a terrifying new weapon. "In all of history we've never had a really clear picture of the spread of a virus," said Joe. "That just changed."

The starting point in the chart is not the San Francisco neigh-

Simplified family tree of COVID-19 strains found in workers and
residents of the Mission District, San Francisco

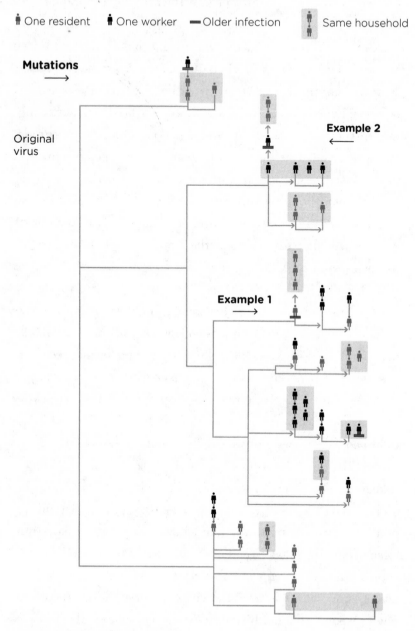

Source: Chan Zuckerberg Biohub

Credit: Elaine He/Bloomberg Opinion

borhood but Wuhan, where the virus originated in December 2019: the original genome, before it changes. Joe liked to think of the subsequent mutations as errors in a medieval manuscript being copied by monks: the mistakes were random but could be incredibly revealing. Drop in on any cluster of figures in the chart and you begin to see stuff that's impossible to see any other way. The household we'll call Example 1, for instance. Three people in the same household were infected with the same virus—that is, the genomes of their viruses were identical. No big news there. One of them likely gave it to the others. The news is how it entered the household—likely from the Mission resident on the same vertical line. He has the exact same virus but contracted it earlier, which is why he has the antibodies and they do not. The advanced age of his infection is conveyed on the chart by the line beneath his feet; the people he may have infected are not just above him but also to the right of him. "This same resident who likely infected the household may have also infected two workers who don't even live in the Mission," said Joe, pointing to another household of workers, one step to the right of those residents. "It's possible there is one degree of separation between them—that he gave it to someone who gave it to them. But no more than that."

Without the genomic information, you might never have any idea that these people had any sort of relationship at all. Even if a test had identified the person who infected the household, and that person were questioned by teams of contact tracers, the connection with the household might never have been made. The person might not even be aware of the connection, or might know it and want to hide it. Once we know that these people must have some social connection, the question becomes: What is it? Do they ride the same bus? Are they having an affair? Do their kids play together? "There are all kinds of rumors," said

Joe. "Kids: Are kids the hidden vector? Or: Can you get it from a handrail? Those guys sitting along the wall beside the park—are they the problem? Or is it the guys playing cards in the park?"

Just then, in early April 2020, it was growing clear to a lot of people at once that the coronavirus did not spread in an orderly way. Just as 10 percent of the people in any company do 90 percent of the work, some small number of people with the virus were responsible for some big number of cases. The human being with the oldest infection in Example 2 has a gift for doing more than his share. He likely infected not only the household above him but another Mission worker, and might even be responsible for the two small clusters to the right of him. The genomic information reveals the urgency of getting him off the streets but it also might lead you, more generally, to whatever he might be doing to spread the disease. All the other little clusters on the charts are of people who are interconnected in ways that might never have been revealed without the genomic information. "It's amazing that all these stories fall into place," said Joe, as he scrolled through that first chart they'd created.

Science was now able to transform a novel coronavirus into little works of narrative nonfiction. Around the same time as the Mission study, up in Humboldt County a meth dealer had tested positive for COVID-19. The public-health nurses had gotten to him soon after he'd been infected, and he agreed to isolate himself. The nurses suspected he was still sneaking out at night, and suspected it even more when a friend of his became infected. That friend lived with his son and daughter-in-law, who worked at Alder Bay Assisted Living, in Eureka. The daughter-in-law had no symptoms, but within a week more than a dozen Alder Bay staff members and residents had been infected. Four died. The public-health nurses could not see the chain of events. Then they received the genome sequencing from the Biohub, and it showed that everyone in Alder Bay had been infected by the daughter-in-law, and that her virus had come from her father-in-law, and that his virus had come from the meth dealer. "It's like the DNA evidence in a crime," said a Humboldt County public-health nurse named Erica Dykehouse. "When we got it we said, 'We're not crazy! We're not crazy!!!!'"

At the heart of any defense against the virus was the creation of safe, defensible spaces. Nursing homes. Schools. Offices. Apartment buildings. Neighborhoods. The genomics allowed you to see whether the virus was transmitting within your safe space—and so the ways that your safe space was not safe. It let you see when and how the virus had infiltrated the safe space—and alerted you to the need to rethink your border control. The distinction between internal transmission and invasion was critical to a society that wanted to remain open. Soon after the Mission study, for example, a pair of workers at a fish-packing plant in rural California came down with symptoms of COVID-19. The Biohub processed their tests and found that both workers had the virus. In an age not all that distant from our own, the fish-packing plant, which believed it had taken the measures necessary to keep its workers safe, would have been forced to close. It would have had to assume that one of the workers infected the other on the job. But the Biohub sequenced the viruses from the two infected workers and discovered that they were genetically very far apart. The workers had contracted the virus independently, outside of work. The fish-packing plant could stay open, and all its workers could keep their jobs.

In late January 2021, the Biohub and UCSF research team returned to the same four-square-block area in the Mission. This time a bit more than a thousand would test positive for COVID-19. One would have a mutation never before seen in the United States. It had been detected only in Brazil, in October 2020, after a thirty-seven-year-old female health care worker was reinfected. The mutation had allowed the virus to escape the antibodies her immune system had produced during its first battle with COVID-19. A strain of the virus that escaped antibodies might also evade a vaccine. "It's a change in a single chemical," said Joe. "And evolution found it." Evolution would find other chemicals, and other strains, especially after people received a vaccine and the virus came under pressure to escape it.

It was not possible for a vaccine maker, or a society, to adapt to an evolving virus without genomic information. And yet nearly a year into the pandemic, in February 2021, the number of genomes being sequenced in the United States was trivial—less than a third of 1 percent of the virus in people who tested positive. (The UK was by then sequencing 10 percent of its positives; Denmark had set a goal of sequencing all of them.) The United States was sequencing fewer of its genomes than any other industrialized country, and the only reason it was sequencing as many as it was is that a bunch of nonprofits had stepped in to do it, haphazardly, for free. In the whole of the pandemic's first year, the tiny Biohub had been responsible for nearly half of all the genomic sequencing in California, and more than 5 percent in the United States. Joe had been shocked by just how slow the society was to realize what science might do for it: it was as if tanks had been invented before the Civil War and the generals couldn't figure out their purpose. "Our federal government should be doing this in a coordinated way," he said. "At the very least, our state government should be doing this. That's what you would do in a rational society. But the system is broken. It's *so* broken."

Looking back on that first year of the pandemic, Joe was able to pinpoint when he felt the last flicker of hope he had in that system. It had occurred on the afternoon of April 29, 2020, when he'd joined a hopeful Zoom call between Priscilla Chan and the state of California. Priscilla couldn't understand why local health officers across the resource-starved public-health system weren't using the Biohub to test for the virus and track it. "I sort of felt like I was speaking out of turn," she said. "But you could already tell that variants were going to be a problem. Joe was like, 'Look! You can see them! And you can see where they come from!' "

She'd written to Mark Ghaly, California's secretary of Health and Human Services, and asked for the meeting. Ghaly had replied with enthusiasm and scheduled it. "I was *thirsting* for leadership to come down from on high," said Joe. "I thought surely the state would have some overall strategy. To better direct us. We're this sharp tool. Use us!" The afternoon of the scheduled meeting, he sat at his desk staring at the Zoom screen. Priscilla was in another box. A few other Biohub people were there, too. There was only one box with a state official in it: Charity Dean was her name. But her box was dark. After several awkward minutes, when it became clear that Ghaly wasn't going to show up, she finally turned on her camera and unmuted herself.

ELEVEN

Plastic Flowers

One of the odd things about American government, circa April 2020, was just how different appearances on the outside could be from the understanding on the inside. Inside California state government, inside even the Trump administration, there was some logic to everything that happened; anyone on the inside could tell a more or less coherent story about whatever they had done, and why. An innocent outsider who turned up and looked at what they had done, however, could be utterly baffled. Paul Markovich was such an outsider. Markovich was the CEO of Blue Shield of California, the health insurer to four million people with a network of sixty thousand doctors. Seeing at the end of March that California ranked last in the nation in the percentage of its residents being tested for COVID, he'd pressed the state to do better—only to be asked by the governor to chair a task force to fix the problem. Gavin Newsom assigned two others to work on it, the venture capitalist Bob Kocher and Charity Dean. Markovich knew Kocher but had never heard of Charity and called around to find out what he could about her.

In early April, the task force set a goal of testing sixty thousand Californians a day by the end of August. They reached that number at the end of May and by late June had doubled it. In three months California went from roughly last in the nation in COVID testing to roughly first, depending on how you counted. To get supplies, the task force had overcome all the logistical obstacles that Joe DeRisi and the Biohub had faced, on a massive scale. Ten million nasal swabs, for example. California enjoyed some advantages—a wealth of private testing labs, maybe the world's finest public university system, a nimble private sector willing to leap into a crisis and help out, a population that agreed that testing was important. Still, no matter how you looked at it, the task force was a triumph. "I don't think we repelled aliens who were trying to invade earth, but it kind of felt like it," said Markovich. Governor Newsom used it as an example of his administration's success. The governors of Illinois and Washington asked Paul Markovich and Charity Dean to brief their cabinets. The White House and assorted federal agencies called and asked them to explain how they had done what they had done. At the end of one call, a staffer in Senator Dianne Feinstein's office had said, "I don't think I've ever been more proud to be a Californian."

Their effort was worthy of a case study on project management, but its details are less important here than its success. For even in success Markovich witnessed the dysfunction of American government. The state's archaic computer systems were clearly unprepared to handle the large amounts of data the new testing would generate. Markovich had offered to replace them for free: he could never figure out why they hadn't taken him up on it. (A COVID testing data-processing screwup in August would be the official reason given for Sonia Angell's resignation.) The state's crusty procurement system wasn't set up to pay for supplies on short notice—Markovich put the Blue Shield credit card down to secure the nasal swabs. And the state's personnel management was bizarre. "There was something seriously awry," Markovich said. "Everyone I called about Charity tells me she walks on water, and it was pretty clear that she was running the show but, like, wait a minute, she's the *assistant* health officer? She's not the head health officer? Where's the head?" He asked around and learned that the head health officer was a woman named Sonia Angell, but he never met her. "It started to be impossible to miss," said Markovich. "This is the biggest public-health crisis ever, and she's nowhere to be found."

As he walked out the door to return to running his health insurance company, Markovich asked Charity what he thought an obvious question. "I asked her, 'What are you going to do when they ask you to take Sonia's job? They can be crazy stupid, but they can't be crazy stupid forever.' And she said, 'I'd need to think about that.'" What she didn't tell him was that she'd already thought about it and was pretty sure what she'd say, and why.

*

Back when she was twenty-four and newly divorced, Charity had rented a small apartment. The place was on the ground floor of a building in a dicey New Orleans neighborhood that got away with describing its units as "luxury" only because they were new. For the first time, she had her own porch. It was protected by an iron fence but visible to anyone who walked by. She felt a need to make it not just presentable but charming. "I was trying to be my mother," said Charity. "I wanted to show I could be a homemaker." She bought wind chimes and flowerpots and flower boxes and dirt and fertilizer and some huge number of brightly colored flowers and turned her front porch into the Luxembourg Gardens. The young professionals and graduate students who lived in the building and passed her porch on the way to their units showered her with compliments. Neighbors came over just to sit on her porch. Even strangers on the street paid her compliments. For a short stretch Charity Dean was the young woman with the porch bursting with flowers.

Then her flowers began to die—though not all at once. The first few deaths left only a bald spot in one of the pots. Charity happened to have a bouquet of plastic flowers. "That's how it started," she recalled, "just to fill in the blank spot in the pot where the flowers had died." From a distance the fake flowers could pass for real; the combover was a success. Then more real flowers keeled over. Charity was studying for two graduate degrees at once and actually didn't have any interest in or aptitude for gardening. She'd imagined that all these flowers needed was to be watered a bit. Now suddenly she was facing the specter of her wind chimes swaying over a Sahara of botanical death. "I finally drove down to Michaels arts and crafts and bought a pile of fake flowers," she recalled. "But when I picked them out I was asking a new question: Which of these flowers look the most real?"

It wasn't easy to make even the most persuasive fake flowers seem real. She had to keep neighbors from getting too close, and invent excuses for keeping them off her porch. Instead of gardening she had to pretend to garden, which was even more difficult. She felt like an idiot waving to strangers while watering plastic flowers, but for months she went right on doing it. "It felt icky," she said. "I just got sucked into it." Every now and then the green shoots of live plants popped up beneath the plastic flowers, then died for lack of sunlight. The metaphor was not lost on her. She knew that her fraud was bound to be exposed, but she kept doubling down on it anyway. Finally, one afternoon, the nice guy who lived down the hall walked into her place and, before she could stop him, walked out on the porch and reached for a flower. His hand recoiled when he realized they were fake.

The pandemic response reminded her of that moment, but on a vast scale. The American institutions built to manage risk and respond to a virus had been engaged in a weird simulation of crisis response that did not involve actually trying to stop the virus. "The greatest trick the CDC ever pulled was convincing the world containment wasn't possible," she said. "Our dignity was lost in not even trying to contain it." She wondered if perhaps they had undergone a process similar to her own—a descent, which ended with them devoting lots of energy to appearing to know what to do when they did not. "In the beginning it's filling in gaps," said Charity. "You let the falsehood continue until slowly the falsehood takes over. By the time you're done, you are no longer just filling blank spots. You have this burden of maintaining optics. It's all optics."

Even as she helped the team of software guys and former Obama officials build the model that persuaded Newsom to shut down the state, Charity had decided that she was leaving. As children, she and her older sister had a phrase to describe the unsettling sensation of fresh doubt about some situation or some person: black smoke. The black smoke had rolled into state government with the virus and never left. In late March she'd informed Mark Ghaly of her plans to resign. He'd asked her to wait and had kept her busy for six weeks fixing California's COVID testing. He then asked her, along with two other women in California's Department of Public Health, to run the pandemic response. There was a catch, however. They'd need to allow Angell to remain the public face of the response—that is, to maintain the illusion that the head of the department, as yet not confirmed by the state senate, actually was in charge. "You can't fire the state health officer in the middle of a pandemic," one high-level state official explained to Charity. Another thought that Ghaly was simply trying to avoid personal embarrassment: he'd hired Angell in the first place. A third suspected that the real worry was Angell's upcoming senate confirmation hearings being used to embarrass the governor. Whatever the reason, the people who ran the state were twisting themselves into knots to preserve the illusion that all was well inside California's Department of Public Health.

For Charity to run the state's pandemic response required the state to formally acknowledge her leadership. She'd need to be given the legal authority that resided with the chief health officer and the chief health officer alone. That clearly wasn't going to happen anytime soon. She'd had to make a pest of herself just to join a Zoom call with the Chan Zuckerberg Biohub. "Ghaly made it really clear to me that this was his turf. He said, 'You can attend. Don't be on video. Keep yourself on mute. And don't say anything.' " Then again, he'd also told her to stay away from the press conference at which Newsom announced his new testing task force, when she *was* the testing task force. Her role, it seemed, was to do stuff the state's chief health officer was meant to do, while not being seen doing it, as that might raise questions about why the chief health officer wasn't. She couldn't just do the job. She needed to be part of an optics machine.

The meeting with the Biohub was meant to start at one thirty in the afternoon on April 29. Shortly after one thirty, Charity unmuted herself and turned on her video and tried to stall by making small talk with Priscilla Chan about their children. At length Priscilla said, "Um, maybe we should just get started?"

Joe DeRisi was in his own box. He had one of those faces that would always look younger than it was, Charity thought. His white-blond hair was out of control even by pandemic standards; he reminded her of Doc in *Back to the Future*. But then he started to explain what he and his team could do for the state of California, if only the state would let them. "There were no pleasantries," said Charity. "It was diving right in." She felt a sensation she had not felt since she was back in Santa Barbara County, gaining control of some disease outbreak. "You know when you pass someone on the street and their cologne or their perfume reminds you of someone you love. It was like that."

It felt to Charity like a second chance to respond to the virus, and to function as a health officer. She'd witnessed the power of genetic analysis when she worked as Santa Barbara's health officer. The links between the five people infected with the hepatitis C virus inside Dr. Thomashefsky's clinic had been made with their genomes. A single mutation in *Mycobacterium tuberculosis* had allowed her to track Agustin Zeferino. But in both cases the genomic sequencing had been slow and laborious and expensive. She hadn't realized how much cheaper and faster it had become—so cheap and fast that it might be used on huge populations to reveal how a virus moved within them in real time. Across the state her former colleagues, the beleaguered local health officers, were trying to control a virus of which they were catching only the briefest glimpses, in random black-and-white photographs. The Biohub could hand them a movie.

The new weapon could do for the state—indeed for the entire country—what it had done in the Mission. It could empower local public-health officers, who could use the genetic connections between viruses to reveal the risky social relationships between people. If a virus mutated into something different, or worse, all the health officers could know at once, and adapt. The new web of information could create a thing that the country badly needed: a true network. Where once they had been a bunch of poorly connected dots on the map there would grow a tight web. A *system*. "It's the future of disease control," said Charity.

The next week she had on her schedule a rare chance to speak with Governor Newsom, when she updated him on the progress of the testing task force. Others were in the room, and she was meant to keep it brief and stick to her assigned subject. But at the end of it, as he was rising to leave, she took a risk. "Can I just tell you about one more thing?" she asked. Newsom sat back down and learned about genomic sequencing. At the end of the lesson he turned to Nick Shapiro, an outside consultant he'd brought in to advise him on crisis communication, and said, *We're going to do this. You two sit down together and figure it out.* Charity spent the next two hours at a whiteboard explaining to Shapiro how it all might work—how samples of the virus from all those in California who tested positive could flow to the Biohub, and the Biohub, free of charge, would perform the analysis, provide it to the local health officers, and train them to use it. In the middle of her explanation, Shapiro had blurted out, "This is fucking awesome!" Here was a chance for the state to lead the country's, and maybe the world's, response to the virus. Here was the chance for the governor to say something that sounded at least vaguely hopeful! Shapiro became so excited that he said, *We're going to announce this tomorrow.*

They hadn't. "It went into the bureaucracy and never came out," said a person close to the process. "I never really understood why." Someone raised the objection that the Biohub had Mark Zuckerberg's name on it and that it might look bad, sort of like the state was handing out people's medical information to Facebook. (Though that's not what the state would be doing.) Someone else worried about the difficulty of routing the positives from various labs to the Biohub. Quest Diagnostics was just then processing, slowly, more of the state's tests than any other lab. You might have thought, as Charity thought, that the testing company would be looking for ways to please a customer it was making hundreds of millions of dollars from. She called the Quest people she'd gotten to know while running the testing task force and asked them to send the specimens from all of California's positive COVID tests to the Biohub. *We'd need to charge you five bucks a sample if we did that,* the Quest people replied. *But we can't because we agreed to send them to the CDC.*

Charity knew, because Joe DeRisi had told her, that the CDC had done little to no genomic analysis for any purpose other than the publication of academic papers. ("We reached out multiple times offering to conduct sequences for them early on and they never took us up on it," recalled Patrick Ayscue, who worked on sequencing in the Biohub. "It was never anything concrete. Just in the spirit of 'thanks, we'll consider it.'") She also knew that it had turned itself into a black box: it sucked in data from others and seldom shared its own, except in the form of academic papers that brought glory to its authors. At this point she had a long list of the ways the CDC, with the help of their former employee and her current boss, had made it more difficult for her to do her job. Now they were trying to add to it, by interfering with the best chance California had to track the virus and limit its damage. Before she could call the CDC to complain, they called her. "They contacted me directly, trying to be friendly but actually wanting to scare me away from routing 'their' specimens to Joe," she recalled. "By the end I was almost screaming. *'YOU JUST WANT SPECIMENS FOR RESEARCH! I WANT THEM FOR ACTUAL FRONTLINE INVESTIGATIONS!!'*" The people who ran the state declined to intervene. They didn't want to get into a spat with the big commercial testing labs, or the CDC.

Joe sensed that he'd found in Charity a person capable of putting him to proper use but unable to, for some reason. "She was somehow forbidden from answering my questions," he said. "And these were matters of life and death." He and the Biohub waited, and waited some more, and finally more or less gave up on the state. "There was something deeply dysfunctional about how the government worked that I never fully grasped," Joe would later say. "There's no one driving the bus." And the CDC—well, the CDC was its own mystery. "God knows what the hell is wrong with them," said Joe.

Charity, like Joe, would later say that their interaction was the last time she felt a flicker of hope that the virus might get anything like the response it required. In late March 2020, when she first announced her intention to resign, she'd made a note in her journal: "one million excess deaths by May 31, 2021." It was a prediction: the number of Americans who would die either directly from COVID or indirectly because of, say, lack of access to an overwhelmed health care system. Nothing had happened to change her view by the time she finally submitted her resignation in June. Walking out the door, she carried with her a list of unanswered questions. Maybe the biggest was: *Why doesn't the United States have the institutions it needs to save itself?*

*

On September 23, 2020, a former director of the CDC, Bill Foege, sat down to write a letter to the current director, Robert Redfield. Foege was eighty-four years old and a legend in disease control—to many "the man who eradicated smallpox." He wore his principles lightly but he had some, and had lived by them. He'd been the last CDC director to rise from within the ranks, propelled by the admiration of fellow experts, rather than through connections to a politician. Later, Jimmy Carter would introduce him as the man he'd handpicked to run the agency, but Jimmy Carter hadn't picked him at all: Foege's peers in disease control had. "Dear Bob," he now wrote, as a disease swept through the American population. "I start each day thinking about the terrible burden you bear. I don't know what I would actually do, if in your position, but I do know what I wish I would do. The first thing would be to face the truth. You and I both know that: 1) Despite the White House spin attempts, this will go down as a colossal failure of the public health system of this country. The biggest challenge in a century and we let the country down. The public health texts of the future will use this as a lesson on how not to handle an infectious disease pandemic."

Points 2 and 3 followed Point 1. The gist of all three was that the CDC, under Robert Redfield, had been disgraced. It had let itself be used by the Trump administration to lead the United States in a direction opposite to the direction the United States had once led the world. ("It was our ability to refocus India from herd immunity to attacking the virus that allowed smallpox eradication to succeed.") But Foege wasn't writing to rehash the details—the lies about the severity of the disease posted on the CDC's website, the public guidance that ignored the science, the cowardly silence. He was writing to urge Redfield to reassert the CDC's independence. "You could upfront, acknowledge the tragedy of responding poorly," he wrote, "apologize for what has happened and your role in acquiescing, set a course for how CDC would now lead the country if there was no political interference, give them the ability to report such interference to a neutral ombudsman, and assure them that you will defend their attempts to save this country. Don't shy away from the fact this has been an unacceptable toll on our country. It is a slaughter and not just a political dispute . . . The White House will, of course, respond with fury. But you will have right on your side. Like Martin Luther, you can say, 'Here I stand, I cannot do otherwise.'"

It was the voice of God, or at least of a different age. That Bill Foege clearly intended for his words to remain private made their effect only more devastating, after someone in Redfield's own office leaked them to a reporter. But the letter hadn't gone as far it might have. It framed the problems inside the CDC as a simple matter of a good agency overrun by a bad president. Foege knew that the story was more complicated than that, as he had lived through more of it than anyone else. The problems inside the CDC had reached some kind of climax with Donald Trump, but they hadn't started with Trump. They'd started with the series of unfortunate events in and around the CDC that had ended with Bill Foege running the place. There were reasons for what had happened in this particular flowerbed.

That story began in 1976. In March of that year, at the end of the flu season, a handful of soldiers at Fort Dix in New Jersey became ill. One died. The CDC gathered samples and found they'd been infected by a new strain of swine flu that appeared to be related to the virus that had caused the 1918 pandemic. The army found that at least five hundred more soldiers had been infected. There was much that the flu experts did not know, and knew that they did not know, but they were not clueless. They'd detected a pattern: roughly every decade the flu genome found some new way to evade the human immune system. They had predicted the previous genetic shift in the virus, back in 1968, and were expecting the next one soon, and believed that it would involve pigs. The sample size was small—1918, 1957, 1968—but each time a new strain of flu had been identified, it had resulted in a pandemic. The severity of the disease was an open question, but it felt to the experts a lot like the one back in 1918—when the first outbreaks had also been mild.

The head of the CDC, David Sencer, convened a meeting of relevant experts in public health and influenza. Bill Foege was included in the meeting. All the people in the room knew the facts of the case and also that they were on a clock, as the swine flu was likely to return in the autumn. While its severity was anyone's guess, everyone agreed that the new flu, if it returned, would be all over the country in a matter of weeks. They also understood that to vaccinate two hundred seventeen million Americans would take months, and you had to add to that the two weeks it took for a body to achieve immunity after vaccination. Finally, they knew that the United States was the only country with the capacity to manufacture enough vaccine to inoculate its citizens before the fall. Public-health people in other countries could take a wait-and-see attitude to this new swine flu because they had no other attitude available. The United States alone had the power to act.

Everyone in the room agreed that a vaccine should be produced as fast as possible. The only disagreement was where to store it: in refrigerators or in people's bodies? Was it smarter to stockpile vaccine, or antibodies? A small minority—composed of academics with little on-the-ground experience of disease control—suggested it might be better to put the vaccine in the fridge and wait. The most credible among them would later admit that he wasn't sure that he had actually voiced his views, only that he'd asked a few questions. The majority, including the greatest disease battlefield commanders on the planet, felt that the country should vaccinate as many people as possible before the flu season arrived.

Flu was more like COVID than like smallpox or polio. It was genetically less stable. The decisions made about it were always going to be tricky. You were always going to be tempted to wait until you were certain of the threat. But to wait was to expose huge numbers of people to the virus before they could be vaccinated. "This is one of those situations where there is a strong argument on one side and almost no argument on the other," recalled Bill Foege.

Sencer heard everyone out and then adjourned the meeting without putting the matter to a vote. There was a clear consensus, albeit with a dissenter or two, that the best thing to do was to vaccinate as many Americans as possible before the flu season arrived. Sencer knew that a mass vaccination program would be costly and controversial: you didn't stick needles into two hundred seventeen million arms without something going wrong. He also knew that there was no way to eliminate the unpleasantness of the decision: the situation was inherently uncertain. As for the matter of why he did not ask for a vote, recalled Bill Foege, "He said, 'This is going to be political, and if it goes wrong I'm going to need to take the blame.'" Holding a vote would have implicated others in the decision and damaged their reputations along with his own. After hearing Sencer's reasoning Foege had a brief chat with himself. "I said to myself, 'This is a person of courage and integrity.'"

Sencer wrote a memo laying out the options but making it clear that the experts at the CDC thought the only responsible course of action was to vaccinate all Americans. He sent it to Dr. Theodore Cooper, an assistant secretary at what was then called the Department of Health, Education and Welfare (HEW). Cooper was actually a bit wary of Sencer, and the CDC, as their location and reputation left them with an unusual independence. But the memo resonated with him. He remembered stories about the 1918 pandemic his father had told him, of the army rolling into their town of Hershey, Pennsylvania, to dig mass graves. He thought that the country needed to work harder at disease prevention. Sencer's memo became Cooper's memo, and was then sent to his secretary and, eventually, to the president.

Then just about everything that could go wrong went wrong. The vaccination program began on October 1, 1976, continued for two and a half months, and reached forty-three million Americans. The goal had been to vaccinate everyone, and

Sencer had known how complicated that would be—which is why he acted with such urgency. But in the event, there was a shocking unevenness across the country in how the vaccine got distributed, because there was no real public-health system to do it. Rather, there were thousands of disconnected local public-health officers. Where those local public officers were capable, people were vaccinated; where the health officer was inept, people weren't.

Two weeks into the program, three elderly people in Pittsburgh died. They'd all been vaccinated at the same clinic. Their deaths made national television news. The vaccine fell under new suspicion, even after heart failure emerged as the cause of all three deaths. A month later, a recently vaccinated man in Minnesota was diagnosed with Guillain-Barré syndrome. Over the next few weeks more cases emerged, until the CDC had counted fifty-four, in ten states. The vaccine was pretty clearly responsible. That made national news again, as did cases of people who'd been vaccinated and become ill for reasons having nothing to do with the vaccine. The vaccine program went from controversial to unpopular to, on December 16, suspended. And the pandemic never came. The new strain of swine flu simply vanished. No one knew why.

On January 20, 1977, the Ford administration gave way to the Carter administration. Two weeks later, the new secretary of Health, Education and Welfare, Joe Califano, instructed one of his deputies to call Sencer and tell him that he was fired. Hundreds of the CDC's employees signed a petition to protest the move, but Sencer himself, who might have put up a fight, stepped aside. The feeling in the air was that Sencer's memo had backed President Ford into a corner and made it impossible for him to do anything but vaccinate everyone. The CDC simply had too much authority for the president to ignore what it said. As a television reporter put it at the time:

CDC was almost the last Federal agency widely regarded by reporters and producers as a *good thing*, responsible, respectable, scientific, above suspicion. This gave Sencer terrific clout. The Presidency after Watergate, the military after Vietnam, physicists, universities, to say nothing of HEW or Congress for God's sake—none of them remotely in the same league! Even a hint that any one of them was blocking Sencer's urgent memo would have been a big story . . . human interest . . . good guys (the best) against bad . . .

That quote appeared in a book called *The Swine Flu Affair*, by a Harvard professor named Richard Neustadt and a graduate student of his, Harvey Fineberg. It had been commissioned by Joe Califano for his private consumption: even though he had already drawn his conclusions, and fired the CDC director, Califano said he wanted to know what had gone wrong.

The short book was very well done. Calling it a "report" made it sound objective and almost scientific when it was really just journalism. From their interviews the authors wove a compelling narrative and delivered it in a tone of lordly omniscience. The story had one clear villain, David Sencer. The villain had one accomplice, Dr. Theodore Cooper, but his role was less central, like a getaway driver's. Sencer for his part came off as at best sneaky and at worst wildly manipulative:

> Sencer was not President. Yet as he did his work this may have been a distinction without a difference. For he evidently thought it was his task to make his constitutional superiors do right no matter what they thought (and so he did). He also made them do it with but little time to think.

Perhaps he'd become intoxicated by his own authority; perhaps, the authors suggested, Sencer was a "hero in his own mind." The book never satisfyingly answered the question of motive: Why exactly would a man who had devoted his life to public health mislead the public about a health threat? But if Joe Califano felt any need to justify how he'd fired Sencer—the first time a CDC director had been dismissed by a political superior—the book slaked it. His immediate reaction to what had been written as a private document was to make it public. "We intended it just for Califano," recalled Harvey Fineberg. "After taking one look at it, he said, 'I have to publish this.'" The book's publication amplified David Sencer's humiliation and put anyone in public health who might stick out his neck to make a decision on notice. It became close to the final word on the episode, at least for people on the outside looking in.

Those on the inside had their own, different understanding. Not long after he had replaced Sencer, Bill Foege was asked by Senator Edward Kennedy during a congressional hearing what he would have done had he been faced with the decision that Sencer made. "I don't know," Foege had said. "I hope I would have the courage to have made the same decision he did." D.A. Henderson, who had given Richard Hatchett and Carter Mecher such trouble on the idea of social interventions, also rose to the occasion. Henderson was just then the only human being walking the planet who might challenge Foege for the title of greatest living disease battlefield commander. And Henderson didn't work for the CDC; he ran the infectious disease unit at the World Health Organization in Switzerland. "It is not customary for me to write to authors in regard to their books and my reactions to them," he began, in a private letter to Neustadt, "but, in this case my anticipations of a scholarly work intelligently shedding light on a complex decision-making process were so rudely shattered that I could not resist writing to you to express a personal bitter disappointment."

The source of the book's many problems, wrote Henderson, was Richard Neustadt's ignorance of "the basic scientific issues relating to influenza epidemiology, virology, vaccine production etc." That failing was "compounded by the clarity with which retrospective judgement is rendered." Unlike David Sencer—but like every person interviewed for the book—the authors had the benefit of knowing that there hadn't been a pandemic, and that everything the U.S. government had done to save lives had been a waste of time, money, and the health of some of those vaccinated. After the pandemic failed to happen, everyone agreed that it was always a lot less likely than it had seemed back when things were uncertain.

Two weeks later Neustadt replied. He was saddened by Henderson's letter, he said. He predicted doom "unless persons of your distinction as public health professionals can be induced to come to grips with the hard issues posed by governmental action through a federal system in a television age, especially after Watergate." Changes in the media and in society had led to changes in the way technical decisions were perceived, and so people with mere technical expertise could no longer make decisions without paying more attention to how they might be made to appear to a cynical public after the fact.

Henderson might have left it at that, but for some reason he couldn't. A month later he wrote a scathing three-page, single-spaced reply. It bothered him that this professor held himself out as a student of battlefield decisions without understanding their most important quality, uncertainty. "I have found that there is an order of magnitude difference between bearing the ultimate responsibility for decision-making and being either an advisor or student of the process," he wrote. "It's one thing to experience an orgasm or an arrow between your ribs and it's another thing to read about it." Sencer had experienced an arrow between his ribs. Neustadt had only read about orgasms—and yet used his vicarious experience to swan about as an authority on the subject. "As an administrator, one is regularly obliged to make decisions based on incomplete evidence," Henderson concluded. ". . . It was a 'no-win' situation in more ways than you have described. From my many conversations with Sencer and the CDC staff during this time, this was only too well appreciated. Thus your portrayal of them as arrogant, arbitrary, single-minded, [and determined] to do good and to prevent disease with a 'public and president be damned' approach is incredibly wide of the mark."

And he was right: *The Swine Flu Affair*, as persuasive as it was, never really faced up to the problem as Sencer faced it. If Sencer had waited until he knew for sure that a deadly new pathogen was circulating, he'd likely have missed the chance to save hundreds of thousands of lives. "Deciding on a swine flu program is like placing a bet without knowing the odds," the authors concluded, without acknowledging that *not* deciding on a swine flu program was also placing a bet, also without knowing the odds. The odds were never knowable. The authors never considered the interesting counterfactual: Given the uncertainty inherent in the situation, how would Sencer's decision have been viewed if the pandemic had occurred? How would American politics and the American public have then treated David Sencer? The public would have seen that theirs was the only country on earth that not only had grasped the threat to its citizens but acted to protect them. Bill Foege thought Sencer would have been seen as a hero.

Foege had followed Sencer as the CDC's director even though he hadn't especially wanted the job. (He preferred working in the field, fighting disease.) And the job was clearly changing, in ways that made Foege want it even less. "The White House meddled more and more," he recalled. The CDC director was then a career civil servant, and when Jimmy Carter was replaced by Ronald Reagan, Foege remained in his job. But now, when Foege testified before Congress, the White House sent minders to sit with him and monitor what he said. They meddled in science that conflicted with the interests of Reagan's base and his financial backers. Any research having to do with AIDS, for instance, had to first be vetted by the White House. The breaking point for Foege came in 1983, after the CDC's researchers established a connection between aspirin and Reye's syndrome in children. When given to children suffering from flu or measles, aspirin could trigger swelling in the liver and the brain and, in rare cases, death. Companies that manufactured aspirin petitioned the White House. "The White House called and told us to cease and desist," recalled Foege. "Do a new study." The aspirin makers had been able to force the CDC to scrap its findings and slow down science.

Foege had resigned after that. "The fact that they would risk the lives of children—it just bothered me so much," he said. He later regretted his decision and wished that instead he had forced them to fire him, as it would have made more of a stink.

The Reagan administration must have noticed the possibility. After Foege resigned, the White House converted the position of CDC director from career civil servant to presidential appointee. Since the agency's inception back in 1946, no one had paid much attention to the party politics of the CDC director. ("No one ever asked me," said Foege.) Henceforth the CDC director would not bubble up from inside the CDC, lifted by the approval of his peers, but would be plucked from the supporters of whichever politician happened to occupy the White House. Foege's replacement, James O. Mason, was an ideological soulmate and good friend of Republican senator Orrin Hatch. If somehow he still managed to displease the White House, the president could fire him on a whim, as he could not have fired David Sencer.* Hence-forth the CDC director would not serve across administrations, as past directors had done, but would be replaced when the pres-ident was replaced, or usually sooner. The entire United States government had been drifting that way for some time—man-agement jobs once done by career civil servants being turned into roles performed by people appointed by the president. One of the problems this created was management inexperience: the average tenure of the appointees fluctuated between eigh-teen months and two years, depending on the administration. Another was the kind of person the job now selected for. There would be exceptions, of course, but the odds favored the pleaser. The person who did not present risks to the White House's polit-ical operation. The person who deferred, rather than made, hard decisions. A Chamberlain, rather than a Churchill.

When she'd come across David Sencer's story, Charity saw in him both inspiration and explanation. She was born the year Sencer was fired, so in that way he felt like ancient history. But the shift inside the CDC that had begun with the Swine

---

* The relationships that Robert Redfield and Tony Fauci enjoyed with Donald Trump give you an idea of the difference between a career civil servant and a presidential appointee. If Donald Trump had gotten up and said, "Fauci, you're fired," nothing would have happened, which is likely why he never did it. The person with the authority to fire Tony Fauci was Francis Collins, the head of the National Institutes of Health. To do it, how-ever, he would have needed to show cause—which is why Fauci was always less likely to be fired than to be reassigned to, say, the Indian Health Ser-vice. Even then Fauci could have appealed the decision, to something called the Merit Systems Protection Board. The Merit Systems Protection Board would not have been able to process his complaint, as it lacked a quorum: Trump never staffed it. But you get the idea. To fire a competent civil ser-vant is a pain in the ass. To fire a competent presidential appointee is as easy as tweeting.

Flu Affair had led it to become a different sort of place. "Now I understood why the CDC was so admired," said Charity. "It was because of people like him." But Sencer had also exposed the price of bravery. After Sencer—or after Foege—the CDC's relationship to disease control had changed in ways that eliminated its need for bravery. It had begun a descent. It had replaced the flowers on its porch with fake ones and hoped no one would notice. But people did notice, at least those who came close to the porch. Rajeev Venkayya had seen things that caused him to exclude the CDC from playing a role in the invention of pandemic planning. Joe DeRisi had seen how little interest they paid to a weapon that might transform the control of disease.

And the need to make hard decisions in public health didn't just go away. It got pushed down in the system, onto local health officers. They had little social status and were thus highly vulnerable, but they also had little choice, if they hoped to save lives. Local health officers across the country paid with their jobs and more in their attempts to control a disease without the help of the Centers for Disease Control. Sara Cody, the health officer in Santa Clara County, had issued the country's first stay-at-home order, after finding the country's first domestic transmission of COVID—and now Sara Cody needed round-the-clock police protection. Nichole Quick, the health officer in Orange County, seeing the virus rampaging through her community, had issued a mask order only to have the CDC waffle about the need for masks. She'd been run out of her job and, finally, for fear of her safety, the state.

Before he was fired, David Sencer had run the CDC for more than a decade and might have imagined running it a decade more. The event flipped a switch inside him. He went from drinking socially, to drinking too much, to being treated for alcoholism. For a decade he'd served as a sort of mayor to the public-health village in Atlanta, but he no longer felt comfortable there. He took a job in New Jersey with a company that made medical devices but hated it. His heart wasn't in business. He applied and was hired for the job of New York City health commissioner. The *New York Times* uncovered the fact that he'd been treated for alcoholism and ran an article about his failure to disclose it. "I've got a disease and I'm treating it," he said in response, but it felt like a second humiliation. His wife would never fully recover from it. Sencer declined so many opportunities to visit Atlanta that it felt to his son, Steve, as if he had exiled himself. When Steve asked him why, he'd say, "You can't go home again."

In June of 2009, two years before his death, Sencer received an email from someone claiming to work at the White House. It invited him to come to Washington and share what he'd learned about decision-making in a pandemic. The White House wouldn't be able to pay his plane fare but would welcome his thoughts. Sencer suspected a prank. He couldn't imagine anyone in the White House caring what he thought. Steve Sencer recalls his father forwarding the email to him and asking him what he made of it. The younger Sencer inspected it right down to the name on the bottom: Richard Hatchett. "Dad, it looks legit," he said. Yet whatever had happened inside of Sencer had scarred him so deeply that even as he stood outside the White House he did not entirely believe that he had been invited to visit.

*

Richard and Carter had both read *The Swine Flu Affair* back when they came together in the Obama White House. Neither was particularly struck by what today strikes a lay reader: the total absence of any strategy to fight a virus, apart from vaccination. At no point in the entire saga did anyone raise the idea

of social intervention of any kind. There was no talk of closing schools, or masks, or social distancing. That's how deep the
accepted wisdom had run. Apart from vaccinating the population, everyone agreed, there was little to be done. Richard and
Carter had helped to change that view; they sort of took it for
granted that a kind of disease fatalism had once been common.
What stuck with them both was how naturally the society had
turned on David Sencer, and how easily they might find themselves in the same position.

Together with a few others, Richard and Carter had come
up with the idea of asking the surviving characters from *The
Swine Flu Affair* back to the White House to talk about what
they'd learned. Richard thought there was a value in history,
and, maybe more to the point, he could see that the president he
served shared the view. "Government—and the value government provides—isn't just the whim of whoever happens to be
elected at the moment," said Richard. "That government provides continuity across administrations and should be the repos-
itory of accumulated institutional experience and wisdom." His
White House bosses agreed, and told him to plan the meeting.
But the moment he had to explain the thing in his own words,
Richard realized that he had a problem.

> In drafting the memo I faced a real challenge coming up
> with a rationale for the meeting. Getting current senior
> officials together with seven officials from the Ford Admin-
> istration sounded like a good idea but what could they
> actually talk about? I couldn't imagine the invited senior
> officials from '76, most quite advanced in age, relishing the
> prospect of coming to talk about how they had assembled
> perhaps the greatest public health fiasco of the last half
> century.... (Hatchett's letter to his son, June 29, 2009)

The meeting, held in the Roosevelt Room, might have turned into a non-event. The Ford administration was never going to tell the Obama administration anything big that it did not already know. The television age had long since given way to the cable news age, which had given way to the age in which every American citizen was a broadcaster. The Obama people knew how quickly and easily mobs formed. They knew how decisions could be made to seem. They could really only nod politely at the biggest point made by David Sencer and the others: to preserve the president's credibility, you needed to keep him as loosely linked to the public side of the decision-making as possible. The enemy was a virus. The enemy's chief weapon was rapid and random mutation. It might well necessitate big changes of strategy, and these were bound to be viewed by the public as signs of ineptitude, and the president would need to seem to be the one to rescue these situations rather than be rescued from them.

President Obama himself took an interest in the meeting, however, and insisted on sitting in. He'd wanted to hear what history had to say. The passage of time allowed for him and everyone else to see that the blame that had been assigned to an individual was more fairly bestowed on a situation. And David Sencer came away with the feeling of having been understood. "It was a beautiful, beautiful thing for our family," said Steve Sencer. "It's in the White House, and someone is actually recognizing what happened."

*

"Not been a good day," Carter Mecher wrote, on November 23, 2020. "My dad started having cold symptoms a couple of days ago, and had a fever today (there is only one cold going around these days). He was back in the ER and tested + for COVID."

The pandemic he'd done so much to prepare the country for had finally come. If Carter had been given a million years he'd never have imagined it as it happened. He'd always kind of assumed that the strategies that he and Richard had cooked up would be used in a smart and targeted way. They'd reduce illness and death so effectively that people might wonder why the government had bothered to intervene at all. "Richard and I used to talk about this all the time," recalled Carter. "What if we do all these things and we close the schools and the result is that we have a very mild epidemic? And people look around and say, 'Why did we do all this?'" They decided that their hides would be saved by the countries that had bungled their pandemic response. They'd be able to point to them and say, "Look! That's what would have happened to us!" They never imagined that other countries would use the United States to demonstrate their own counterfactual. "We are the bad example for the rest of the world," said Carter. "That's what is so embarrassing."

What puzzled Carter maybe more than anything was how people who should have known better had downplayed the risk. Donald Trump was one thing; scientists were another. Carter couldn't get over that an actual medical professor at Stanford named John Ioannidis became a sensation on U.S. cable news in the spring of 2020 by claiming the virus posed no real threat. Ioannidis predicted that no more than ten thousand Americans would die. He condemned social distancing policies as a hysterical overreaction. That was all that those who wished to deny the reality needed to be able to say, Look, we have experts, too. To say: See, all the experts are fake. Carter had received threats in the mail from such people, who had learned of his role in the strategy.

Carter's father was the first to be diagnosed. The next day his mother became ill with the virus and followed his father to the hospital. Carter arranged for his father to return home with a supply of oxygen. "If he is going to die, I don't want him to die alone and away from family," he wrote. The doctors put his mother on steroids and started her on antivirals. "All we can do now is wait," said Carter. And his father rallied—and told his son that he was going to beat the virus. "Then he started to cry—a little because of happiness for beating the virus but also sadness because my mom was so sick," wrote Carter, then continued:

> It is hard to fathom all the pain the virus has brought. The virus is truly a demon from hell ... I think deep down inside we all sensed this—it was why we tried to get leaders to take early aggressive action to minimize the pain that we knew would come.

Eighteen days later Carter's mother died. Carter sat down and wrote a long letter to his family. His theme was gratitude, for the lives they had shared, but his words were suffused with other emotions. "Over the past several days I felt like a balloon that lost all its air," he wrote at the end. "But I know that with a little time I will re-inflate." He was like the surgeon, famously described by a writer, who had inside himself a small cemetery where he buried his failures and, from time to time, went to pray. And so he went to pray.

The Sin of Omission

t took her longer than it should have to find the grave. Except for the names on the stones, the plots were identical. In every direction stretched the dead, side by side, in long rows, like houses in a new development. Eight thousand or more precisely drawn rectangles, each marked by the same flat granite head-stone, perfectly preserved by the California desert. Delius Oscar Johnson, 1866–1959, obviously had been here for some time, but his final resting place still looked brand-new. It was indistin-guishable from the rectangles freshly carved at the edge of the graveyard for sale to the future dead.

Something was coming. Something bigger. Charity Dean did not know if the next pathogen would leap from an animal or a laboratory—she didn't actually *know* anything. She just sensed it, the way she'd sensed that Mrs. Lorenzen, her second-grade teacher in Junction City, whom she adored, was pregnant before she'd told anyone—and completely panicked the woman by blurting it out in class. "Oh no I'm not!" her teacher had exclaimed, leaving Charity feeling hurt and confused until, a few days later, the woman pulled her aside and asked, "How did you know?" It had always been part of the story Charity told herself about herself: that she knew things before she knew why. That she had a nose for things about to change. And for risk.

A year into the pandemic, she thought of COVID as Mother Nature's gift to the country. The hardest part, to a public-health officer trying to control a communicable disease, was that you were always looking in the rearview mirror. COVID had given the country a glimpse of what Charity had always thought might be coming—a pathogen that might move through the population with the help of asymptomatic spreaders, and which had a talent for floating on air. Airborne and Asymptomatic. Now that we knew how badly we responded to such a threat, we could begin to prepare for it. "Mother Nature has given us a fighting chance," she said. "She's tipped the odds in our favor."

The graveyard was empty. The February sun was setting behind the desert mountains and a new chill was in the air. She picked up the pace and walked up and down the long rows in search of what she'd come for.

Even before she'd quit her job she'd had that odd thought, that the country didn't have the institutions that it needed to survive. In particular, it did not have what it needed to battle a pathogen. The pandemic had given America's enemies a clear view of the country's weakness: its inability to respond to a COVID-like threat. On her calls with the Wolverines, she'd ask: "What does the country need?" She was really asking herself, as no one had the answer. Her conclusion had pained her some. Once she'd become a public-health officer, she'd imagined an entire career in public service. Now she did not believe that the American government, at this moment in its history, would ever do what needed doing. Disease prevention was a public good, but the public wasn't going to provide anything like enough of it. From the point of view of American culture, the trouble with disease prevention was that there was no money in it. She needed to find a way to make it pay.

The problem was a crazy problem. It wasn't going to have a non-crazy solution. Still, she'd sort of shocked herself. She'd never had the slightest interest in business. But if she wanted to save the country, she'd need to become an entrepreneur, and create a company—though in business, she quickly learned, she couldn't talk like that. When she said she wanted to build a tool "to save the country," people just smiled and thought she was goofy in the head. But when she said things like "I'm going to create a data-based tool for disease prevention that companies can use to secure their supply chains," serious business types nodded. "Five smart people have replied with confusion when I said the company was to save the world and protect our country," said Charity, after her first attempts to explain her vague idea. "Then when I said, 'We're going to do private government operations, like Blackwater,' their eyes lit up and they said, 'Oh wow, you could take over the world.' "

She'd entered the private sector with the bizarre ambition to use it to create an institution that might be used by the public sector. She'd already hired twenty people, among them public-health nurses and some of the team at the Chan Zuckerberg Biohub responsible for genomic sequencing, including Josh Batson and David Dynerman. Joe DeRisi had signed on as an adviser; Carter Mecher was about to. She'd raised millions of dollars in capital. Venrock, a leading health care venture capitalist, had taken a stake in the new company. As a local health officer, she hadn't been able to get the tens of thousands of dollars she needed for some new disease-stopping machine. In the private sector, people would throw tens of *millions* at an idea: if she failed, it wouldn't be because investors wouldn't give her the money to try. The Public Health Company, she'd called it.

It was still unclear what The Public Health Company might become. The person with the most curious view of the possible future was Todd Park, the former White House chief technology officer. After he'd seen Charity in action in Sacramento, Park had told her he'd help her with whatever she wanted to do. He'd created three separate billion-dollar health care companies himself, and in each case his idea was to find the person who was the very best in the world at a given task and, effectively, turn them into software. For example, in 2004, he'd found a woman named Sue Henderson, who, for reasons no one could understand, was the single best person in the country at getting insurance companies to pay doctors' bills. The country had hundreds of health insurance companies, each with its own rules, which they'd change capriciously. Sue Henderson somehow knew them all, along with the language that got them to pay a bill. Todd's brother, Ed, had sat in a room with her and coded her reaction to various situations. It had taken them five years to finish the job. By the time they were done, the company, athenahealth, had become the country's leading medical biller because thousands of doctors used Sue Henderson to deal with insurance companies.

Todd Park thought that The Public Health Company might do the same kind of thing, by turning Charity into the local public-health officer for everyone who needed one—a group that suddenly included just about every big corporation.

At length Charity found the grave she'd come for. Jerald Scott Jones. May 23, 1958–December 8, 2015. He'd been found dead on a Santa Barbara street corner at the age of fifty-seven. The official cause of death made for a long list, but what its items had in common was neglect. When he died, the United States had just entered a three-year period during which the life expectancy of its citizens had fallen every year—the first such stretch since the First World War and the 1918 pandemic. And so Jerry was, in his way, a representative case.

He'd first turned up in the emergency room at Cottage Hospital when Charity was a resident. She'd treated him for years, first in the ER and then on the trauma floor, then in the ICU and, after she'd become the health officer, in the basement at the Santa Barbara county clinic. She'd finally treated him on a street corner, after he refused to visit the room she worked in at the homeless shelter. "Too many drugs there," he'd said. "I don't do drugs. I'm an alcoholic." She'd thought, *Me too*, but she'd never said it. She had been too worried about preserving her status—about keeping the flowers seeming real. But she'd loved the guy; she thought of him as maybe the most honest person she'd ever met. "Dr. Dean, I'm not going to stop drinking, so no need to start," he'd say, and that was that. Jerry never knew it, but he'd taught Charity about the disease, and where it ended if left untreated.

What Charity always regretted most was not what she had said or done but what she hadn't. Sins of omission. She had left him with a false impression of who she was. It was unlike her not to have told him; she felt she had left something unsaid. So now she said it. Then she made an incision in the ground, buried a piece of herself, and moved on.

ACKNOWLEDGMENTS

Five years ago I met a man named Carl Kawaja, who said, "You need to meet this guy named Joe DeRisi, because you really should write about him." I was dubious. Carl was persuasive. I met Joe for a sandwich and came away wishing I had an excuse to write about him. Then, in late March 2020, I did. Around that time, Max Stier introduced me to Richard Danzig, who not only offered lots of great advice but introduced me to the Wolverines. Within about three weeks several of them, plus Joe, plus DJ Patil, had said, "You need to meet this woman named Charity Dean." I'm grateful to everyone involved in this chain of events.

A bunch of people read all or part of the manuscript and said things about it that were helpful to me: Tom Penn, David Shipley, Jacob Weisberg, Adam McKay, Doug Stumpf, Elizabeth Riley, Scott Hatteberg, Tabitha Soren, and Quinn Lewis. Elaine He at Bloomberg News invented a new way to depict a phylogenetic tree that is probably not respectable to experts but spares the viewer much pain. Christina Ferguson not only hunted down information for me but prodded me in useful ways with her own ideas.

I don't think anyone in my life has saved me from myself as many times as Janet Byrne. I think her formal title is copyeditor, but she's more like a human mosquito net who keeps a billion bugs from biting my books. Finally, there's always someone you are sort of writing these books for—the person you sort of imagine reading it. That would be my editor, Starling Lawrence. His flowers are still the freshest in town.